Women in social work

International Library of Social Policy

General Editor   Kathleen Jones
Professor of Social Administration
University of York

Arbor Scientiæ
Arbor Vitæ

A catalogue of the books available in the **International Library of Social Policy** and other series of Social Science books published by Routledge & Kegan Paul will be found at the end of this volume

Women in social work

Ronald G. Walton

School of Social Work,
University College, Cardiff

Routledge & Kegan Paul
London and Boston

First published in 1975
by Routledge & Kegan Paul Ltd
Broadway House, 68–74 Carter Lane,
London EC4V 5EL and
9 Park Street,
Boston, Mass. 02108, USA
Set in Monotype Times
and printed in Great Britain by
Unwin Brothers Limited
The Gresham Press
Old Woking, Surrey
A member of the Staples Printing Group
© *Ronald G. Walton 1975*

ISBN 0 7100 8041 7

For Pam

For Pam

Contents

Acknowledgments   xv

Introduction   1

Part I   **Women pioneers and early social work organisations 1860–1914**

1   Employment and education for women   11

Family patterns and entry to professions   11
Teaching, nursing and philanthropy   13
Miss Parkes and the English Woman's Journal
employment bureau   15
Philanthropy and higher education—Emily Davies   16
Josephine Butler, Octavia Hill, Mary Carpenter   18

2   Women as innovators in social work   20

Male creative influence in new welfare developments   20
Female initiatives   22
*Contrasting approaches—Octavia Hill, Josephine
Butler, Mary Carpenter*   24

3   Women in social work organisations   27

Introduction   27
The Charity Organisation Society   28
The Poor Law: visitors and guardians   30
*The Poor Law: employment under the Poor Law—
institutional staff and relieving officers*   32
Women inspectors: the Poor Law   36
Women inspectors: prisons and reformatories   38
Women inspectors: factories   39
Moral welfare   40
Almoning   43

| | *Probation* | 47 |
| | *Settlements* | 50 |

4	Women and social work education	57
	The need for training—Charity Organisation Society concern and policy	57
	Tension between the Charity Organisation Society and university courses	59
	The School of Sociology and the spread of social studies teaching	61
	Academic and practical work	61
	Women's changing choice of training opportunities	63

5	Women social workers, women's suffrage, and social reform	66
	Introduction	66
	Attitudes to the women's suffrage movement—Octavia Hill, Josephine Butler, Mary Carpenter	67
	A new generation of women linking nineteenth- and twentieth-century social work—Violet Markham, Eleanor Rathbone, Cecile Matheson	72
	Patterns of involvement	77

6	Overview 1860–1914	80
	Main trends	80
	Social work as a career for women	81
	Professional identity and the ideal of service	82
	Marx, Engels and Veblen—theoretical views	84

Part II Emergent profession 1914–39

7	The First World War	91
	Impact on social work	91
	Munitions work	92
	Training and opportunities for paid social work	93
	Almoning	95
	Probation	96
	Moral welfare and housing management	97
	Mental hygiene and American links	98

8 Women's social position and career prospects
   1918–39   102

   Limited emancipation for women   102
   Employment problems   103
   Low pay and poor prospects in social work   107
   Class and social work   108

9 Women in social work organisations 1918–39   112

   General or specialised social work   112
   Almoning   114
   Probation   122
   Psychiatric social work   128
   House property management   137
   Moral welfare   139
   Settlements   141
   Women inspectors   143

10 Overview 1918–39   146

   Training patterns and problems of recruitment   146
   Women and professional development   149
   Five women   157

Part III Social work 1939–71: an expanding mixed profession

11 The Second World War   167

   War and welfare   167
   Almoning   168
   Psychiatric social work   170
   Probation   174
   The Caxton Hall Conference, 1942   177
   Voluntary effort in wartime—women in action   181
   Venereal disease   183
   Child welfare, women and social work   184

12 The demographic background after 1945   188

   Marriage, family and work   188
   Trends in the balance of men and women in social
   welfare   189
   Social welfare, teaching and nursing   191

A*

13 Social work under the microscope 1945–51   196

    *The welfare state and the significance of child care
service*   196
    The state of social work—Younghusband and Simey   198
    Social work and the vanishing Poor Law   202
    Universities and social work   203
    *Developments in probation, almoning and psychiatric
social work*   206

14 Two decades of training 1951–71   209

    New demands and limited resources   209
    Women in social studies departments   211
    The Younghusband Report, 1959   211
    Training in child care and health and welfare   213
    Generic training   215
    Fieldwork teaching   216
    *Central government reorganisation and the National
Institute for Social Work Training*   218
    Training as a special field for women   219

15 Women in social work agencies and the social work
    profession: the male threat   221

    The wider pattern of recruitment and employment   221
    Psychiatric social work   223
    Medical social work   224
    Child care   226
    Probation   228
    Local studies   231
    Directors of social services   235
    Social work inspectors   238
    Voluntary social work   239
    Professional organisation   241

16 Problems of women's employment in social work   246

    Defining the issues   246
    Married women and part-time work   247
    Hesitant responses to women's position   251
    Women's liberation and social work   255

17 Conclusion 257
Motivation for social work 257
Differentiation of male and female social work roles 258
Leadership and administrative abilities of women in
social work 258
Future trends 260
Maximising women's contribution 260
Reinterpreting the history of social work 261

Notes 264

Bibliography 295

Index 304

Tables

1. 1	Women's employment, 1891	12
8. 1	Number of occupied women, 1881 and 1901	102
8. 2	Occupations of women graduates, 1930s	108
9. 1	Persons on probation, England and Wales, 1910 and 1930	127
9. 2	Work setting of psychiatric social workers, 1930s	133
12. 1	Occupied women, 1951 and 1961	188
12. 2	Women social studies students, 1909–49, age of marriage	189
12. 3	Social welfare and related workers, 1921–61	190
12. 4	Social welfare and related workers, rate of increase	190
12. 5	Female social welfare workers, marital status 1951–61	191
12. 6	Teachers, nurses and social welfare workers, 1951–61	191
12. 7	'O' and 'A' level passes	192
12. 8	Female workers in teaching, nursing and social welfare, 1951–61	193
12. 9	Male workers in teaching, nursing and social welfare, 1951–61	193
12.10	Numbers of first-degree graduates entering further training	194
13. 1	Occupied males and females 15 and over, 1951	200
15. 1	The most popular forms of social work training, 1940–60	222
15. 2	Employment status of social welfare workers, 1951–61	222
15. 3	Women social welfare workers aged 35–44 and 45–54, 1951 and 1961	223
15. 4	Wastage in the child care service, 1969–70	227
15. 5	Senior appointments in children's departments, 1970	228
15. 6	Senior appointments in the probation service, 1965	229
15. 7	Staff structure of the probation service, 1961 and 1969	230
15. 8	Staffing of social work departments in a northern county borough, 1957 and 1969	232
15. 9	Social workers in different departments by sex and position	234

15.10 Seniority and qualifications   234
15.11 Men and women in the probation service inspectorates,
       1950 and 1969   239
15.12 Men and women representatives, Standing Conference
       of Organisations of Social Workers, 1963   243
15.13 ACCO presidents, 1950–69   244

Acknowledgments

I am indebted to many individuals and organisations for help in gathering material for the parent study which formed the basis of a doctoral thesis in 1972 at the University of Manchester. Mrs B. N. Rodgers, formerly Reader in Social Administration, and Dr Jean S. Heywood, Reader in Social Administration, encouraged me to combine research into the history of social work with a study of the position of women in the profession. Mrs Rodgers supervised my research and her intimate knowledge of social work and social services was of enormous help in stimulating and guiding my work. During the early stages of my work I was particularly aided by interviews with Dame Eileen Younghusband, Lady Mary Stocks and Professor Noel Timms. Later Miss S. Clement Brown discussed the development of social work in the inter-war years with me and kindly allowed me to borrow a number of manuscripts and pamphlets which were invaluable in understanding the state of social work in Britain between the wars.

The British Association of Social Workers gave permission to use their records as did the National Association of Probation Officers and the Josephine Butler Memorial College. I owe a particular debt to the Fawcett Library and the Librarian, Miss M. Surrey for help in tracing early sources. Also I was able to use the library of the National Institute for Social Work Training, another valuable source of records dealing with the early development of social work.

The study was undertaken during the period 1969–72 whilst I was a social work tutor in the Extra Mural Department at the University of Manchester and I am grateful to Professor E. G. Wedell, Director of Extra Mural Studies, and Mrs N. Lingard, Senior Staff Tutor, for permission to study on a part-time basis. Mrs Lingard and my colleagues at Manchester were tolerant, supportive and helpful throughout the period of my research.

The manuscript was prepared by Mrs L. Seden, to whom I am specially grateful for her care and attention which has eradicated many drafting errors. Any remaining faults or inaccuracies in the text are my responsibility alone. Finally I would like to express my thanks to my wife for her support and encouragement, without which my research would have been extended over a much longer period.

Introduction

The aim of focusing on the position of women in social work 1860–1971 is to introduce a further degree of clarity and understanding of the social processes activated when a society is faced by social problems of the kind existing in England and Wales during that period. These problems arose from three related basic forces in British society: increasing population, industrialisation, and urbanisation. In 1801 the population was just under nine million; by 1851 it had increased to almost eighteen million reaching thirty-two million in 1901. By the mid-nineteenth century half the population was living in urban areas, rising to four-fifths of the population a century later. In 1851 agriculture occupied 25 per cent of males aged twenty and over but this had dropped to 10 per cent by 1900. There was vast social disorganisation resulting from this powerful population explosion and the process of establishing modern industrial capitalism in the spreading cities. To cope with the nightmarish results entailed the creation and articulation of new systems of government agencies to replace inadequate institutions which had served a rapidly passing age. Public health and education were the earliest functions to be recognised as public responsibility coped with through *ad hoc* boards. Later came the restructuring of local government to match the shifts in population and the problems accompanying them.

Alongside these positive functions of health and education was the seemingly permanent problem of pauperism being coped with by the Poor Law and voluntary bodies. A plethora of organisations and an army of voluntary helpers fought a losing and often unorganised battle against social evils, of the causes of which their individualistic approach had little knowledge or understanding. It is out of these individualistic approaches that social work was conceived and the time of conception has earned the criticism of many who condemned it for being born in a class-ridden society. These critics—who usually favour large-scale revolution—make the logically false assumption that because social work was largely started by middle- and upper-class people, many of whom were

1

resistant to fundamental changes in society, social work can only exist as an impediment to broad changes in society. This thesis, which has a Marxist ring about it, has appeared in many guises, the latest of which is the sociological emphasis on social work as an agent of social control. It also accounts for the critical attitude towards the Charity Organisation Society because of its resistance to social insurance.

Any division of a historical period into parts tends to be arbitrary. But some division is necessary to organise our perception and test our longer-term sense of trends in the light of shorter periods which appear to have more cohesion. My division lines are simple and correspond with those used by a great many other historians. Thus the periods I discuss will be 1860–1914, the First World War and 1918–39, the Second World War and 1945–71.

Social work has evolved not only as an outcome of industrialisation and problems of urban growth, but also as a career for women. In its early growth it was an expression of social service by women and the social forms in which it was realised reflected demographic factors, the class structure and the social position of women. It is the main aim of the present study to describe and analyse the roles that women have played in social work and to argue that such an approach yields an increase in understanding when applied to twentieth-century social work as well as nineteenth-century philanthropy. Although reference is made to women's movements it is not intended to give a full account of these, but to refer to particular points of contact with the field of social work; similarly demographic and occupational data are used to connect the social position of women with their employment in social work and other careers. Because economic, family and social welfare institutions vary greatly throughout the world I have studied the situation in England and Wales, with some mention of the position in America. It would be a corollary of the evidence about this country, that the development of social work in other countries could be related closely to the demographic structure and the social position of women.

The historical material used in the study and arguments derived from it do not depend upon any particular view of the psychology of women. Much opposition to women's emancipation was a result of essentialist notions of the mental characteristics of women and the case for women's advancement put by Mary Wollstonecraft and John Stuart Mill was based on general principles of social justice, almost treating women as a particular example of a group heavily discriminated against in society. Cultural investigations in many parts of the world have shown how, given women's biological characteristics, there is an enormous variety in characteristic personality traits, family and social roles.[1] Men have been particularly forceful in their pronouncements about women's character. Their interpretations, as in the case of Freud and D. H. Lawrence, have frequently met with less than enthusiasm from women themselves and I therefore prefer extreme caution in making statements about the personality and character of women in general. As also with men, society should be prepared to accept a variety of temperaments in women. This study, as many others have done, confirms the unhealthy influence of rigid stereotypes about women's psychology and social position. An emphasis on social justice leads to the conclusion that equality of the opportunity to share in all social aspects of life and to enter a full range of occupations is the right aim. This aim, echoed throughout the nineteenth and twentieth century, does not entail the sameness of men and women, but the chance for women to develop fully as persons for self-enrichment and the enrichment of society.

The present study has incorporated material dealing with the general development of social work so that the contribution of women can be related to it. A difficulty exists in using the term 'social work' as it may have many different connotations. As a result the inclusion or exclusion of particular organisations or individuals from the field of social work tends to be arbitrary. The definition of social work by its methods is doomed to failure as methods may change or be discarded. Any statement 'social work is . . .' must accommodate the fact that social work, like any other specialised human activity, is developing all the time. Thus any attempt to define social work by listing organisations at one point in time or by listing techniques in operation at one point in time invariably leads to difficulty. Harriet Bartlett sees these problems clearly:[2]

> Until the distinguishing characteristics of social work are better
> understood it will be difficult to identify its basic role in society.
> While social work should not be regarded as excessively
> dependent upon the other professions, its role should be
> perceived in relation to their roles, that is as distinct from and
> not duplicating their activities.

Because of these problems a historical investigation seems specially valuable. Noel Timms expresses this view well: 'Because social work is the product of many changing forces, a historical approach provides the most serviceable approach to understanding its operation.'[3] Our difficulty with social work is that until recent times its functions have been incorporated into the functions of the family, the community, and religious, judicial, medical or business institutions. This difficulty, however, yields a positive way of studying social work, as Bartlett observes: 'The only way to relate social work to our society is to perceive it as a social institution, like medicine and education.'[4] It is the failure of the latter institutions to cope with some of the problems associated with the emergence of modern industrial society which led to the slow birth of modern social work as a special form of human endeavour.

For the purpose of this study I have not studied all social work organisations. But the organisations and individuals included would all be accepted under the umbrella term of social work on a pragmatic basis. A large enough group of individuals and organisations has been dealt with to give conclusions which could readily be applied to organisations and individuals not included.

Before embarking on the main study it will be helpful to consider some of the broad attributes of social work in society as a framework into which particular developments may be set. As in considering the psychological and social position of women, I take the view that too fixed an idea of the nature of social work leading to a neat definition is inappropriate; social work is a diverse social institution whose functions will vary as society develops.

If we look at the range of activities commonly called social work—work in settlements, systematic visiting of the poor, sick or troubled, medical social work, probation, child welfare, psychiatric social work, social work in schools, moral welfare—we see that they have certain attributes in common:

a   compassionate response to human suffering;
b   the people being helped feel that their personal or emotional difficulties cannot be solved from their own unaided material, social, intellectual or emotional resources and they ask for help, and/or some individual or group in society perceives the state of one or more people and believes that it should be improved in some way—help is offered;
c   the help is personalised and mediated through direct contact between the social worker and whoever is being helped.
d   In the early days the first social workers most frequently

offered material help because the problems were of poverty, but they also offered human warmth and concern. The efforts were sporadic, diffuse and unorganised: 'The older type of social worker was mainly endeavouring to deal with results; he saw that people were hungry or ill-clad or sick, and his first impulse was to provide food, clothing and medicine.'[5]

 e During the course of the nineteenth century social workers created an enormous variety of voluntary organisations. The housing activities of Octavia Hill and child welfare work of Barnardo and Stephenson are typical of the individual response to human suffering becoming institutionalised in an organisation:[6]

> By social work we do not mean social reform, though some   .
> social workers have necessarily become social reformers. Nor
> do we mean social services. We use the term social work as
> referring to the personal efforts of individuals who assist those
> in promoting their own.

 f During the course of the late nineteenth and early twentieth century, the development of broadly based insurance, housing, education, and medical welfare services, and the gradual break up of the Poor Law put many social workers into the position of helping people to use the available services effectively and this has remained one of the key functions of social workers to the present day. Rodgers and Dixon expressed this in their definition: a social worker is 'someone employed at the consumer end of a social service, who is in personal contact with those using it, and who is able to appreciate them in their family and social background.'[7]

 g Whereas social workers were mainly working in voluntary organisations until the first quarter of this century, since the last war the numbers and proportion of social workers in statutory social services has greatly increased.

 h From the nineteenth century there has been a developing drive to establish and broaden the scientific base of social work method. Charles Loch was a passionate advocate of this. In spite of great advances in the disciplines which social work depends on— sociology, psychology, administrative and political science— research methods have been little applied to the observation and analysis of social work methods. This has been one of the major factors hindering the acceptance of academic study of social work as an applied social science.

 i Social workers and their organisations have consistently acted as agents of broad social change, that is as social investigators and reformers, often putting political pressure on government. The evolution of modern industrial society has created stresses and problems for individuals, families, and societal groupings of various kinds. Gradual understanding of the problems and pressures from politically powerful groupings led to the establishment of comprehensive welfare services as a matter of community obligation and individual right. Social work as a part of the total welfare system (whether provided statutorily or voluntarily) shares many of the value elements common to all welfare services. The high value of the individual, the desire to provide an environment for self-realisation as well as useful and creative social participation, are held in common.

Belief in democratic processes and Christian ethics are often in evidence in Europe and America as part of this value system, but not necessarily so. Nor is the belief in social work as an agent of social change. Attlee saw this very clearly when he wrote:[8]

> Our attitude to social service will be different according to the conception that we have of society. If we regard it as at present constituted on the whole just and right, and approve of the present economic structure, social work will seem to us as it were, a work of supererogation, a praiseworthy attempt to ease the minor injustices inevitable in all systems of society. We shall see a set of disconnected problems not related to any one general question. On the other hand we may see as the root of the trouble an entirely wrong system, altogether a mistaken aim, a faulty standard of values, and we shall form in our minds more or less clearly a picture of some different system, a society organised on a new basis altogether, guided by other motives than those which operate at the present time, and we shall relate all our particular efforts to this point of view.

Attlee also provided a clear philosophy for the social worker to carry as part of his function in social investigation, the pioneering and discussions of new social groupings and political or social agitation:[9]

> The social worker must have definite views—must have formed some clear conception of what society he wishes to see produced —and I think it is a mistake for him to hold aloof from reform

movements . . . the social worker has as much right to make clear his view as anybody else.

Thus Attlee poses the dilemma which social workers in England and America have felt keenly in the last decade. Many local authorities and other organisations of which social workers form a part have not reached that state of adulthood where they can accept agitation for change as a necessary part of social work.

From the context of the list of attributes and comments on social work as a part of total social welfare, I would suggest the following definition for social work: social work is work with people entailing specialised knowledge and skills. These are used in a direct relationship to enable individuals or groups regain or maintain certain social roles, which they would otherwise perform inadequately and which society considers should be performed at a certain level of competence.[10] As well as this the knowledge and skills may be used to promote emotional well-being even when normal role-functioning is not considered inadequate. A social worker is someone whose main function is social work.

There are several corollaries from this definition:

a Social workers accept a minimum core of commonly held values of the society within which they work. If this were not so their conflict would be so acute, that it might be resolved by engaging primarily in reform or political agitation. It implies working within the rules of society when attempting to change social conditions and methods of dealing with social problems. Conflict is not taboo but illegal modes of dispute are.

b These commonly held values are embodied in systems of legal and administrative procedures which are embodied in organisations usually called social work agencies, for example, probation departments, children's departments, child guidance clinics, family service units. The agencies may be statutorily sponsored or voluntarily sponsored.

c The values and norms implied by the wish to see that certain social roles are fulfilled may vary from time to time in the same society or in different societies at the same time but this does not alter the style of analysis. The values may be characterised by stressing the efficient functioning of society or by advocacy of various norms of conduct for their own sakes.

The existence of social work and social workers is the direct result of the existence of some individuals in society who are unable to live satisfactorily within the community without some help. Social workers are concerned with behaviour or personality adjustment of the individual to community norms and may be regarded as enabling individuals to use other welfare services or to give an individual overall competence in the business of living. The impact of sociology in recent years has emphasised that social work is a form of social control. This is particularly evident in the probation service, child protection services, and mental health services. Yet those who by implication criticise social work for this do not emphasise that minimum conformity to social norms achieves great freedom for an individual in arranging his life to suit himself. If social work measures are unsuccessful this often means that their clients pass on to provisions where the controls are less normative and more coercive. It should not be forgotten that the aim of enabling people to become more masters of their fate and more capable of exercising choice in any aspect of their lives entails the possibility that individuals or groups after social work help may be less accepting of their lot and become more effective in changing it through dealings with social service agencies and through political activities.

The definition I have used avoids the pitfalls arising from posing such questions as: 'Is social work an art or a science?' and 'Is social work love or skill?' As in engineering, architecture and medicine, motivational factors, scientific knowledge, ethical considerations, skill, and imagination all play their part in social work. It is the particular manifestations which are of interest not the question of whether they are present or not present.

The original study dealt with the period 1860–1971. During the past two years much of interest has taken place in the field of women's rights and brief reference is made to these developments in the concluding chapters. Much still remains to be accomplished and I hope that this study of the contribution of women to social work will add to the growing consciousness that if social work is to realise the full potential of its women workers, special efforts will need to be concentrated on their problems in employment. There is less likelihood of this happening if the present generation of women social workers remain unaware of their predecessors' contribution to social work and the relationship to women's rights movements.

Part I

Women pioneers and early social work organisations 1860–1914

1   Employment and education for women

There are three main themes in tracing women's role in the development of social work. The first theme is the social status of women and the struggle for women's rights. Second, there is the theme which deals with women's entry into various spheres of employment and the professions. Third, there is the theme of women's contribution to the development of social work as a particular profession. Each of these three themes varies in relative importance at different times during the period being considered and vigilance is always needed to guard against explaining developments in social work by reference to differences between men and women rather than much larger social changes. Therefore we may find that women in social work may have exerted strong searching influences on its development within a pattern where the primary determinants have been factors such as industrialisation, the growth of professions, and increasing state welfare provision. The kind of questions which are thrown up by looking at the development of social work from this standpoint are: 'How did social work as we know it today begin?' 'Why did women enter social work rather than engage in other work?' 'How concerned were women social workers with the women's rights movement?'

Family patterns and entry to professions

In mid-Victorian England families were large and women were very much tied to child-bearing. The average age of marriage was higher than in this century and there was a high proportion of single women. Industrialisation had removed the economic and educational functions of the family unit at the same time as providing an ever increasing variety of occupations. Simultaneously with these developments women and men engaged in the battle for the emancipation of women, incorporating the struggle for birth control without which it is impossible for large proportions of women to be released from the home for work. For the working-class women there were many appointments for work often at pitiable wages and under

11

atrocious conditions. But for middle-class and upper-class families the situation was different. As the middle-class grew in size the wives of successful husbands often spent their time in supporting good causes and visiting the poor. At the same time as cities were growing rapidly, creating problems of sewage, housing and poverty, there was a reservoir of unoccupied women with all the advantages of wealth and education. For some of these women their aim was 'chiefly to be an ornament to her husband's home and a living testimony to his wealth' [1] but others set their sights rather higher and engaged themselves more seriously in the business of living.

As an indication of the direction and scale of processes occurring during the first decade of our period we can examine some of the changes in England and Wales between the censuses of 1861 and 1871.[2] The population increased from twenty million to just under twenty-three million. At the same time the number of towns increased from 781 to 938 and the population in the towns increased from almost eleven million to fourteen million. There was an excess in the ratio of women to men at both periods and an increase in the number of spinsters and widows from 3·2 million to 3·6 million. As an example of increasing prosperity, the number of 'gentlewomen independent or annuitant' increased from 87,429 in 1861 to 143,385 in 1871. Although the number of schoolmistresses only increased from 37,669 to 38,774, the category described as 'teacher professor, lecturer, governess' increased from 42,324 to 55,246. Apart from the educational field, in spite of the large increases in

Table 1.1   Women's employment, 1891

Employment category	Number of women	%
National government, Civil Service (officers and clerks)	8,546	21
Local government, municipal, parish, Union and district officers	5,165	27
Missionary, scripture readers, itinerant preachers	4,194	45
Nun, Sister of Charity	4,678	100
Church, chapel, cemetery officer, servant	1,781	23
Physician, surgeon, general practitioner	101	0·5
Dentist, dental apparatus maker	345	7
Sick nurse, midwife, invalid attendant	53,057	99
Schoolmaster, teacher, professor, lecturer	144,393	74
Hospital and institution service	15,301	68

the decade the number of other 'professional' workers in 1871 was only 13,000.[3]

The achievements of women in entering more professional employment as the century progressed can be shown from census information in 1891. Numbers of women in various professions are given, together with their proportion in each employment category, in Table 1.1.[4]

The total number of women in the professional class was 328,393 but this included 70,650 women students. It is clear that the bulk of the expansion at this period was in the lower professions, with any significant inroads in the higher professions yet to come. Only nineteen women were employed as architects and the only women employed in the legal profession were 166 law clerks.

Teaching, nursing and philanthropy

For the mid-nineteenth-century woman of leisure there was the possibility of seeking out marriage as portrayed in the novels of Antony Trollope, Mrs Gaskell and Jane Austen. Whilst playing the marriage market there was occupation in domestic management, sewing and visiting. For the unmarried woman looking for an occupation there was teaching or nursing, but these professions were still in their infancy and often not considered suitable by the wealthy middle classes or aristocracy. An indication of the pent-up demand for suitable avenues of employment is given by the fact that during 1849–59 the proportion of female pupil teachers rose from 32 per cent to 46 per cent.[5] It is clear, however, that it was initially most attractive to the lower middle-class or respectable working-class woman for whom teaching gave employment, income and status. Many would hope to have been married later. A clear example of the predicament of the young single women from a respectable but financially poor background is found in Charlotte Bronte's *Villette*. The heroine, Lucy, first goes as a private companion to an old lady and then seeks employment as a teacher in a private school. The young woman of humbler origin often had a better educational grounding than the daughter of middle-class parents, and the latter were sometimes unsuccessful in their attempts to enter the field.[6]

Nursing evolved from even humbler origins and in the early nineteenth century represented little more than a specialised form of charring,[7] certainly not an occupation for ladies. By the middle of the century the situation was changing and nursing was becoming more respectable, but it was not until the second half of the century that nursing became better established with the first register of nurses being established by the British Nurses Association in 1889. New entrants were to undertake a three-year training course but 'lady' pupils who had only had one year's training with three years' experience were admitted to the first register.[8] The Royal Charter was granted to the British Nurses Association in 1893, but the register was not strictly administered and remained unsatisfactory until the twentieth century.

Before examining women in social work at the same period, we may notice three key differences between social work and the two other professions of teaching and nursing. In both teaching and nursing women were moving into a situation where men were already established. Already in the 1830s and 1840s there had been a growth of many local schoolmasters' associations and at a different level the male-dominated universities had a long history and an established part in our national life. Registration had been achieved for doctors in 1858. In both teaching and nursing women were mainly engaged at a level which was inferior to that of men, in teaching younger children and giving medical care and attention under the direction of a doctor. In social work there was no such pre-set pattern. Furthermore, in teaching and nursing there was an identifiable task recognised from earliest times. With social work there was no such accepted task except in terms of the traditional concept of philanthropy or charity. This was an attitude of mind rather than the set of identifiable techniques which were so important in the development of training for teachers and nurses. A third difference was that of scale. The need for education and health affects all people. Thus even with the incomplete and patchy development of education and health services in the mid-nineteenth century, the scale of the problem exerted considerable pressure towards the development of standard organisational and administrative structures, in particular the standardisation of 'pattern of training'. When we turn to the development of social work in the mid-nineteenth century there is abundant evidence of an enormous amount of effort being expended on giving help to those in need, this being largely done on a voluntary basis. The main forms of help were material—money, food, clothes—or friendly visiting. Material help, often given indiscriminately and from a multitude of different societies was, often severely criticised,[9] but friendly visiting such as that of Elizabeth Cadbury to prisons and Louisa Twining to the inmates of workhouses, which often included an element of material aid, remains in the mainstream of later developments by social workers because of the emphasis on constructive character building and its reaching out to those despised by the general community. In the community the pioneering efforts of Dr Chalmers were a prototype of the family visiting agency albeit on a voluntary basis and with a church structure for its organisation (Chalmers 1912). With these pioneer women there is an element which remains important to the present day. Their visiting was concerned with inmates and aspects of living most closely linked to their domestic roles of child care and nursing care. Moreover, the sharp differentiation of sexual and social roles meant that only women should talk to women about womanly things and that men should not have to deal with inmates over domestic matters.

Miss Parkes and the English Woman's Journal employment bureau

How the situation for the employment of women appeared at the start of our period is preserved in an account of how the *English Woman's Journal* established an employment bureau in 1859–60.[10] The *Journal* had been increasing in circulation, and when advertisements for posts had appeared in the *Journal* they had been deluged with applicants. As a result a register was started 'for noting applications for the more intellectual and responsible departments of female labour'. Miss Parkes recalled

> one Friday in the month of March, when twenty women applied
> at our counter for work whereby they could gain a livelihood—
> all of them more or less educated—all of them with some
> claim to the title of a lady.

The *Journal's* secretaries dealt with the applications, but, as many of the women had letters of introduction to her as co-editor, Miss Parkes interviewed many herself:

> I had to ask them what kind of work they wanted, and indeed,
> a very important question, for what kind of work they were
> fitted. In this way we may certainly lay claim to have heard
> more of women's wants during the last year than any other
> people in the kingdom, and that just because the demands were
> so indefinite—the ladies did not want to be governesses, they
> wanted to be something else and we were to advise them. In

this way I have conversed with ladies of all ages and conditions:
with young girls of seventeen finding it necessary to start
in life; with single women who found teaching undesirable
as life advanced; with married ladies whose husbands were
invalided or not forthcoming; with widows who had children
to support; with tradesmen's daughters, and with people of
condition fallen into low estate.

Two registers were kept, one dealing with the semi-mechanical
occupations women might enter, and the other dealing with 'the
benevolent institutions of the country, so as to provide workers to
the one, and matrons and female officials to the other'.

After discussing openings in teaching, Miss Parkes concentrates a
good deal of attention on openings in benevolent work:

Now there is work which really clever and energetic women
are wanted to perform and which people are everywhere
beginning to say they ought to perform: all work involving
moral superintendence over women, and physical care of the
sick and infirm of both sexes.

One of the main obstacles was that apart from training in religious
orders, there was no adequate training to equip ladies to take such
posts and Miss Parkes emphasised that exceptional people such as
Florence Nightingale, Mary Carpenter and Elizabeth Blackwell
had generally received some regular kind of training. She complained:

Thus we find in every department of benevolent exertion the
want of efficient machinery for teaching those who are to help
others. And this knowledge is necessarily of two kinds—
intellectual and practical.

With a flash of insight Miss Parkes saw that training for benevolent
work could not be achieved without

receiving pupil teachers, as it were, into all our institutions, and
this can only be done by the consent and co-operation, in
many cases of Government, in all cases of the men who control
our institutions in England.

Philanthropy and higher education—Emily Davies

Miss Parkes's argument immediately connects the movement for
the education of women with the impetus towards social work as a
career for women. A more theoretical statement from the educational

viewpoint is given by Miss Emily Davies in her book *The Higher Education of Women*, published in 1866. She describes the haphazard education of young girls at home or at inferior schools, and then perhaps at a finishing college, from which, even if they were lucky enough to have had good tuition, they were removed at the age of sixteen to eighteen years, leaving an interval of at least three to four years before marriage. Miss Davies states as a general principle that (1866, p. 73)

> the education of a lady ought to mean the highest and the finest culture of the time. The accurate habits of thought and the intellectual polish by which the scholar is distinguished, ought to be no less carefully sought in the training of women than in that of men.

In thinking of the uses to which an educated woman would use her talents Miss Davies is led to give special consideration to benevolent or philanthropic work as spheres of activity, whether voluntary or paid (pp. 77–8):

> How far it may be desirable or justifiable for women to take part in political affairs is a vexed question, into which it is the less necessary here to enter, inasmuch as it is evident that the same kind of intellectual training which forms the groundwork of the education of a statesman is needed for other purposes. Women who think at all can scarcely help thinking about the condition of the poor, and to arrive at sound conclusions on so vast a subject involves an acquaintance more or less complete with almost every consideration which comes within the range of the politician. Unpaid work, such as the management of hospitals, workhouses, prisons, and reformatories, and charitable societies, naturally devolves upon the leisurely classes and offers a field in which cultivated women may fitly labour. And the moment they enter upon such work, or attempt in any way to alleviate the sufferings of the poor, they find that a strong, clear head is as necessary as a warm heart. The problem of how to deal with pauperism—the very same difficulty which has hitherto baffled the wisest of our statesmen—meets them at the threshold of their work. The encouragement or discouragement of the proper spirit depends in a great degree on the discretion of district visitors and other charitable agents; and the women who act as almoners of the rich and the advisers

B

of the poor need for their difficult task something more than gushing benevolence.

Miss Davies refers to the paid posts in workhouses, hospitals, reformatories, and penitentiaries, where the superintendence of nurses and the offices of matron and schoolmistress were already undertaken by women, but which could be developed further in all institutions where women were employed in a subordinate capacity. The general arguments she uses in favour of her cause are the wastefulness to society of keeping any class or members in idleness, and the fact that, apart from the care of infants, men do all the things that women are supposed to be generally suited for and yet remain men; women, would, therefore, not become men by doing work at present limited to men.

Josephine Butler, Octavia Hill, Mary Carpenter

All women who had an interest in the entry of women to particular professions had a uniting interest in the development of higher education of women,[11] and the development of the women's colleges in the last three decades of the century was contributed to by key figures in the development of social work. Social work then benefited from the increasing number of women educated to university standard. Josephine Butler's presidency of the North of England Council for Promoting the Higher Education of Women 1867–70 was important in helping to secure the institution of special examinations for women at Cambridge and London universities.[12] The North of England Council stimulated the growth of grammar school education for girls and in Bradford, a member of the council, substantial improvements in the middle-class education of girls occurred in the 1870s.[13] The Girls' Grammar School opened in 1875 and many of the girls who attended became future voluntary workers. They were for the most part 'daughters or wives of small businessmen or men in the professions, comfortably off with a modest household'.[14] One such woman, Margaret Law MA, became a city councillor and a JP. The Grammar School 'inculcated in its pupils a tradition of voluntary service to the community' and strongly influenced many pupils.

Octavia Hill was not an activist in the same way as Josephine Butler but nevertheless supported the development of improved education for girls. She had had much experience of finding governesses for people and was interested in the subject. Emily Davies had approached her about a petition for the extension of university examinations to girls in 1864 and Octavia replied, giving support in gathering signatures. An extract from her reply shows careful deliberation:[15]

> These like all examinations require careful and noble use; people
> must look beyond them, or they cannot look at them rightly.
> There are better things to be learnt than ever come out of an
> examination. And to work for one is dangerous; learning for
> the sake of learning and knowing is the only ultimate course,
> but a standard, that will test our knowledge at last, is
> almost invaluable. . . . But there is a still greater value in these
> examinations. Some such plan must be adopted before the
> education of our girls will improve.

Mary Carpenter, although not able to be active as a speaker, watched the progress of the movement for the higher education of women keenly. Her own excellent experience gave her an appreciation of the value of a fine education and J. Estlin Carpenter commented that[16]

> she possessed a large store of observation and experience;
> and these were always at the service of the leaders who were
> striving to carry out on a large scale principles of education
> with which she had been familiar since her earliest years.

In the last two decades of the century the establishment of women's colleges at universities was linked with settlement work, starting with the involvement of Mrs Barnett and, gradually, Octavia Hill. A further link between social work and higher education was established with the representation of heads of women's colleges on the Hospital Almoners Council before the First World War. Throughout the period there is strong evidence of the mutually supportive relationship between the development of women's education and of social work as a potential avenue of work for educated women.[17]

2 Women as innovators in social work

Creativity is not the sole prerogative of men in spite of the fact that in the fields of art, music, literature and science, it is difficult to find women who would be commonly agreed to have achieved greatness through their ability to initiate ideas or movements. In western society with its dominantly patriarchal culture the conditions under which creative discoveries are made have favoured men; we see this in their freedom from the chores of day-to-day living and their better access to education and systematic studies over a long period of years. Wealth, position and influence by themselves do not ensure creativity but can be of great importance in the transformation of ideas into action. Considerations like these would lead to the expectation that in the nineteenth century there would be little opportunity in the creation of social institutions and that where this was possible the hand of some man would not be far away.

Male creative influence in new welfare developments

In this section I shall examine the start of several branches of social work to see the relative parts played by the men and women involved. The developments I shall consider are the Charity Organisation Society, hospital alming, probation, social work with deprived children, work with delinquents, settlements, housing management, and moral welfare work.

Of these, only three—moral welfare work, housing management and social work with delinquents—owe their inception to women. All the others owe their beginning to men. The Charity Organisation Society was formed in 1869 and accounts of its beginnings are given by C. L. Mowat (1961) and Helen Bosanquet (1914). The ideas which formed the basis of organisation were presented in papers by G. M. Hicks in 1861 and by Dr Solly and Dr Hawkesley in 1868. That the new organisation had financial backing was largely due to Ruskin's £100 subscription and to the help of Lord Lichfield who provided premises. Octavia Hill was the only woman member of the first Charity Organisation Society Council. Hospital almoning was the brainchild of Charles Loch,[1] although concern about the state of medical charities had been felt for many years before the appointment of Miss Stewart, the first almoner at the Royal Free Hospital. Similarly, when we turn to the development of settlements we find the initiative being taken by Canon Barnett, who founded Toynbee Hall in 1884 and delivered a paper at Oxford in the same year describing the concept of the settlement.[2] The close relationship with the university extension movement and the influence of philosophers such as T. H. Green and Bernard Bosanquet were extremely important, and the attempts to establish a systematic political philosophy embracing the definition of the proper obligations of the state towards its individual members had its social counterpart in the attempts to realise in action the obligations of a moral system.

The probation movement is generally accepted to have been originated by Mr M. Davenport Hill, who after his experience in Warwick as recorder of Birmingham for 1841, got parents to sign in a book and initiated a system of social enquiries before release combined with supervision by the police after release. Later in 1876 it was a working printer, Frederick Rainer, who urged the Church of England Temperance Society to appoint missionaries to help those who appeared in court for the first time as the result of drink. The first missionary to be appointed was Mr G. Nelson who worked at the Southwark, Lambeth and Mansion House Courts from August 1876.[3] The establishment of probation as a statutory service owes much to Howard Vincent, who saw the workings of the probation system in Boston, Massachusetts, in 1884 and campaigned for the introduction of probation work on his return to this country. In addition the Howard Association put much pressure on successive governments to introduce an effective state service. As part of its publication activities the Howard Association brought out a book by Miss E. P. Hughes in 1903 entitled *The Probation System of America*. Miss Hughes had been a principal of a Cambridge College for women teachers, and spent the winter of 1901, part of which was spent making investigations on behalf of the Howard Association, in America. Another woman, Rosa M. Barrett, won the Howard Medal Prize Essay in 1900 with the topic 'The Treatment of Juvenile Offenders'.[4]

Social work with deprived children involved a number of organisations and each of these was initiated by a man—Dr Barnardo's, The Church of England Children's Society (Prebendary Rudolf) and the National Children's Home (Dr Stephenson); the crying need seemed to call forth a response from these men who set on foot organisations which rapidly grew in size towards the end of last century.[5] We must also note that the National Society for the Prevention of Cruelty to Children also owed its inception to a man, Benjamin Waugh,[6] following the provincial work of Frederick Agnew in Liverpool.

Female initiatives

In all these organisations the dominating initiative was from men. We now turn to the aspects of social work which owe most in their beginning to women: house property management, moral welfare, and social work with deprived children, associated with the names of Octavia Hill, Josephine Butler and Mary Carpenter.

Octavia Hill (1838–1912) came of a good family, and in spite of her father's reversal of fortunes in 1825, she belonged to the prosperous middle classes.[7] Her father's radical nature and inclination in politics, and family connections with Dr Southwood Smith and others in the progressive movement in mid-Victorian England, ensured that she was aware of important social movements during her formative years. Her lively mind and precocious ability enabled her to take an imaginative part in running a ragged school and, later, a working women's college. Belonging to a social élite which included Ruskin, her wish to become a landlord was made possible by Ruskin's generosity in making a gift from his inheritance; thus she was able to buy the three courts near Nottingham Place in 1865. We see here the great importance of male patronage in enabling the realisation of a new idea. Yet in recognising this there is no lessening of Octavia Hill's contribution to social work, but the acceptance that it would have been extremely difficult for a woman without financial means to have made a significant innovation in the development of social work.

Mary Carpenter (1807–77)[8] was the eldest child of a Unitarian minister, Dr Lant Carpenter, headmaster of a Bristol boys' school. After receiving a sound classical and scientific training at her father's school she opened a school for girls in Bristol in 1829. When the American philanthropist Dr Joseph Tuckerman visited Bristol in 1833 Mary Carpenter met him and he drew her attention to the condition of a poor boy in the city, urging that something should be done. In 1835 Mary Carpenter started a Working and Visiting Society in Bristol and remained its secretary for twenty years.

Eleven years later she began a ragged school in a Bristol slum and it was this undertaking that led her towards her most important work in establishing reformatory schools and industrial schools, and in influencing public attitudes towards the treatment of children. The results of her experience and visits to Europe were contained in two major books;[9] her public influence led to the Reformatory Schools (Youthful Offenders) Act 1854 and the Industrial Schools and Reformatory Schools Acts of 1857; the practical realisation of her ideas in action was by the founding of Kingswood School just outside Bristol in 1852. The money to buy the property for the school was given by Mr Russell Scott of Bath, who had himself visited the Rauhe Haus in Hamburg. She had a keen analytic brain but in her early years this was allied to personal shyness and intensity of religious feeling. In her middle and later life her religious commitment was as intense as ever but her work gave her immense satisfaction and personal fulfilment which led to much greater confidence in public affairs.

Born in 1828 of Northumbrian stock, daughter of John Grey of Rilston, Josephine Butler had an extremely happy childhood, being brought up on her father's country estate.[10] She enjoyed to the full the social life in the district and had a great love of animals. At the age of twenty-four she married the Rev. George Butler, then at Oxford University. She had a powerful intellect and a deep Christian commitment. When George Butler moved to Liverpool she started visiting the workhouse and prison and became well acquainted with helping women in depressing surroundings. She was concerned about the position of women in society, and in securing their access to education. She and her husband helped Anne Clough to organise university extension lectures to women in Liverpool in 1866. The following year, when Anne Clough established the North of England Council for Promoting the Higher Education of Women, Josephine Butler became president and held this position until 1870. This was because her work in opposition to the Contagious Diseases Acts had taken an increasing amount of her time, particularly after 1869. She provided the leadership for the movement which resulted in the repeal of the Contagious Diseases Acts in 1886. Although Josephine Butler was a prolific writer, the two principal books mirroring her philosophy were *Women's Work and Women's Culture* (1869) and *The Constitution Violated* (1871). Her significance for social work was not that she set on foot a particular pattern of help, because there were many penitentiaries and homes for women and girls already in existence, but that her legislative and protective aims illustrated a concern for preventive measures and embodied clear analysis of a social situation in society, rather than an unthinking provision of relief measures. She altered the whole social context within which work for women and girls was undertaken.

Contrasting approaches—Octavia Hill, Josephine Butler, Mary Carpenter

Any charitable enterprise needed support from public subscription and wherever possible support from ecclesiastical opinion; therefore committees were composed of aristocrats, businessmen and church leaders. Where women were initiators a number of preconditions were almost invariably present: strong religious commitment, leisure, and male patronage or support. These conditions were met for each of the women we have briefly mentioned and between them they represent a range of approaches to social problems. Octavia Hill emphasised work with the individual and was opposed to large-scale welfare enterprises. Generally, she steered clear of political machinations and legislation, preferring to extend the work with poor tenants, when the opportunity presented itself to purchase more houses, and when there were workers available to undertake the necessary work with tenants. In 1884 she gave an address to the Kyrle Society in which she indicated something of this attitude:[11]

> I have been asked to add a few words about the homes of the people, but what can I say? There has been so much said. Is it not better just now silently to do? If after all the talking and all the writing, you are meaning henceforward quietly and naturally to draw a few poor people as your friends, you will soon learn how to help them, and how they help you. . . . much has been said lately of Miss Octavia Hill's plan of managing homes for the poor. There is no plan in it at all . . . only somehow, if we set our desires on trying to help, and lose thought of ourselves in others, our mistakes and failings seem to sink into insignificance, and the great purpose we have at heart prospers, and little by little as the years go on steady progress is made in the outward things, and the sense of affection and relationship between us and our tenants deepens, and out of our imperfect work our Father leads us, and all we love, onward towards His own perfection.

Mary Carpenter had undertaken practical social work and also battled for legislative change, writing and speaking extensively about her work and ideas, having a foot in the active part of social work and creating a framework within which character reform could be carried out in a humane way. It would be an error to suppose that because of this Miss Carpenter had advanced views about women's position. In discussing reformatories for convicted girls Miss Carpenter was firmly of the view that girls should be prepared for domestic life at home or in the homes of 'the respectable portion of society'.[12] She maintained '. . . we must endeavour to make our reformatories such that Christian women may fearlessly seek for girls from them as servants in their own families'.

Although women should be the managers of girls' schools,
. . . they may need to be sustained by the power and business
habits of men, especially in the relation which these institutions
bear to Government. The actual working which I have
witnessed for a quarter of a century of a united committee of
gentlemen and ladies, with a sub-committee of the former
for business details, and one of the latter for domestic
management, would lead me to advise it strongly, but where
this cannot be done, everything which they can do should be
left to the lady managers; it is probable that experience will
teach them to do everything which is really necessary under
ordinary circumstances, having a gentlemen's committee
to refer to.

Thus Mary Carpenter, whilst to some extent accepting the *status quo* in terms of the roles of men and women, perceived that the roles were not inviolate and that women could do the things normally expected of men, given experience. But not all women! She did not consider that ordinary matrons or schoolmistresses, 'however excellent in their own department' could undertake full responsibility for management of the reformatory. A lady capable of understanding and interpreting the principles and intentions of the managers should live in as a superintendent or live close by.

Whereas Mary Carpenter principally involved herself in the theory and practice of child welfare and related social reform, the bulk of Josephine Butler's efforts were in championing the rights of women by altering the legislative and social framework, whether it be in removing the Contagious Diseases legislation, extending opportunities for women's education, or enabling women to vote.

B*

Her main work was carried on in her development of an international movement, but throughout it all was the assumption that women and men should co-operate on an equal basis in the family and in all other social institutions. The social aims were incorporated in her private life, and the Butlers, as did the Barnetts, demonstrated a partnership as fruitful as that of the Webbs.

These three women showed at this formative period the variety of approaches to social problems which could exist, and should sharpen our awareness of the variations in women's characters as well as uniformities. In social work, as in the women's suffrage movement, the women's education movement, and the entry of women to the medical profession, one could discern gradualists, revolutionaries and middle-ground participants.

Through looking at the origins of these different branches of social work one comes closer to understanding the development of social work in society. Where clear initiatives came from women they had private means or financial and moral support from husbands and friends. Mary Carpenter and Octavia Hill both received money from friends for their first practical projects; Josephine Butler's family was wealthy, and her marriage to George Butler consolidated her position in the upper middle class. The reasons for male dominance are not far to see. Command of public life in the nineteenth century was in their firm grasp; it was they who had the greatest access to information about social problems and the best trained minds to apply to the task of finding solutions. Exclusion from business activities denied women economic power except by inheritance and marriage. Yet skills in domestic management in their own households gave them experience in managing people, and if they had ideas and convictions they could influence the male members of their circle. This was a reactive process because of the background of religious and liberal ideals in many of the families, which produced women sensitive to the conditions of their time.

3 Women in social work organisations

Introduction

When organisations are initiated and expand, full-time staff become necessary and sooner or later paid staff. In identifying the stages of growth and professionalisation of social work, key factors are the introduction of paid staff and training. At the beginning of our period the most common contribution of women was as committee members of voluntary organisations and visiting of various kinds. It is a central hypothesis of this study that in spite of the changing position of women in society and the presumption that social work is a woman's profession, women have predominantly been the lower participants in social work organisations.

In the Charity Organisation Society it was often usual to have as a chairman a man of title, and many other members, including some of the local clergy. There was an honorary secretary and honorary treasurer; in some districts there might be sub-committees. Many women were members of hospital relief committees. The attitudes of many women involved in this way must have been very similar to that of Johanna Chandler, honorary secretary to a ladies' hospital committee in London who in the course of writing to Miss Ridley to say that her father was entitled to six recommendations commented:[1]

> but of this I am sure, helping others is the sweetest of all pleasures. When my own heart has been heavy with domestic cases, and this year has been especially trying to me owing to my dear brother's severe illness, I have found something to do for some afflicted one, and the burden has grown lighter. Just now my collection is in hand for the poor disappointed candidates after the election on the 10th, and a quantity of clothing to prepare for distressed outpatients. The thought of both seems quite to gladden me—but my words may perhaps seem only foolishness to you.
> With every sentiment of esteem, believe me
> dear madam. . . .

Not all women were active in their committees as the following letter shows later in the century. Mrs Ellen Frances Pinsent (later Dame Ellen Pinsent), honorary secretary to the NSPCC wrote to a Miss Hughes on 20 March 1896, inviting her to join the committee:[2]

NSPCC
Ladies District Committee

Dear Madam,

At the last meeting of the above committee it was proposed by Mrs Hugo Young and seconded by Mrs W. H. Ryland that you should become a member of the committee and I was requested to ask you if you would kindly consent to serve.

The chief object of the committee is the collection of funds for the NSPCC and from time to time we help to arrange an entertainment for the same purpose. Good may also be done by spreading knowledge of the society and its work. We are greatly in need of a few more *active ladies* on our committee and I trust that you will be able to give us a favourable reply.

Yours truly,

Ellen F. Pinsent, Hon. Sec.

Miss Hughes,

Don't you think you had better join the active ladies?[3]

Both these letters illustrate the possibilities of committee work in the late nineteenth century and convey a fervent application to good causes. The letter to Miss Hughes shows that the quality of committee membership was variable. We should not conclude from the lives of the charismatic women pioneers of nineteenth-century social work that all women so involved were as clear thinking, industrious, and imaginative.

The Charity Organisation Society

Yet the dominant influence on the organisational side was male. M. Rooff in her study of the Charity Organisation Society (1972) describes how in the nineteenth century it was mainly an upper middle-class foundation with eminent men in law, business and medicine giving substantial service in time and money to give this new organisation a firm footing. The first Charity Organisation Society Council was mainly a combination of aristocratic and ecclesiastical figures with Lord Lichfield taking early initiative and finding the first offices at 15 Buckingham Street; Octavia Hill was the only woman member. C. P. B. Bosanquet (secretary 1870–5) and Charles Loch (secretary 1875–1914), who were both paid, provided the main drive and purpose of the Charity Organisation Society and gave it its central importance in the development of social work. The Charity Organisation Society had twelve district offices open by 1870, thirty by 1871, and thirty-six by 1872; in 1913 there were forty-two district committees. In the provinces by 1879, eighteen provincial societies were in correspondence with the London Charity Organisation Society; in 1913, 135 societies in the United Kingdom were in correspondence with the Charity Organisation Society in London.

The fast expansion of the Charity Organisation Society led to the need for administrative ability of a high order. When Bosanquet resigned in 1875, Lord Lichfield told him that a man was needed (Helen Bosanquet, 1914, p. 51)

> whose administrative ability will enable the society to do for
> London as a whole what has already been done with so much
> success for some districts. We cannot expect to secure the
> services of such a man for less salary than the requisite
> qualifications would command in any of our government
> departments.

Six years later in 1881 the lack of men and women of leisure to engage actively in the work of the district committees had led the Charity Organisation Society to hold a special conference of honorary secretaries and district delegates to strengthen the district committees by paid superior officers if necessary (Mowat, 1961, pp. 102–3). This was agreed and Mr A. Dunn-Gardner (already assistant secretary to the council) was appointed to Hackney in 1881. The title district secretary was first used in 1883 and by 1889 there were ten district committees with district secretaries. Miss Stewart (Fulham) and Miss Sewell (Camberwell) were the only women secretaries, but in 1897 there were six women district secretaries out of fourteen. This growth of paid work both for men and women in a social work organisation was important, although very small in scale compared with the large number of voluntary committee members and visitors. It contained the seed for a growth and recognition of special skill and knowledge essential in the development of any profession.

Other ways in which women gradually became involved in welfare work were within the structure of the Poor Law, in local authorities and as inspectors.

The Poor Law: visitors and guardians

Involvement of women in the operation of the Poor Law took several forms. They visited the inmates of the workhouses, worked within workhouses and served on Boards of Guardians.[4] Visiting in the mid-nineteenth century had been sporadic at first but gradually became more structured with the formation of the Workhouse Visiting Society and the efforts of Louisa Twining. Visiting the sick women and girls in the workhouses, especially in the lying-in wards, and concern with the living arrangements within the workhouses and after care, were principal concerns of the women visitors.

It was soon realised that changes of fundamental importance could not be achieved without women's representatives on Boards of Guardians, and it became a major aim of Miss Twining and others to secure the election of women as guardians—Miss Twining had told the 1861 Select Committee on the Poor Laws that women should be elected as guardians though not suggesting that they should interfere in the 'gentlemen's province'. She brought up the matter regularly at meetings of the Social Science Association which in 1869 passed a resolution that women should have a voice in the education of children and the conditions of the sick.

An abortive attempt in 1850 by the clerk of the Ludlow Union to test a woman's eligibility for membership of the Poor Law Board had failed because of convention and reluctance of men guardians to alter precedent, in spite of there being no legal obstacle to the election of women guardians. It was not until 18 April 1875 that the first woman guardian, Miss Martha Crawford Merrington, was elected to the board of the Kensington Union. She was appointed to the workhouse visiting committee with a special responsibility to supervise the female scrubbers and washers, and also to a district relief committee. The focus of many men had centred on the inexperience and over-zealousness of some women, but Miss Merrington did her job well and was placed on the infirmary visiting committee, two schools committees and an asylum visiting committee. Westminster and St Pancras Unions appointed a woman guardian in 1876 and Wenover Union in South Wales in 1878. It was 1881 before the first married woman was elected guardian—Mrs Harriet McIlquahan in Tewkesbury—and her husband was publicly abused for letting her stand.[5] In 1881 a Society for Promoting the Return of Women as Poor Law Guardians was formed with Miss Twining as a member of council and its chief financial support.

In 1898 there were 950 women guardians (90 on metropolitan boards and the rest on provincial boards); yet there were still 383 boards without a woman on them. By 1910 there were 1,165 women guardians but still 234 boards had male members only. The Society for Promoting the Return of Women as Poor Law Guardians was dissolved in 1904 as it was considered to have achieved its aims and its papers and publications were transferred to the Women's Local Government Society of which Louisa Twining was president.

Although there had been much initial resistance to women, once women had established themselves they and their work tended to be accepted and appreciated. It is significant that their functions and achievements tended to be in areas where they were not competing with men and where women's experience of family life and domestic skills was most valuable. Ross evaluates their achievements in the following passage:[6]

> They [women guardians] worked consistently for the removal
> of children from contact with adult paupers; either through
> the use of boarding out or cottage homes or through sending
> them to local elementary schools; for the education of paupers
> nurses and the employment of trained nurses in workhouse
> sick wards and infirmaries; and for the increase in comforts for
> the aged. Their work among the female paupers was
> accomplished without the support of the Local Government
> Board Orders; they alone were responsible for rescue work, and
> for the creation of the many Workhouse Girls Aid
> Societies and Workhouse Magdalen Societies to help young
> unmarried mothers.

The women who took up work as guardians tended to be of a higher social class than the men, the wives or daughters of upper middle-class business and professional men, whereas the men tended to be drawn from the ranks of the lower middle-classes. It had not always been easy to persuade women to stand for election as many were more willing to undertake the more congenial work under the School Boards established in 1870. The Women's Local Government Society had conducted an enquiry in 1908 which revealed that of 837 women guardians surveyed, 405 were married women most of whom were eligible for election by their residential qualifications.

Whilst the women who became guardians did not seek to achieve fundamental reform of the Poor Law they, together with enlightened men, secured important advances in liberating and humanising Poor Law care for non-able-bodied paupers. In doing so another area of activity previously exclusively male had been opened to women thus contributing to the battle for emancipation. Yet it was possible to have moved forward in this direction without envisaging any fundamental change in social structure or the methods of dealing with poverty.

The Poor Law: employment under the Poor Law—institutional staff and relieving officers

Within the workhouses in the mid-nineteenth century the majority of the staff were untrained and much of the nursing was done by adult paupers themselves. Abel-Smith (1961, p. 4) describes the position as: 'In the workhouses, nearly all the nursing of the sick paupers was done by such able-bodied paupers as happened to be available. There were hardly any paid nurses until after the middle of the nineteenth century'. Later in the same study Abel-Smith describes the expansion of nursing training which took place in voluntary hospitals, but comments on the much greater difficulty in reforming the workhouses. The majority of the nursing staff would tend to be from working-class backgrounds. But increasingly during the latter part of the century there were attempts to encourage 'ladies' to take senior posts within the Poor Law.

Mrs Nassau Senior exemplifies this attitude in a letter she wrote to Mrs Hubbard on 4 October 1874 following publication of her report of which she enclosed a copy. Mrs Hubbard wrote and campaigned extensively on behalf of women's potential as employees, and edited the journal *Work and Leisure* which devoted itself to describing new developments in careers for women. The extract is as follows:[7]

At all the Meetings on Pauper Schools, except one, the Superintendent and Matron are man and wife. At Sutton the superintendent is a married man, but his wife is, I am told, mad, and Mrs Howes the matron, is a widow. As far as I can remember her salary is from £100 to £120 a year; but I gave all my statistics when my report was done, to some New York friends who wanted all the information they could get on Poor

Law matters. At the other schools, where master and matron
are married people, the salaries vary according to the size of
the school and the ideas of the guardians. But at the larger
schools the combined salaries are never less than £200 a year,
and at the smallest school the initial salary is over £100
and you must remember that salaries are clear gain. The
superintendent and matron are lodged and boarded and lighted
and warmed and washed: and so, even the smallest salary is
excellent pay. The post of school mistress would be well suited
for a lady, but of course she *must* be a certificated teacher.
The post that *I* should like better than all, would be matron
or head nurse in the Infirmary. The largest schools have
detached infirmaries. But then I positively enjoy hospital work,
and many people do not share my taste—But you may
consider that there are, in all schools, 2 places at least, in
which any lady might be perfectly happy (at least I could).
Matron, and Schoolmistress, and for big schools Matron, and
Infirmary Matron (i.e. head nurse) and Schoolmistress and
Infant Schoolmistress, and Work mistress.
For the post of infant schoolmistress a lady ought to
thoroughly understand the treatment of children—she ought,
in my opinion to have tended children herself, and she ought
to thoroughly make herself mistress of Froebels Kindergarten
system. For matron, she must be capable of keeping an eye
over *every* department of household work as she is expected
to visit each department once a day to know whether all is
going satisfactorily—she has to give out shoes and linen, or to
superintend its being given out and she has to see people
applying for servants. Of course there are many other
incidental duties. The matron of a large school, must be (if
she is to be equal to the situation), a *really* capable woman.
Then there is a delightful post in all the larger schools, Head
workmistress—her duties are to cut out or superintend the
cutting out, of all the wearing apparel, to understand sewing
machine, and patching and darning, etc. This would be a
delightful post in my opinion and would give a woman the
chance of getting great influence over the girls—for instance
in the evening there are generally 2 hours of needlework for
the elder girls before going to bed. Think what an opportunity
for good; if the work mistress knew and cared how to utilise it!
Reading aloud, teaching poetry, etc. Most ladies would not

like it I fancy but *I* should not at all object to being the 'training cook' in one of the big schools. The training cook is supposed to teach the girls in turns, how to cook in a small way. A woman of ordinary household experience, and a couple of courses at the School of Cookery would be able to fill a post splendidly. The salary is about £20 a year—but all is found and there is great opportunity for influencing the girls. *I* would not mind the post but then I don't care what I do. . . .

The letter demonstrates great insight into the appointments which the various posts describe for social work with young children in pauper schools, both for married couples and single women. Looking more broadly at workhouses the kind of attitudes in this letter must have been more widespread, for we find a leader article in *Work and Leisure* in 1888[8] stating that

> it is one of the happiest results of the greater independence and activity which prevail among educated Englishwomen that many of them now occupy posts and perform duties which it would never have occurred to the neediest of their grandmothers or great-aunts to undertake. It is a matter for public congratulation that, for instance, almost all positions of authority and superintendence in English institutions are occupied by women more or less belonging to the ruling classes, on whom the possession of power has not the disturbing effect which so often unbalances the judgements of officials who have been raised from the ranks, and who therefore can display that arrogance and want of judgement which has gained for such persons the sobriquet of 'Jacks in Office'. While far from asserting that there are not exceptions to this rule in both directions . . . we do not think we are wrong in expecting that, all else being equal, a lady will prove a more efficient head of an institution than a servant.

The leader goes on to regret that not more ladies have become matrons of workhouses in which 'vast powers for good and evil may be wielded'. In this passage the élitist view of society is presented, within which the development of social welfare based on humanitarian principles exactly mirrors the class structure in the wider society. This is exactly comparable to the position in the Charity Organisation Society in which from the earliest days paid workers, usually men of the respectable lower classes, were employed to deal with cases; they were called collectors, enquirers, or inquiry agents. Little mention was made of these working-class men in the affairs of the Charity Organisation Society and some committee's lists distinguished them from the members who were of a higher social class (Mowat, 1961, pp. 27–8).

The need and pressure for women of a higher social class to involve themselves in the workings of the Poor Law arose from the generally low quality of staff in them. It was the normal practice to appoint the wives of masters as matrons and many of them were quite unsuited to posts of responsibility, adopting attitudes of scorn and disgust towards female paupers. Thus, however much one jibs at the social and intellectual arrogance of some better-class women, there was no doubt that the recruitment of a higher class of woman held prospects of improving workhouse management as well as providing further job opportunities for middle-class women. Generally, women of better-class calibre had been recruited to hospitals and schools rather than to workhouses but Ross's study confirms that gradually some better women were appointed, particularly as school matrons, as their husbands tended to be of a higher social class (Ross, 1956, p. 234).

The appointment of women as relieving officers was slower, the first woman, Mrs Price, being appointed in 1893 in Oswestry. Her husband was a relieving officer and when he died in 1897 she was given a permanent post, but this was not accepted as a general precedent. It was 1900 before the second woman relieving officer was appointed in Suffolk, also to take the place of her late husband. At the time of the 1909 Royal Commission on the Poor Laws only three additional female appointments had been made as full relieving officers, but eight women were employed as assistants.

In reviewing the impact of women on the operation of the Poor Law, Ross[9] picks out several elements as important. First, there were the direct results of modifying the Poor Law system and its treatment of the 'deserving' non-able-bodied; there were the developments in the non-institutional upbringing of children, the care and protection of girls leaving Poor Law Schools, the rehabilitation of unmarried mothers, the training of nurses for workhouse sick wards and infirmaries, and the providing of comforts for the aged and infirm. Second, distinguishable from the day-to-day work as visitors, guardians, or officials, women 'played a major part in causing the central authority to modify its policy regarding nearly all the able bodied poor in its charge'. Thus the central authority became increasingly involved in functions other than its primary responsibility of relieving destitution. Third, 'Poor Law institutions became the training ground for many branches of social service, and in them women gained experience of great value to future generations of voluntary and professional social workers.' In the context of the career opportunity for women we can add that women's infiltration into Poor Law services, although slow, provided an expansion in paid employment opportunities. Resistance was met from men who distrusted women, but also there was difficulty in recruiting women of the right calibre. This may well be because of a feature of social welfare pointed out by Abel-Smith: 'The status of those who are caring for other people is often related to the status of the other people.'[10] Thus, at the beginning of our period those who worked in workhouses were not rated much higher than the inmates. This may be seen particularly in institutional care of all kinds where even a hundred years later staffs of hospitals for the mentally subnormal, prison, and children's homes carry a relatively low status. This applies particularly to the direct caring staff rather than the senior administrators who are cushioned from direct contact with low-status inmates except in carefully pre-scribed situations. Within the Poor Law women took on duties which used their domestic skills and experience and as happened so much in the employment sphere division of labour developed along lines dictated by sex-roles and characteristics.

Women inspectors: the Poor Law

Although the first woman inspector was within the Poor Law, it is more logical to deal with this along with the development of other inspectorial appointments of women. The first employment of women in the Civil Service had been in 1870 when women in the telegraph service became government employees following the Telegraph Act of 1869. By 1875 they were also established in the Returned Letter Office and the Savings Bank.[11] Although there had been much opposition, the principle was established and when the Local Government Board was formed in 1870 with responsibility for the administration of the Poor Law it was at least a possibility that a woman official might be of value, particularly where pauper children were concerned. Louisa Twining had long argued that women inspectors should be appointed to deal with women and children under the Poor Law and to be concerned with health and domestic arrangements. She had raised the matter in evidence to the Select Committee on Poor Relief in 1861, and the matter had been raised at a meeting for the National Association for the Promotion of Social Science in 1866.[12]

Mr James Stansfield, a man in favour of sexual equality, was made president of the Local Government Board and in 1873 he was daring enough to appoint a woman inspector to obtain a woman's point of view on the education of girls in pauper schools.[13] The woman appointed was Mrs Nassau Senior, daughter-in-law of the economist and sister of Thomas Hughes. It was an extremely unpopular appointment with the men in the department who resented bitterly a woman Poor Law inspector. Mrs Nassau Senior accordingly kept strictly to her terms of reference in looking at the physical, moral and domestic training in the schools. Her report was published in 1874, but she had to resign later through an illness which was fatal in 1877. Mrs Nassau Senior's feelings about her appointment are made clear by a further extract from the letter of 4 October 1874 to Mrs Hubbard:

> There is not the *smallest* chance of my having any 'subordinates'. If the Tories don't abolish me I shall be thankful:[14] I am quite certain that they will not put up any other woman, officially, to help me. But even if they would, you see Miss B. says that she should not like subordinate work. However, there is no sort of post connected with Local Government Board, or Poor Law Board which is now filled by a woman. I am the only woman employee. Had Liberals stayed in it might have been otherwise, after a short time. But now it will be years before there is the smallest chance of another woman being appointed to any official post.

Mrs Nassau Senior's fears were realised and it was not until 1885 when Miss M. H. Mason was appointed as a boarding-out inspector that another woman filled a similar official position. The expansion of boarding out necessitated the appointment of a second woman inspector in 1898 and a third in 1901, Miss Mason becoming the senior inspector. Miss Mason retired in 1909 and her work, reported on regularly in the reports of the Local Government Board, was widely known and had a strong influence on public opinion. Her pattern of supervision of the work of voluntary women's committees in rural areas and of inspection of foster homes created a tradition of high-quality social work and an inspectoral tradition which were to extend through the first half of the twentieth century. But although Miss Mason proved the value of women in the overseeing of boarded-out children she was not an activist in campaigning to extend the range of opportunity for women's employment in the Civil Service (Martindale, 1938, p. 34).

Miss Twining's efforts to improve Poor Law administration and the Workhouse Nursing Association had both influenced public opinion in the direction of accepting the need for a woman inspector, especially in relation to the sick wards. As a result Miss Stansfield was appointed as assistant Poor Law inspector in the metropolitan district. She worked for thirteen years as the only woman engaged in this part of the Poor Law administration. Little is known of her work, but she gave evidence to the Royal Commission on the Poor Laws and showed wide knowledge and experience in the care and treatment of women and children in Poor Law institutions. It became increasingly clear that additional female help was needed and in 1910 four fully-trained nurses were appointed as inspectors under the Local Government Board. Their duties were the inspection of Poor Law children's homes, certified homes, the administration of Poor Law institutions, particularly sick wards and separate infirmaries, and supervision of boarding-out committees. Miss Martindale describes how difficult it was for them to work as they were assistants to the men general inspectors and were dependent on them for their work. Some men resented the intrusion, others were glad to share the overall workload. But even though their workload was controlled by the men general inspectors on the district, their reports were initially sent to Miss Stansfield, who was made superintendent of women inspectors in 1910 after Miss Mason's retirement. Miss Martindale comments that[15]

> the position of the women inspectors was a difficult one, and
> in comparison with the practice adopted in some of the other
> departments, the use made of them under the Local Government
> Board was disappointing. Still the calibre of these women
> was such that their work, hampered as it was in some directions,
> cannot have been without effect. Their standards were high;
> their knowledge extensive, and their desire to improve
> conditions, which indeed needed improving, was heartfelt.

Women inspectors: prisons and reformatories

Although the proportions of men and boys in prisons and reformatories far exceeded those of women and girls it gradually became evident that women inspectors were needed. Progress was very slow because although the Rev. Sidney Turner, a prison inspector, had been given responsibility for inspecting reformatories and industrial schools in 1857, it was not until 1904 that a lady sub-inspector, Mrs H. E. Harrison, took up duties as inspector of girls' schools. Her work was valued and an additional appointment was made in 1914. Interestingly the 1913 report of the Departmental Committee on Reformatory and Industrial Schools recommended a woman should visit boys' schools as well as girls' schools.

On the prison side of the Home Office it was not until 1908 that a woman inspector was appointed. Until then all the members of the Prison Commission and inspectorate were men, in spite of the numbers of women in prison. This was fourteen years after the report of the Departmental Committee on Prisons (1894) had advised the appointment of a woman inspector who would also be responsible for female prison industry as well as general inspection of women's prisons. The recommendation did not meet with approval from the prison commissioners, who favoured an extension of voluntary philanthropic visiting by ladies and increasing the numbers of women on visiting committees and aid societies.

Women inspectors: factories[16]

With the growth of women's employment in industry there was much pressure to appoint women inspectors of factories, but it was not until 1893 that the first two women inspectors were appointed. In the 1870s and 1880s the movement had had strong support from the TUC[17] and the patronage of men such as Lord Shaftesbury, but the final impetus had been the appointment of the Royal Commission on Labour in 1891 and the appointment of four women assistant commissioners (Miss Orme, Miss Collett, Miss Abraham and Miss Irwin) to investigate women's questions in industry and produced a highly praised report. Mr Asquith, as Home Secretary, in January 1893 promised an increased factory inspectorate and in the spring of that year Miss Abraham and Miss May Patterson became the first two women factory inspectors. The men inspectors had opposed the appointments, but fortunately from the first the women inspectors were given all the powers and duties of an inspector in the field of women's trades and not made subordinate to men inspectors. By 1914 there were twenty-one women inspectors. In 1896 the women's inspectors were organised into a district branch in the factory department, and in the decade before the First World War senior posts were created and a regional form of organisation of the women inspectors was adopted.

The increased number of women in central government inspectorates was enormously important in humanising welfare services, influencing policy and ensuring that the needs of women and children were given adequate attention. It can only be regarded as a tragedy that so often they were confined in their scope of operation. In every case there was initial resistance to the introduction of women into an existing service by the men already in post. It pays tribute to the high quality of their work that government reports often singled it out for special praise. For a contemporary assessment an extract from a paper by Mrs W. P. Byles read at the 1899 International Congress of Women[18] evaluates women's achievement. After following the same sequence as H. Martindale's account she concludes with a passage dealing with training:[19]

> Long and serious study of the economic causes which have
> produced the industrial, social and physical conditions of the
> people is of the first importance. For many inspectorships
> a medical course would be a most valuable part of the training;
> and when we get, as I hope we may before long, a woman
> inspector of prisons, a knowledge of psychology, as well as
> of sociology will be necessary to her. No women are discharging
> graver, more responsible duties to society than these inspectors.
> The future legislation which is to make some of the crooked
> things straight, will be to a large extent, inspired and moulded
> by them. The organisation of industry and the homes of England
> alike in years to come will bear the impress of their insight,
> their intelligence, their devotion.

Moral welfare

Welfare work for the unmarried mother and her child already had a long history before the second half of the nineteenth century[20] with the evolution of homes—penitentiaries and refuges—for the unmarried mother and her child. Also there was the unsatisfactory care provided within the Poor Law. The attitudes of society towards unmarried mothers and the related social institution of prostitution, provide a case study of a problem group where the response of society was determined by the sex of the group. Also Christian ideals, at the heart of much of the reformative and rescue work during the nineteenth century, found a special expression in the care and treatment of fallen women and girls and the actual work of dealing with them was undertaken by respectable women.

In London and the other expanding cities prostitution was rife, and the rapid growth of rescue homes during the middle years of the nineteenth century led to an increasing awareness of the need for co-ordination. In 1851 the Church Penitentiary Association was formed and in 1856 the Reformatory and Refuge Union came into being. This latter body established a Female Penitentiaries Special Fund in 1858 to promote rescue work in homes and to help women and girls in need. Under the title of the Female Mission to the Fallen, street missionaries were appointed, and accommodation for mothers with their babies provided. The paid women missionaries were each responsible for an area of London, under the general direction of a 'lady supervisor'; the missioners provided tracts and talked kindly to the women they sought out, giving advice on where to find shelter or employment 'in service'.

This remained the pattern of provision in the 1860s and 1870s, but during the last two decades of the century the work became organised on a more structured basis within the diocesan framework and gradually dioceses began to appoint women organising secretaries for preventive and rescue work—London and St Albans in 1890 and Rochester in 1894. As the work grew and developed beyond the aim of saving souls, there was a growing pressure for training, particularly as women in poor background and quality were finding their way into the work. Most new workers were simply attached to experienced workers, whether in the rescue homes or on the streets, but in 1898 St Agnes' House was opened in London, as the Central House of the Order of Divine Compassion and as a training home for students. In 1911 this was followed by the training scheme at St Monica's in Liverpool by Miss J. E. Higson who was the worker in charge of the refuge and the first organising secretary in the Liverpool diocese.

How the rescue work of women developed at a provincial centre has been described by J. C. Scott in her account of women's organisations in Bradford (1970). A Female Refuge was founded in 1860, which eventually closed in the 1870s. Later, in 1885, a Refuge for Women was established and remained open till 1904 when it closed through financial difficulties. The ninth annual report commented: 'The Committee feel that this is peculiarly a woman's mission. It is a woman's hand in its gentle tenderness which alone can reach those who have been taught to distrust mankind.'[21]

The régime at the refuge was based on a strict daily routine of work, worship, and educational activities, but quite a number of women spent time with the girls, reading with them, singing, playing games or simply talking. Two years after the Women's Refuge closed a church committee for rescue work was formed. Thirty-four ladies and ten gentlemen formed themselves into a working committee with the aim of raising money to employ a lady member and to buy premises for girls in need of shelter and help.[22] Later the committee was reformed into an executive committee of fifteen women and two men and the Bradford Church Committee appointed Miss Sara Sharp as paid worker at the salary of £40 per annum. Miss Sharp's sister, who was a doctor, provided medical services for the committee. The welfare work involved finding accommodation for unmarried mothers, dealing with the courts over paternity and maintenance, securing medical help, and giving lectures to senior girls' schools on purity.

In addition to the work of rescue, preventive help was given in Bradford by the Ladies Association for the Care of Friendless Girls (1881–1910) and the Women's Home and Shelter, established in 1893 because of the problems of vagrancy. The membership of the committees of these and other women's organisations was extremely stable, both married and single women contributing their services.

Alongside the work of reclamation and reformation was the battle to alter social attitudes being undertaken by Josephine Butler and Ellice Hopkins. Although both these women accepted the usefulness of immediate help to women and girls who were victims of prostitution, their energies were channelled into prevention, which in this case meant the changing of fundamental attitudes:[23]

> Their concern was a more radical one, the creation of a society
> with a single moral standard for both men and women, and
> closely allied to this a legal and judicial system which should
> be impartial as between the sexes.

They were also concerned with humanising the treatment of 'fallen women' which was often severe and uncompromising; the fragmented structure of provision with many small committees caused wide variations in standards.

Josephine Butler's campaign against the Contagious Diseases Acts has already been referred to. Ellice Hopkins,[24] under the influence of Dr James Hinton, devoted her life to campaigning for improved moral standards and legislative changes. Her efforts led to the formation of the Church of England Purity Society and the White Cross Army in 1883; the two organisations were amalgamated into the White Cross League in 1891. The aim of the movement, which attracted large numbers of men, was to cultivate high moral standards and a respect for women. Her propaganda work was combined with a practical involvement in the founding of Associations for the Care of Friendless Girls in the larger towns, whose work was similar in outlook to the Metropolitan Association for Befriending Young Servants.

Within the beginnings of the moral welfare movement one can distinguish the process of voluntary committee work and visiting gradually being supplemented by paid visitors and organising secretaries. Religious commitment was a vital motivation, revealing, however, an ambivalence in action, leading to reprobation and severity as well as kindness and friendly advice. As the work expanded so the first efforts at providing training germinated. The legislative reforms and attitude changes which Josephine Butler and Ellice Hopkins fought for demonstrated a stage in dealing with social problems of large-scale shifts in social values, rather than palliative measures. Yet it is extremely doubtful whether either of them would have espoused the Marxian analysis which was in many ways similar to their own. *The Communist Manifesto* analysed the situation thus: 'Our Bourgeois, not content with having the wives and daughters of their proletarians at their disposal, not to speak of common prostitutes, take the greatest pleasure in seducing each other's wives.'[25] The communist critique which would have taken the causative nexus one step back, to economic relationships rather than moral ones, was not appreciated and because of its anti-religious tenets was not welcome in a church-based movement. Apart from the propaganda work of the White Cross League, and some help on committees, the practical work of helping women and girls was in the hands of women. Those who had 'fallen' should be kept at a distance from the sex which had wronged them, reformed, and ultimately find a position of service suitable to their class.

Almoning

The development of almoning has a special interest for the historian looking at the evolution of social work by being an exclusively women's career. Loch's imaginative mind had become aware of the disarray of medical charities in voluntary charities and also the problems of meeting patients' social and material needs if medical treatment was to be fully effective.[26] The confusion of medical charities was attacked by the launching of the Metropolitan Provident Dispensaries Association in 1879, independent of the Charity Organisation Society and with Sir Charles Trevellyan playing a large part in its founding (Mowat, 1961, pp. 60–1). The attention to individual social needs was met by the appointment of Miss Stewart to the Royal Free Hospital in October 1895. One of Miss Stewart's early priorities was training and by 1898 St George's Hospital had appointed an almoner trained in this way and by 1902 the Westminster Hospital had also appointed an almoner (Young and Ashton, 1956, p. 109). Development was slow because every appointment had to be the result of convincing hospitals of the need for this kind of appointment, even though the results of existing almoning work were encouraging.

The connection with the Charity Organisation Society was close. Almoning inherited the tradition of social work within the Charity Organisation Society and one of their main functions was to prevent abuse of medical services and to distinguish the deserving from the undeserving.[27]. Because of the incidence of poverty it was natural that the work of the almoner should be related to the problems of paying for medical treatment:[28]

> The far-spreading abuse of hospitals is a fact too well known to need comment. For a long number of years the public has become aware that funds given for this form of charity have been constantly spent on patients totally unsuitable for charitable relief in any form; and that the patients who most need medical relief fail to benefit because their home circumstances are such that it is impossible for them to carry out the doctor's recommendations.

In 1901 the Charity Organisation Society had advised the district committees to do friendly visiting and inquiry on behalf of almoners to verify the patients' statements.[29] Thus the almoners were placed in an institutional setting and their function was largely determined by this—that is, to support the efficient working of the hospital as a whole by forming a link between hospital and the community. Their status depended on the attitudes of the medical profession and the characteristics of the women almoners. Like many other charitable organisations the almoners needed to have the blessing of the traditional establishment, and the composition of the vice-presidents to the first Hospital Almoner's Council reflects this. The vice-presidents were:[30]

Bishop of London	Sir Frederick Milner Bart
Bishop of Southwark	Sir Edward Bradbrook CB
Lord Elcher	Sir William Dennet KC VC
Earl of Stamford	Sir William Watson Cheyne
	Bart CB
James Goodhart esq MD FRCP	Mrs Scharlieb MD
Thomas Eden MD	

Thus only one woman was a vice-president. However the members of the Hospital Almoner's Council were more balanced although both the chairman and the secretary were men:

Chas. Gray esq MD (chairman)	Miss Richmond
Mrs Eden	D. R. Thorne esq
Miss Mudd	E. J. Urwick esq
Miss Cummins	Captain A. S. Morse (secretary)

To become established almoners needed the patronage and support of the medical profession. Unlike the Charity Organisation Society which could raise funds and establish itself, in new districts or towns the expansion of almoning depended on the willingness of voluntary hospitals and doctors to employ them. The almoners had proved their value to doctors and to be acceptable colleagues to them. Miss Brummel was gratified by the 'kindness and courtesy of the medical staff'[31] and it is clear that the first group of almoners were 'a carefully chosen and closely knit group of women, powerful in personality, able in administration and planning and, above all, prowess in social work' (Cherry Morris, 1955, p. 86).

They had organised themselves into the Hospital Almoners Association in 1903 and established the Institute of Hospital Almoners in 1907. It was this latter body which was responsible for recruiting and training almoners and they expected the women they recruited to possess many qualities:[32]

It is essential that an Almoner should be a woman of sound judgement, tact and discrimination. The successful supervision of an out-patient department, the establishment of satisfactory relationships with charitable bodies outside the hospital, the

maintenence of a good understanding with the managers and
staff of the hospital itself, all these call for a variety of
qualities not always found in combination.

These qualities, it might be thought, would be best found in 'ladies'
and thus would cut out many applicants. In the institute's first year,
of fifty-eight candidates given information, twenty-four did not
proceed; of the thirty-four who did eighteen were unsuitable; of
the sixteen accepted five were appointed to hospitals, three were
adversely reported on during training, three withdrew and five were
still training.[33]

Interest in the movement was widespread in the year before the
First World War and there was a heavy demand for speakers on
the subject of almoners' work from women's colleges and charitable
bodies all over the country.[34] Thus the slow spread of the employment of almoners (it was only in 1910 that Miss Mudd was appointed
almoner in Leeds, the first provincial city to employ an almoner)
must be explained by the slow process of converting each individual
hospital and its doctors and the short supply of almoners with their
high standards for admission to training; even in 1914, of forty-five
women interviewed only twenty were accepted for training.[35] Fees
had risen as well. Only women of independent means could be in a
position to undertake training and it was even more the case by
1913 when the fees were twenty guineas compared with five guineas
at the start.

The emergence of almoning was an important development in
that from the start it was a paid career for women in contrast to
much of the visiting of prisons, poor law institutions and hospitals.
It was not an administrative post in the sense that held good for the
paid secretaries in the Charity Organisation Society even though a
good deal of administration was necessary. It also posed all the
problems of social work practised in an institutional setting whose
main function was different from social work; we are still grappling
with the difficulties of locating social workers in prisons, children's
homes and schools. The basic precondition of success was accept-
ability to the existing hierarchy in this case of the male-dominated
medical profession and the hospital structure. It was the almoner's
task to ensure that the doctor's directions were not thwarted because
of the patients' home circumstances and that the hospital's facilities
were not abused. Preoccupation with financial and material matters
was necessary because the hospitals were voluntary and charged

fees; with the level of poverty so high it was not surprising that almoners in out-patient departments concentrated on ensuring that the benefits of medical treatment were not lost through unfortunate social circumstances. It was not until the passing of the 1911 National Insurance Act that the possibilities of shifting the emphasis emerged. But the almoners were clear about their institutional role and recognised 'that whatever effect the National Insurance Bill may have, the problem of the outpatient department will remain to be faced, and there will be the same necessity for its supervision and control'.[36]

By this time, almoning was spreading internationally, particularly in the USA where Dr Cabot greatly assisted the development of the work there by his writings and fervent advocacy. Dr Cabot introduced medical social service at the Massachusetts General Hospital in 1905. The developments in America differed from those in England in that before 1905 the impetus had been closely associated with experience of voluntary and paid family visiting, particularly of mothers with young children.[37] A further difference was that many of the almoners in America were drawn from the nursing profession, whereas this seems not to have happened in England. Nevertheless, there were similarities in that the same process of gaining acceptance from the medical profession was gone through: Lubove writes: 'In the critical first two decades, when medical social work laboured to define its place in the hospital hierarchy, its survival depended upon the prestige and power of sympathetic physicians and administrators'.[38]

Probation[39]

The male propensity for crime compared with women meant that following the appointment of the first police court missionary in 1876 it was several years before the first woman was appointed and that their number has always been far less than that of men. By 1910 the number of male police court missionaries had increased to a hundred with an additional nine missionary women. The first woman seems to have been appointed in Liverpool in 1884 after the Liverpool Society reported to the Church of England Temperance Society the need for a woman worker in the court. In London the first woman was appointed in 1886. The Liverpool Society had justified the need for a woman worker in the following way:[40]

> The sad increase in drunkenness amongst women, testified to
> by all the police statistics of the country, makes it absolutely

necessary that the Society should extend its work amongst
our female population, and the council have decided to ask
for such an increase to their funds as will allow of their
appointing a lady . . . to engage in Rescue Work, believing
that women will best be reached by their own sex.

The Probation of Offenders Act 1907 strengthened the work of
the police court missionaries who were generally appointed probation officers to the courts under this Act. The Act consolidated the
earlier Summary Jurisdiction Act 1879, the Probation of Offenders
Act 1887 and the Youthful Offenders Act 1901. Section 5.3(2)
of the 1907 Act encouraged the appointment of special children's
officers 'where circumstances permit' and two appointments were
made, both women. Miss Ivimy and Miss Croker King were ladies
of independent means and received a part-time salary. They were
working in London, but the appointment of special officers did
not spread quickly either in London or the provinces. In 1910 Miss
Ivimy changed to full-time work and received £200 a year, much
more than male missionaries at the time. This was an anomaly
which was rectified later; even at the time ordinary women missionaries would not have received such a salary. It seems to have been
accepted that women missionaries should deal with women, girls
and young boys, but the Act was very unevenly implemented and
there were many courts without the services of a woman probation
officer. Another feature was the debate about voluntary and paid
court work. The large number of part-time appointments, the fee
system and the close links with voluntary effort in the past militated
against a fast growth of professionalism in the service.

Nevertheless, the extent and growth of the probation service led
to the formation of the National Association of Probation Officers
in 1912. Conferences had been held in Croydon for two or three
years previously and the Town Hall at Croydon was the venue for
the inaugural meeting on 22 May 1912. The meeting was addressed
by Mr S. G. Edridge who pointed out the necessity for the formation
of an association of probation officers.[41] An association was formed
and a provisional committee elected with Mr Edridge as chairman
and most of the committee members from London. When the
elections were held in December 1912 the committee remained
substantially the same. Mr Edridge was elected chairman, the other
officers also being men. The president was the Right Hon. the Earl
of Lytham. But there were four women out of the executive com-

mittee of sixteen, two of them married (Mrs Carey, Mrs Curtis) and two of them single (Miss Ivimy and Miss Lance). This was a significant contrast to the almoning departments where all the women involved were single. In the following year Mrs Curtis was elected to be a member of a team of three who were to give evidence at the Home Office's Enquiry with Regard to the Remuneration of Probation Officers, and Mrs Carey, and four men, as a member of a Journal Sub-Committee. In 1914 Miss Ivimy was appointed secretary of a sub-committee to be formed to deal with children's work.

It is interesting that the first appointment of a woman as secretary of a professional sub-committee, should have been related to work with children. In probation from the beginning there existed a division of labour based on sexual characteristics. Women probation officers would deal with women, older girls and young children whilst men would deal with men and youths. However, there were not enough women probation officers and Miss C. Matheson, a Birmingham settlement warden, when talking to a meeting of the Birmingham branch of the National Union of Women Workers, expressed the need for 'more women probation officers and women police to attend certain cases'.[42]

An indication of women's role in the court in a voluntary capacity is given by an account of an experiment in Cambridge started in January 1913.[43] Mrs Hutchinson and a friend had felt it unsatisfactory that

women when on trial, or when called as witnesses in police
or law courts, should not only be without one of their own sex
in the court; but should also be without one of their own sex
in the court during their trial or examination.

The two women gathered a group of eighteen women who were prepared to take their turn in daily attendance at the town's courts; the work was carried out as a part of the Vigilance Sub-Committee of the Cambridge branch of the National Union of Women Workers. The aims were fourfold:

  (i) To give support to women by our presence in court
 (ii) Incidentally to help individual cases
(iii) To watch the local administration of the law as it affects women and children
(iv) To watch the procedure of the law as it affects women and children

c

The women volunteers involved passed women on to other agencies if available, and only gave assistance if none other was possible. Nevertheless, they were asked to talk with women prisoners, help girls with affiliation orders and to visit women after release from prison—exactly the problems which women missioners would tackle if serving a court.

In probation, therefore, we may note several distinctive features in the early stages. There was not the same degree of aristocratic patronage as within the Charity Organisation Society and almoning. Male probation officers relied on their work for their living and from the start of their professional association were keenly interested in salaries. They were not generally from the upper class themselves and likewise the women do not seem to have been 'ladies'. The extension of their service in relation to the courts was reinforced by legislation, whereas there was no such impetus to almoning within the voluntary hospital system or to the Charity Organisation Society as a voluntary community agency.[44] Women were accepted from the start but, as in the inspectorates, certain areas of activity stemming from social attitudes towards sex were prescribed for them. In a situation of overall shortage of probation officers it was natural that they should undertake exclusively work their sex equipped them best to deal with. Within the professional association women were active from the beginning but were encouraged particularly to concentrate on aspects of the work they were dealing with practically.

Settlements

Attlee, looking back at the development of the settlement movement in 1920,[45] and himself having participated in the movement commented that it

> may be said to have opened a new era in social service, with
> the conception of originators that the chief thing needfull was
> not the mere giving of relief, but an active sympathy and
> co-operation between classes that could only be gained by the
> well to do going down to the districts where the poor
> congregated and getting to know them as friends and neighbours.

Canon Barnett's experience as a parish priest in St Jude's, Whitechapel had convinced him that[46]

> The poor need more than food: they need the knowledge,

the character, the happiness which is the Gift of God to this age. The age has received His best gifts, but their blessings have fallen mostly on the side of the rich.

Barnett's close contact with Octavia Hill, one of whose assistant workers, Miss Rowlands, he married in 1873, and his knowledge of the Charity Organisation Society and other relief organisations, led him to give out a *cri de coeur* at the inadequacy of scientific charity to solve the problems of the poor:[47]

> Thus it is that the poor miss the best things (e.g. travel, knowledge), and those who have cared for them are not content with the hope offered by 'scientific charity'. They see that the best things might be common, and they cannot stand aside and do nothing . . . No theory of progress, no proof that many individuals among the poor have become rich, will satisfy them; they simply face the fact that in the richest country of the world the great mass of their countrymen live without the knowledge, the character and the fullness of life which is the best gift to this age, and that some thousands either beg for their daily bread or live in anxious misery about a wretched existence. What can they do which revolutions, which missions, and which money have not done?

It was as a reply to this question that Barnett evolved the idea of a college mission. He wanted the university to share its cultural riches with the poor by its members living in poor areas, befriending the inhabitants and running extension classes and other cultural activities. Its conception was a complement to and not a complete alternative to charity, but in the long term Barnett argued that a settlement could contribute to the solution of poverty in a different way:[48]

> In-as-much, though, as poverty—poverty in its large sense including poverty of the knowledge of God and man—is largely due to a division of classes, a university settlement does provide a remedy which goes deeper than that provided by popular philanthropy . . . I am afraid that it is long before we can expect the rich and poor again to live as neighbours: for good or ill they have been divided, and other means must, for the moment be found for making common the property of knowledge. One such means is the university settlement.

Barnett conceived the settlement as being run by a man who would be paid by a university college:[49]

> He must have a good degree, be qualified to teach and be endowed with the enthusiasm of humanity. Such men are not hard to find. One of these, qualified by training to teach, qualified by character to organise and command, qualified by disposition to make friends with all sorts of men, would gladly accept a position in which he could both earn a livelihood and fulfil his calling; he would be the centre of the University Settlement.

But although Barnett had originally conceived the settlement ideal as for men, the steadily growing movement for the entry of women to higher education, made the concept equally applicable to women. Helped by the influence of Mrs Barnett,[50] following the admission of women to all classes at Cambridge in 1889, the Women's Settlement at Nelson Square was established in 1887. The value of settlement work was quickly recognised and many other settlements were established: Caius in 1887, St Hilda's for women in 1889, Mansfield House 1890, Bermondsey Settlement 1891, Canning Town 1892, Browning Hall 1895, Cambridge House 1896, and Passmore Edwards 1896. Attlee in 1920 listed twenty-four women's or mixed settlements in London and the provinces.[51] In America settlements were established on a larger scale. Jane Addams had visited the Barnetts, initially in 1887, and again in 1889, and from their inspiration established 'that most wonderful of all settlements, Hull House, where men and women work together'.[52]

By the time Barnett died in 1913 it was estimated that there were four hundred settlements in the USA. Jane Addams's work itself became internationally renowned and, although administration and social reform increasingly took her time in the early years, she engaged in domestic work and helped to tend babies.[53]

The happy collaboration of Mr and Mrs Barnett was itself an example of the potential creativity of men and women working together in social work. Mrs Barnett managed Toynbee Hall for seventeen years, even though on three occasions the male settlement residents formed their own management sub-committee, asking her on each occasion to take on the job again. Mrs Barnett commented: 'But men—young men especially—always think that the male brain can accomplish everything better than the female brain. . . .'[54] She herself exercised a civilising influence on bachelor lives and her partnership with her husband showed an ideal of married life which many may never before have experienced. Both she and her husband wrote prolifically about social work, reform and socialism, but were financially secure enough to refuse a salary for their work at Toynbee Hall. Their social circle was wide and they delighted in giving dinner parties with contrasting personalities and beliefs; simple fare was served 'so that none should be embarrassed'. Guests included Mr Jowett, James Russell Lowell, Henry Ward, Mr Asquith, H. H. Stanley, Mark Wilks, Walter Besant, Dr Abbott, the Duke of Devonshire, Tom Mann, Herbert Spencer, William Morris, Ernest Hart, Ben Tillott, Lady Battersea, John Burns, Lord Croachen, Frederick Rodgers, Lord Bryce, Octavia Hill and Emma Cons.

Alongside her work in the settlement movement and for socialism, Mrs Barnett engaged in social work with women and girls. She played a central part in the formation of the Metropolitan Association for Befriending Young Servants in 1877, and had arranged classes for women and girls in Whitechapel. From 1875 to 1897 she was a member of the Board of Managers for District Schools and had helped with women and girls in the Poor Law infirmaries. In 1894 she was the only woman appointed as a member of the departmental committee 'to inquire into the conditions of Poor Law Schools' and worked hard for two years gathering evidence and helping to prepare the report of 1896 (the Mundella Report). That same year Mrs Barnett helped to found the State Children's Association and became its honorary secretary. She was a campaigner against the large barrack schools and for the introduction of scattered homes; related to this she was in favour of more women inspectors being appointed.

Within the settlement movement the women's settlements differed from the men's. For the men who were resident, settlement experience was a broadening-of-life experience to be brought to bear in other careers, whether the church, law, business or politics. For many of the women it was a training for social work, whether in a voluntary or paid capacity. The range of activities was large. For instance, in the Birmingham Women's Settlement in 1910 activities included: Mothers' Guild (health, hygiene, sewing, etc.); kindergarten; children's care committee; employment registry; play hours for children; youth activities; women's social.[55] The women's settlements had brought the idea of the whole-time service for residents which had made possible the training developments which emerged and led to the collaboration in training with the Charity Organisation Society in the last decade of the century. Women's settlements saw their training function as an important addition to the ideals of Barnett but this did not always meet with approval. E. J. Urwick, in an article in 1903, observed that short-term voluntary work, which he particularly ascribed to women's settlements, 'tends to destroy the settlement proper, and to substitute for it a training college'. He continues:

> I do not think it unfair to say that most women's settlements ought to be called by the latter name and not the former. I don't say that they are therefore inferior—the object may be as good or better—only it is something quite different from the object of a settlement. It is to be noted further, that the training idea is likely to occupy a much more important part in a women's settlement than a men's. In the latter (this, by the way, is very dangerous ground) there is possibly less need for specific training. I do not know whether this is due to constant discussion of theory and practice in social, political and charitable matters, or to a more general familiarity with economic principles or to more arrogant self-confidence among the men.

Also Urwick was not impressed by the many organised activities of the women's settlements but pleaded for an ideal of 'undifferentiated helpfulness' as a settlement's aim.

Barnett was in favour of women's suffrage and the full participation of women in public life; he had canvassed to get Dr Elizabeth Garrett Anderson on to the first School Board in 1870 and wanted the removal of all legal restrictions on the occupations and voting powers of women. Yet when he wanted to bring men closely together he believed in excluding women on the grounds that they were too distracting for themselves and the men; thus the pals parties (of settlement members) consisted of men only. Yet this was a slight aberration compared with his overall attitudes to women, and the partnership between him and his wife reflected the wider relationship of men and women in England where they were both working for social improvement and also women's rights—George and Josephine Butler were another such pair.

Mrs Barnett's strong and independent mind conflicted with Octavia Hill's approach even before her meeting with Barnett; the contemporary critique of social casework by sociologists is condensed in some remarks of Mrs Barnett's about Octavia Hill (1921, p. 30):

> She [Octavia Hill] was strongwilled—some thought selfwilled—but the strong will was never used for self. She was impatient in little things, persistent with long suffering in big ones; often dictatorial in manner but humble to self effacement for those she loved or admired. She had high standards for everyone, for herself ruthlessly exalted ones, and she dealt out disapprobation and often scorn, to those who fell below her standards for them, but she somewhat erred in sympathy by urging them to attain her standards for them, instead of their own for themselves. 'His standard is only getting drunk once a week instead of every day. Let us begin on that' I once said to her of one of the tenants of Barnett's Court where I was the volunteer and inefficient rent collector; whereupon she scorned me. On the other hand I thought that her demands for the surroundings of her tenants were not high enough. She expected the degraded people to live in disreputable surroundings, until they proved themselves worthy of better ones, whereas it can be argued that for most folk, decent environment is essential to the promotion of decent life.

Although Mrs Barnett advocated a more radical approach to social reform than Octavia Hill, both women were conscious of the dangers of officialdom in organisations in the face of the bleakness of much Poor Law provision. As the Metropolitan Association for Befriending Young Servants grew, Mrs Barnett, 'fearful lest friendship should be lost in officialdom', decided to hand over each year's girls to two ladies who would befriend them, with guidance and support from the full-time organiser, Miss Townsend. Nevertheless, advocacy of state pensions and development of other state help were an essential part of the Barnett's philosophy. The need for the transfer of the Poor Law functions to local authorities was a long-held conviction which they were pleased to see in both the 'Minority' and 'Majority' reports in 1909. If Mrs Barnett had been a member of the Royal Commission on the Poor Laws she would have supported the 'Minority Report' approach but might have had a more integrative effect than Beatrice Webb.[56] She tells how her husband, having refused an invitation to serve as a member of the commission, took a keen interest in the commission's reports and emphasised the common factors in them.

The realisation of the settlement idea brought two major contributions to social work of the pre-1914 period. There was first the theoretical standpoint, as valid today as then, that ultimately separation of classes and changes of attitude towards people in another class can only be broken down by constructive social contact not of the one-way relief kind. How important this was for the social development of this country is immeasurable. Without the settlements in their pioneering period many statesmen and civil servants would never have come into contact with ordinary people or had their thinking shaped by the social conditions they saw from the settlement base.[57] The second contribution was a further development of the district social work approach exemplified in the district organisation of the Charity Organisation Society. Settlements could be viewed as a new technique, offering the opportunity for greater awareness of community and neighbourhood needs and for the location of a range of services at an accessible point in the community. A major problem, as already indicated, was that of a tension between the latter aspect of settlements, tending towards professionalisation of workers and training, and the former, which emphasised neighbourly help. This tension expressed itself in the divergent development of men's and women's settlements. The men's settlements indirectly provide supporting evidence that men of good social standing would only enter social work in an organising capacity, or as members of committees, whereas many of the women in settlements had in view some area of social service as a career, thus giving the women's settlements their distinctive association with social-work training. In London and some of the major provincial towns the women's settlement, university Social Studies Department, and local Charity Organisation Society formed a triple alliance in the battle to develop an adequate training for social work.

4   Women and social work education

The creation of any social work organisation, whether in residential institutions or for individual families in the community entails eventually some systematic training. The picture we have of the third quarter of last century is of a large number of voluntary workers, mainly women, who were mainly occupied with disbursing relief. We find written of voluntary workers in the East End of London at this time:[1]

> The great number of East End Clergy have converted themselves into relieving officers. Sums of enormous magnitude are collected annually and dispersed by them either personally or through district visitors, nine-tenths of whom are women, and the bulk ignorant and silly women.

When more purposive visiting was started by Octavia Hill in 1864 with her rent-collecting activities she began to teach new recruits her methods. Similarly in her work of the Women's Settlement at Southwark Miss Margaret Sewell saw the need for training new recruits, particularly through the medium of group instruction and lectures. These two women joined forces in 1890 and more systematic training for settlement workers and rent collectors was given by lectures at the settlement and practical work in either of these two settings.[2]

The need for training—Charity Organisation Society concern and policy

Concern over the training of visitors in the Charity Organisation Society was apparent very early in the life of the organisation and was a matter for discussion amongst the staff and district committee members. This may be illustrated by an anonymous correspondent's views in a letter to the *Charity Organisation Review*, 1 March 1877. After saying that an inexperienced visitor needs to have a specific object and should not have to bear the responsibility of making decisions about relief to make a safe beginning, the letter proposes the following system of training:

57

These conditions would be realised if the District Committees of the Charity Organisation Society would associate with themselves ladies or visitors. These might in some instances be found working already in the District, in connection with the Clergy and other agencies. Whenever a case had been taken down at the office a 'visitor' would be told off to attend to it. Resident visitors might, if they preferred it, take charge of a particular spot, but to assign cases to visitors in rotation would secure a better distribution of work. A combination however of both methods would very likely to be found desirable. There would be no vague, formal, objectless visiting. The visitor would acquaint herself at the office with all that was known about the applicant; she would visit the latter with the definite purpose of talking about the application; she would, when possible be the instrument for carrying out the decision of the committee; she would keep up her acquaintance with the family, she would get gradually to know other persons in the house, the court, the street; she would activate friendly relations with all whom she found working amongst the poor, and thus she would form a connecting link of a pleasant sort between the Committee and other agencies, with which at present the Society has little to do. At the same time she would be a member or associate, without vote, of the Committee and thus by occasional attendances learn its principles without becoming responsible for its action.

In this manner a body of trained visitors would gradually be formed able in turn to train others and thus preparing the way for the ultimate institution of that house visitation which, I believe, under present circumstances, to be inexpedient; and which is, on a large scale impossible.

This letter shows the difficulties of the Charity Organisation Society in providing training and the apprenticeship ideal. It also demonstrates that the visitors were of lower status than the committees, most of whom had men as chairmen. It was out of this kind of preliminary thinking about the organisation and structure of district visiting that much of the later Charity Organisation Society training policies developed. Thus in the 1890s the district committees were heavily involved in the training of voluntary social workers. After Miss Dunn Gardner's paper in November 1894, read to the Charity Organisation Society Council, emphasising the need for training and suggesting methods of practical work training, a joint lecture committee was established in 1896 with representatives from the Women's Varsity Settlement, the National Union of Women Workers and the Charity Organisation Society. The first series of lectures was delivered by Miss Sewell and Miss Miranda Hill, followed by Miss Sophia Lonsdale, Miss Bannatyne and Miss Sharpley, who was the first paid lecturer. In June 1897 the Charity Organisation Society had set up its own special committee on training, which submitted its first report in December 1898, relying heavily on the thinking of Miss Dunn Gardner's paper and suggesting that the society should become the basis of a university training. However, the existing organisation of this first formalised course of training did not lead directly to the development of a university training. Although lectures were given in some of the outer London districts, the structure was concentrated in London and when the idea of extending a pattern of training beyond London was being floated the Women's University Settlement withdrew from the joint lectures committee which was disbanded in 1901.

Tension between the Charity Organisation Society and university courses

The problem was to find a form of organisation which would not leave the control of the courses with the Charity Organisation Society, which would be too narrowly based, and would not leave the university solely in control, which might make courses too academic. Members of the Charity Organisation Society having nurtured the delicate seed of social work education so far were reluctant to leave it to the care of unsympathetic hands. The Charity Organisation Society Special Committee on Training, formed in 1897, had only had one woman member, Miss Bruce. But the lecturing was fairly evenly spread between men and women, the latter tending to concentrate on the teaching of social work method and on provisions relating to children, thus establishing a pattern which still persists to some extent. The honorary secretary of the joint lectures committee was Mrs G. F. Hill who 'seems to have devoted an immense amount of time and work to the cause of training social workers' (Smith, 1965).

Nevertheless, the move towards the university was promoted from within the Charity Organisation Society with Charles Loch as the initiator, with slightly different results in London and Liverpool.

Some university members were circularised in 1901 inviting them to become members of a general committee to extend lectures and for universities and agencies to combine in establishing a pattern of social education for social workers. The Charity Organisation Society formed a new 'Special Committee on Social Education' and in October 1902 convened a conference to discuss the whole question at which were several university members. Professor A. Marshall delivered the opening paper on 'Economic Teaching at the Universities in Relation to Public Well Being'. This left the universities' door open, but did not give a positive welcome to practical social work training only emphasising that there[3]

> is a need for a larger number of sympathetic students, who have
> studied working class problems in a scientific spirit, and who,
> in later years, when their knowledge of life is deeper, and their
> sense of proportion is more disciplined, will be qualified to
> go to the root of the urgent social issues of the day, and to
> lay bare the ultimate as well as the immediate results of
> plausible proposals for social reform.

In the end the reluctance of university members such as Professor Chapman (Manchester) and Professor Foxglove (Cambridge) to have anything to do with practical social issues combined with the wishes of those like Mr Medd (who wanted a School of Social Work such as that at Amsterdam) to induce support for an independent trust leaving the issue unsettled. Miss Sewell, who had withdrawn from the original joint lectures committee herself, made a strong plea for the combination of theory and practice. She referred (Smith, 1965, p. 43)

> to her personal experience as a student at Newnham and as
> Warden of the Women's Settlement in Southwark. There was
> an increasing number of women with leisure and sympathy who
> were anxious to do really useful social work, and would
> welcome opportunity of fitting themselves for it, not only by
> economic study but also by practical training under experienced
> workers. It was essential to combine theoretical and practical
> r aining.

The issue was not just between women and men, although the male professors disdained practical work[4] and university teaching was and has remained a dominantly male profession. The universities were extremely suspicious of the possibility of a scientific approach to personal relations—which in the field of psychology led them to distrust Freudian psychology and to concentrate upon problems of perception and physiology; similarly, the universities were only just beginning to involve themselves more closely with problems of industry and other social questions besides pure economics.

The School of Sociology and the spread of social studies teaching

Following the conference the Social Education Committee drew up plans for a university course with a two-year syllabus and transferred itself into the School of Sociology in 1903, independent of the Charity Organisation Society. Mr Urwick was the first lecturer and tutor.[5] As with the lectures under the joint training committee, the most applied subjects were lectured on by women. Mrs Frank Ogilvy lectured on 'The Principles Underlying Social Work' and Miss Plato ran an introductory course for those mainly interested in practical work. This is not to say that women did not also lecture in other subjects. Miss Newell lectured in social legislation and Miss E. Pearsons lectured on economics and social ethics and philosophy. Yet men rarely entered into the teaching of social work methods. The School of Sociology was assimilated into the London School of Economics in July 1912 with Mr Urwick as professor.[6]

The other development was in Liverpool—the establishment in 1904 of the School of Social Science formed as the outcome of arrangements between the University of Liverpool, the Victoria Settlement for Women and the Charity Organisation Society. This was the direct result of Charles Loch's suggestion to Professor Gonner at Liverpool.[7] As with the School of Sociology, the School of Social Science was not fully incorporated in the university. This incorporation finally took place in 1918. It fell to Birmingham University in 1908 to be the first British university to register social students as internal students of the university and to take full responsibility for their training, to be followed later by Bristol, Leeds, Manchester, Edinburgh and Glasgow.

Academic and practical work

Towards the end of the first decade of this century there was a good deal of consensus about the nature and purpose of social work training and in 1910 a conference of representatives from all the leading British 'social schools' drew up a suggested programme of lectures to which all their syllabi approximated.[8] It was recommended that any course of social study should include:

Modern industrial and social history   (20 lectures)
Economics   (10 lectures)
Social philosophy   (10 lectures)
Local government and institutions   (20 lectures)
Problem of poverty   (20 lectures)

There was also general agreement that there must be concurrent theoretical and practical work experience, with the practical work giving opportunity for 'controlled experience' that 'shall serve as a preliminary and independent work'. A wide range of agencies were recommended as providing a good base for training, particularly the Charity Organisation Society, medical or employment committees, care committees, and club work. Settlements were singled out as being particularly well suited both for observation and actual work. There had not always been an easy acceptance of the role in training, for in 1910 we find Elizabeth Macadam telling a Conference of the Federation of Northern Settlements that 'the advantages of the training now given in the settlements were now recognised and applauded by persons who a few years ago scoffed at their efforts',[9] E. J. Urwick, in 1903, as we have seen, had maintained that it was not 'unfair to say that most women's settlements ought to be called by the latter name [training college] and not the former [settlement proper]'.

Thus the responsibility for social work training gradually slipped from the Charity Organisation Society to the universities, who found it difficult to find the right balance between theory and practice. The Charity Organisation Society was not altogether satisfied that the training was adequate for their workers and by 1915 had organised its own twelve-month training course and in 1916 entered a co-operative scheme with Bedford College. Within the Charity Organisation Society the district committees continued to be the practical school for many intending social workers. For example in 1909–10 the St James committee was said to have helped with the training of twenty-five men and women (for weeks or months) at the district office, seven of whom were preparing for district secretaries, three for Charity Organisation Society work elsewhere, and four for hospital almoning. Three students were from the School of Sociology and eight others were gaining practical experience for any social work which might come their way (Bosanquet, 1914, p. 101). Any contribution to training was important at this stage in the development of social work because the scale of operations was so small. Between 1903 and 1918 only 269 students had qualified for diplomas or certificates offered by the six universities which offered training, and of these only thirty-one (12 per cent) were men.[10] The pattern of training had been set which was to exist until after the Second World War with the exception of training for psychiatric social work. Also the ambivalence of the universities towards social work training was already clear. But the small foothold gained was held on to and university training for social work was to become the only branch of university teaching where women outnumbered men. This was in line with women's involvement in formalised social work training during the latter part of the nineteenth century. Yet it seemed tragic that the development in social legislation during the first decade or so of the twentieth century did not lead to a more systematic policy on training for social work and that by far the majority of those occupied in social welfare, whether in voluntary or statutory agencies, were untrained.[11]

Women's changing choice of training opportunities

An important indication of shifts in emphasis in the attitudes of women wishing to enter the social service field between the 1860s and the decade before the First World War is by the preference for some women to gain experience in school care committee work rather than the Charity Organisation Society or housing management. To understand this entails a further brief consideration of Octavia Hill's work and the development of welfare work in the educational field. Between the start of Octavia Hill's training schemes in the mid-1860s and the Charity Organisation Society schemes, the natural way for a young woman to get started in social work was to become one of Octavia's 'young ladies', notable examples of whom were Emma Cons, Miss Peters (later Mrs Charles Loch) and Miss Rowlands (later Mrs Barnett). As the century drew to a close, however, developments occurred in the educational system which were to affect this.

The Forster Education Act in 1870 created School Boards to which women could be elected, and this, as well as election as guardians, provided an additional sphere of work for women of leisure. Some of the major problems in schools systems were of attendance, health and nutrition of the school child. Although attendance was the responsibility of the boards' male officers, the welfare of the school child became a major concern of many women. Mrs Barnett's school-board work has already been mentioned. Other notable pioneers, were Miss Lydia Becker, who was placed in the Manchester School Board in 1870 at the first election and also played a key part as secretary of the Manchester Society for Women's Suffrage; and Margaret Frere, a manager of Tower St Board School, Seven Dials, London, and member of the LCC Education Committee. At both levels, as members of School Boards and managers of particular schools women exercised a strong welfare role.[12] After 1902 the functions of the School Boards were transferred to local authorities. In Bradford in 1894 Margaret McMillan was elected to the School Board and her work had important consequences; in Bradford she established a Cinderella Club to provide supplementary meals for children and the first school baths.[13] Margaret joined her sister Rachel in London in 1902 and it was largely through her efforts that the 1906 Education (Provision of Meals) Act and the clause relating to medical inspection in the Education (Administrative Provisions) Act became law. These provisions gave the opportunity for the school care committee system, mainly in London, and when Margaret opened the first school clinic in London in 1908, its work was supported by a local school care committee, and one of the clinic nurses was a member of the school care committee. The LCC backed the venture and the system of care committees became established as a part of its educational provision. Miss Morton, formerly a Charity Organisation Society worker, became responsible for the organisation and development of the work which involved the support of volunteers by full-time secretaries.[14]

How this worked out in the case of an individual young woman entering the welfare field is described by Mary Stocks in her autobiography (1970). Octavia Hill had wanted her to get experience of Charity Organisation Society work but at the age of seventeen in 1908 Mary Stocks decided to embark on work as honorary secretary to the Saffron Hill Elementary School Care Committee. She recounts Octavia Hill's displeasure, because the care committees were a statutory body, and the argument that followed. Margaret McMillan was a founder member of the ILP party in 1893 and it seems likely that a number of women to the left of the political spectrum and convinced of the need for larger state provision of social services and broader reforms turned to work in the educational field rather than the Charity Organisation Society.[15] However, this should not lead us to ignore the fact that the style of operation of the care committees was very similar to the Charity Organisation Society pattern of full-time secretaries and volunteers. Had the system of voluntary aid committees advocated by Charles Loch been implemented following the report of the 1909 Royal Commission on the Poor Law, there might have developed a statutory basis for the Charity Organisation Society which would have transformed the long-term future of social work in this country.[16]

5 Women social workers, women's suffrage, and social reform

Introduction

Social work—defined very broadly—was a developing career of work for women during the second half of last century. Apart from the volunteer committee member and visitors, however, it provided employment only for a small minority of women. It is, perhaps, unrealistic to speak of career in the singular, as what we see is the development at several points in our social life of a reaction to the suffering caused by low income, bad health and housing. There were a number of key individuals who established new forms of help which gradually became institutionalised. The part that women played at each of these growth points was determined by the particular administrative and social context. Formal leadership was heavily invested in the aristocratic, ecclesiastical and upper middle-class businessmen with their connections, influence and financial power. Creative women such as Octavia Hill, Mary Carpenter and Josephine Butler came from similar families, and depended on liberal-minded men for acceptance and the furthering of their ideals.

Every achievement for women, in social work and other fields of work, contributed to the emancipation of women, but women social workers were by no means all fighters for women's rights. Their very family backgrounds made it hard for many of them to feel free to criticise the old order and to fight tooth-and-nail for the new. It is very clear, for instance, that Louisa Twining (1820–1912) was neither a campaigner for women's rights, or of more radical social reform, than her labours on behalf of workhouse conditions and treatment implied; she had been happy to ensure that tasks which needed women in the workhouses were gradually allocated to them. The same limited vision could be said to have been held by many of the philanthropic women in the middle and late nineteenth century. Yet the scene was changing. There must have been a substantial minority of women such as Violet Markham's mother of whom she writes in her autobiography (1953, p. 21):

My mother came to maturity at a time when great ideas were

stirring in the world. *The Origin of Species*, published in 1859 had set on foot a revolution extending far beyond the scientific matters to which Darwin's work was primarily directed.
Ruskin in 1860 had flung 'Unto this last' full in the face of the laissez-faire school; Carlyle, Herbert Spencer,[1] Sir Henry Maine, T. H. Green, were weaving new patterns in thought . . . My mother with her keen intelligence, adventured eagerly among these new ideas, but there was no-one in her immediate surroundings to give her much assistance with the doubts and questions of the hour.

Attitudes to the women's suffrage movement—Octavia Hill, Josephine Butler, Mary Carpenter

There is generally little mention of the question of women social workers' attitudes to women's suffrage in the literature about social work, but we do know that some of the early social work pioneers had clear views on the subject.

Octavia Hill, although interested in furthering the education of women, had no taste for political life and her skills were in directly dealing with the poor. She regarded political campaigning as luring women away from useful work. Thus—to use Maurice's phrase—she regarded the female suffrage movement as 'a sort of red herring' drawing women out of an involvement with the work for which they were specially fitted[2] (Maurice, 1914, pp. 263–4). Another factor influencing Octavia Hill was her abhorrence of self-advertisement, of which she thought that suffragists were guilty; they would be better employed in some fitting regular work. Only once did Octavia help in an election campaign and that was to support a friend, Mr Thomas Hughes, who was a candidate in Marylebone in 1874.

Josephine Butler was a major protagonist for the emancipation of women, her work being extremely diverse in approach. As mentioned earlier, she played a significant part in the history of the North of England Council for the Better Education of Women. In the battle for enfranchisement and writing as president of this council she wrote on 1 July 1869 to a Peer (probably Lord Crewe) about Mr Hibbert's Bill proposing to enfranchise women for parochial purposes:[3]

It is no doubt somewhat difficult for persons residing chiefly in London and in country houses to realise the fact that the

population of these large provincial towns in the North of
England are composed of very different elements from those
which form the chief part of the London Society. There are
few, scarcely any women in these towns who live a simply
fashionable life. They are often humble middle classes
chiefly, and are for the most part sensible, earnest, working
women. A very considerable number are trading in their own
names. The *men* of these towns are apt to be a little too
much absorbed in business and money making, and the women,
who have somewhat more of leisure, are frequently, as it is,
called upon to supply to members of Town Councils opinions
on all the matters with which Town Councils deal. They are
matters which concern women and children equally with
men, and in which the advice and practical help of women
will be needed more and more. The question of pauperism
alone, including that of nursing out of pauper infants is one
in which men will require all the help they can get from women
of insight, and delicacy of perception, for it is a question which
has to deal with human beings of all ages and both sexes.
Again all such questions as those of public health, prison
government, the details of expenditure in large institutions,
etc., are questions in which the united common sense of men
and women is required, and in which women could be granted
a greater share of responsibility with great advantage to the
whole community.

After discussing the increasing number of self-supporting and
working women, Josephine Butler goes on:

Many would marry if they could, but are driven of necessity
to self support. These are facts which should not be ignored
by our Government, for this mass of female ratepayers and
breadwinners is becoming nationally a more independent,
intelligent and enquiring class. They bear their fair share of
the world's work, and are a very considerable contingent
among ratepayers, and it is felt that it would be consistent
with the principles of our English Constitution that such
ratepayers and breadwinners should have a voice in local
arrangements and regulations which daily press upon them no
less than upon men, and of which their enforced condition of
independence and activity enables them to form a shrewd
clear judgment.

Parts of the letter are strongly reminiscent of passages in J. S. Mill's writing on the position of women in his essay *On Liberty* and in *The Subjection of Women*.[4] Josephine Butler had, however, edited a series of essays—*Women's Work and Women's Culture*—in 1869, the same year as the publication of *The Subjection of Women*, and she was at pains to point out in her editorial introduction that although the essays covered much the same ground, they had been produced independently. In her introductions she was critical of whose who pauperised the community 'by their old fashioned, Lady Bountiful way of dispensing alms and patronage'. Yet she was not happy with the tendencies leading to large-scale management and organisation:[5]

> The tendency at present is to centralisation of rule, to vast
> combinations, large institutions and uniformity of system. I
> have a doubt about any wholesale manipulation of the poor,
> the criminal, scholars in schools, etc. . . . I believe it to be so
> far from founded on a philosophical view of human nature and
> society, that if carried to extremes the last state of our poor
> will be worse than the first. For the correction of the extreme
> tendencies of this reaction, I believe that nothing whatsoever
> will avail but the large infusion of Home elements into Work-
> houses, Hospitals, Schools, Orphanages, Lunatic Asylums,
> Reformatories, and even Prisons: and in order to do this
> there must be a setting free of feminine power and influence
> from the constraint of bad education, and of narrow aims, and
> listless homes, where they are at present too often a superfluity.
> We have had experience of what we may call the feminine
> form of philanthropy, the independent individual ministering,
> of too medieval a type to suit the present day. It has failed.
> We are now about to try the masculine form of philanthropy,
> large and comprehensive measures, organisations and systems
> planned by men and sanctioned by Parliament. This also will
> fail, if it so far prevails as to extinguish the truth to which the
> other method witnessed, in spite of its excesses. Why should
> we not try at last a union of principles which are equally true?

In this passage Josephine Butler touches on a feminine distaste for large-scale organisations in common with Octavia Hill and Mrs Barnett, and a search for organic growth. She counselled her fellow workers[6]

> to repress impatience by considering well the motive of an

organic change. Organic growth cannot be healthy except
under conditions of freedom from constraint; from the pressure,
on the one hand of the swaddling clothes of the past, in the
shape of bad or worn-out laws or customs, which must be
torn off and put away before there can be any free growth;
from the pressure, on the other, of too great an urgency.
Growth cannot be hurried or forced, any more than it can be
cramped, without injurious consequences.

Where Josephine Butler had proceeded on several fronts of the
women's movement, Mary Carpenter's work in social reform
followed a much narrower line and she was rather more cautious
about women's suffrage. Her sense of the qualities of women made
her initially unresponsive to campaigns for attaining the vote, but
gradually her attitude changed. In 1867 J. S. Mill had written to
her to urge that she take a more attacking attitude within the
suffrage movement:[7]

> You will see from this that I cannot agree in the wish you
> express that the right should rather be given to women by
> those who deprived her of it, than from her own demand.
> Because, even if any sentiment of generosity should make
> one feel it is a more beautiful thing to receive a legitimate
> power unasked than asked, there can be no generosity and
> nothing noble or beautiful in waiting to have a duty thrust upon
> one, instead of asking to be allowed to take it upon oneself
> for the good of everybody concerned.

Mill therefore encouraged Mary Carpenter to put any doubts
which she had about the rectitude of agitation to one side. Although
she never participated in the women's suffrage movement in any
way more involved than signing a petition, she became firmly
convinced that women should have equal voting power with men
if social legislation were to be established on a 'true basis'. Mary
Carpenter firmly supported the temperance movement and the
movement for the repeal of the Contagious Diseases Acts. Within
the latter movement she joined Mrs Butler, Miss Nightingale and
Mrs Harriet Martineau in signing the appeal for the formation of
the Ladies National Association, and subsequently became a vice-
president of the National Association, attending meetings of both
associations.

Another area of interest which linked some of the early reformers was the improvement of life in India. Mary Carpenter wrote to Mill in 1867[8] asking him to join a deputation on the position in India and sending pamphlets. Mill replied saying that he could not join the deputation and thanked her for the pamphlets and her 'valuable efforts to improve the very defective jail management of India'.[9] Mary Carpenter was also in touch with Professor Fawcett, another champion of women's rights, over the question of India in 1876–7; she wrote asking for an appointment and to ask his advice.[10] Her campaign linked her with Florence Nightingale, who wrote to her in 1868 enclosing two books to read on her journey to India commenting that the *Notes on Nursing* (chapters on 'Minding Baby') were applicable in Africa and Asia.[11] India gave a further link by interest to Josephine Butler who was also very concerned with Indian affairs.[12] These women had a span of concern which embraced direct care and welfare of individuals, the rights of women, and the empire.[13] Their family and class connections gave them access to key public figures and the centres of power. Mary Carpenter and Josephine Butler had a wide range of contacts and used them to full advantage. For instance, in July 1869 Mary Carpenter received a letter from Lord Houghton apologising for the lack of chivalry of the Lords in having no ladies' gallery and inviting her to lunch with himself and Asquith.[14] The National Association for the Promotion of Social Science had welcomed women members and Mary Carpenter had delivered important papers to the association. It should be remembered that this was an important breakthrough— even in later years there was a strong feeling that women should not speak at public meetings. Whilst people like Mary Carpenter and Louisa Twining were accepted as speakers the more forceful younger generation of women were not.[15]

In spite of the forward-looking and wide-ranging activities of some of the major women social workers of the late nineteenth century, it is as well to remember Violet Markham's comment on the 1870s and 1880s (1953, p. 7):

> There was a genuine desire amongst thoughtful men and women to improve education—it was not sufficiently widespread to rouse the fears that it was later to excite—but looking back to the 'seventies and 'eighties it seems to me that there was little or no attention paid to social questions as we understand the phrase today. Employment had few frills and welfare was a word yet unspoken in factories and works.

A new generation of women linking nineteenth- and twentieth-century social work—Violet Markham, Eleanor Rathbone, Cecile Matheson

Violet Markham's experience of growing up and experiencing social work provides a bridge between the extreme attitudes of social conservatism and quick radical social and political reform. Born in 1872 at Brimmington Hall, near Chesterfield, her mother was the daughter of a successful businessman and her father an engineer, being managing director of the Stavely Coal Company from 1863 till his death in 1888. Violet was brought up at Tapton House near Chesterfield where the family had moved a year after her birth. From her mother and aunt she received an intelligent and lively introduction to human affairs and learning and within the family there were streams of discussion about public affairs or books. In addition she received a perfunctory gloss of formal education at a private girls' boarding school in London for eighteen months, part of which was 'an occasional address on some charitable subject'. Her social conscience was stirred whilst reading Ruskin's 'Unto This Last' when twenty-three years old and was influenced in the direction of social welfare. In 1899 after she 'had found intolerable the life of a young lady of leisure at Tapton', Violet took her first steps in public life as a school manager under the Chesterfield School Board; she continued to sit on the Board and Education Committee almost uninterrupted until 1934, for many years as vice-chairman. Two years later in 1901 Violet was left a legacy which enabled her to be financially independent and establish a small home in Gower Street, London. She decided to 'fling some contribution into the scales in which the prosperity of the few was balanced so unevenly against the meagre life of the many' and sought advice from May Tennant, who encouraged her to start a small settlement. In her own words: 'The idea appealed to me at once because it linked up with the teaching of Ruskin and Arnold Toynbee and the work of the Barnetts at Toynbee Hall.' So the die was cast and the Chesterfield Settlement, an old home in a back street, came into existence in 1902. During the first decade of the new century Violet had had little experience of public work outside Chesterfield, and at the suggestion of a close friend, Miss Lyttleton, she became honorary secretary to the Personal Service Association in London. Her mother died in 1912 and for seven years she looked after the affairs of Tapton.

Violet Markham had in this first decade a wide circle of friends, including John Buchan, Leo Amery and Sir Geoffrey Milner, and also travelled to South Africa. Her childhood and early adulthood show that, although she developed a keen social conscience, she managed to balance this with an appreciation of the values of the old order. She managed to justify privilege on the grounds of its cultural and civilising effects and because a privileged position could be used to influence the welfare of the poor. She was not a suffragist at first and initially supported the anti-suffrage movement to the extent of signing (along with Beatrice Webb,[16] Mrs Creighton, Mrs T. H. Green and Mrs Arnold Toynbee) a Protest against Women's Suffrage, drafted by Mrs Ward in 1889 when a Private Member's Bill on the subject was before Parliament. However, much of this opposition had evaporated in the years before the First World War.

The emergence of independent women who were becoming much more interested in changing society and in spite of having experience of Charity Organisation Society work were turning away from this as an adequate solution is exemplified in the early life of Eleanor Rathbone, also born in 1872.[17] It has already been seen that it was a Liberal government which appointed Mrs Nassau Senior as an inspector under the Poor Law, and Eleanor was nurtured in a family and circle which embraced the leading disciples of Gladstonian liberalism and was heavily involved in charitable work in Liverpool. As with Violet Markham her early formal education was limited, with a succession of governesses and tutors and a period at Kensington High School, but this was counteracted with eminent people and discussion. The family's wealth, based on the shipowning business, enabled it to undertake charitable work and gave it considerable influence in public affairs. Eventually she went to Somerville in 1893 and had among her contemporaries Margery Fry, Lettice Ibert (later Mrs H. A. L. Fisher), and Hilda Oakley. Her select group of friends discussed the problems and philosophies of the day, convinced of the power of the individual to make an impact on social evils and only rejecting communism outright following a reading of *Das Kapital*.

In 1897 she became a visitor with the Liverpool Central Relief Organisation, a manager of Granby Street Council School, and honorary secretary of the Liverpool Women's Industrial Council. As a visitor she became disenchanted with the little impact the Central Relief Association seemed to have, and thought that it could be doing harm. She diagnosed that the seat of the problem was that the Liverpool visitors were of worse quality than in the

London Charity Organisation Society and were untrained lower middle-class people of limited education; training should be the answer. She wrote to her friend Hilda Oakley (Stocks, 1949, p. 55):

> That is why I like the despised Charity Organisation Society work so much. If one's large schemes fail, if dock labour is never properly organised, or the executive power better guided, or any system of philosophy elucidated, it will be a satisfaction at the end of life to know that at any rate some poor bicycle-maker and his children were set on their legs and saved from the House and made respectable citizens through my agency.

Eleanor became a member of the committee of the Victoria Women's Settlement after the turn of the century and came into contact with Elizabeth Macadam, a Scottish social worker with experience in London settlement work, when she was appointed warden in 1904; Elizabeth Macadam was later to become a lecturer at Liverpool University and exercise a strong influence on social work thinking during the inter-war period. Eleanor developed her welfare activities with research into casual labouring and the conditions of widows under the Poor Law.

Unlike Violet Markham, Eleanor Rathbone had not opposed the women's suffrage movement and indeed became heavily involved in it. As early as 1897 she had become parliamentary secretary to the Liverpool Women's Suffrage Society which adhered to the National Union of Women's Suffrage Societies of which Mrs Henry Fawcett was the president. In 1911 Eleanor became president of the newly formed regional Federation of Suffrage Societies (covering Lancashire and Cheshire) and was later elected to the executive committee of the national body. Her activities did not end there—she became the first woman member of Liverpool City Council in 1909, and in 1913 founded the Liverpool Women Citizens Association and was its president. Also she played an active part in establishing the School of Social Service at Liverpool University.

Both these women combined the ability to look broadly at social problems and also to engage in more immediate social work. They bridged the emotional and philosophical gap between Octavia Hill and Beatrice Webb, the latter having turned completely away from the Charity Organisation Society methods and philosophy.[18]

During the period leading up to the First World War it would be difficult to find a clearer expression of the middle road than that of Miss Cecile Matheson, warden of the Birmingham Women's

Settlement 1909–15, when discussing the equipment of the social worker in 1908:[19]

> It is a peculiarity of 'Social Service' that the ground work of equipment necessary for large and small efforts and for voluntary and paid work is the same: first a human sympathy and imagination that will enable us to understand ideals and sufferings from our own, and secondly, a knowledge of present social and economic conditions together with the history of race-development that has made these conditions possible. The more we insist on the necessity for this two-fold equipment, this union of heart and head in social work, the more we shall rid society of two present dangers. We aim at the elimination of the social reformer who mistakes illustration for principle, who cannot look beyond the details of case-work or personalities and whose one idea of enlisting public sympathy or national reform is by means of inflammatory and sensational appeals, issued in defiance of history or of national interests. On the other hand we must check the supply of armchair idealists who would legislate for a Utopia before they have learnt to understand human nature with its manifold and varying virtues and vices, aspirations and temptations.

Miss Matheson was born in Hampstead, London, and educated at private schools and Bedford College.[20] She was brought up in a home atmosphere of interest in public service. On leaving school she took up teaching and secretarial work. In her spare time she took an interest in evening classes and clubs. Later she did work for the Special Enquiry Department of the Board of Education, having been appointed to make two special enquiries into the teaching of domestic subjects in Switzerland, Germany and Austria. She went to Birmingham in 1904 doing club work and undertaking social investigations, being a co-author of *Women's Work and Wages*. In 1906 she went to work at the Women's Settlement and became warden in 1909, developing many new departments and experiments. She gave evidence to the Royal Commission on the Poor Laws and Relief of Distress, the Parliamentary Committee on Pensions, and the Birmingham Council Housing Enquiry. Also she played a prominent role in women's organisations, for example the National Union of Women Workers and the National Union of Women's Suffrage Societies. She lectured widely and was a frequent writer on social work and social policy.

Although written during the First World War it is relevant to consider here an important article by Miss Matheson entitled 'Why Social Workers Want Women's Suffrage'.[21] She begins with the following words:

> When Social Workers meet an anti-suffragist, their usual
> recourse is to try to interest her in social work. Well, they all
> know that certain prominent social workers are ardent 'antis',
> but they know also that such workers are few and far between
> and that the great majority of modern social workers are also
> strong suffragists. As a class social workers probably feel their
> un-enfranchised position more keenly than any body of women,
> for social workers have all the instincts of reformers, and to
> such political helplessness must be galling.

Miss Matheson's argument is clear and in the tradition of Josephine Butler, that women must be allowed to play their full part in solving the problems of human misery. Enfranchisement was a means to an end. Until this was achieved women would not be able to have their fullest impact on government at the highest levels. Yet Miss Matheson gives eloquent expression to the tension in the social worker between giving present help and fighting for broader social reform to which women's enfranchisement would contribute:

> They [women social workers] are not comforted by the oft
> repeated adjurement to recognise how much women can, and
> should, do, and to busy themselves faithfully with the present
> substance rather than waste time and energy in pursuit of an
> uncertain advantage that will surely prove to be but a shadow
> . . . And yet—how many social workers have one by one given
> up their work and gone over to the active suffragists, and the
> recruits that should take their place are joining them instead,
> and one and all give the same answer to the over-pressed
> social worker calling for more and yet more help. 'Not yet',
> they cry, 'Not yet'. 'Our hearts are with you in your struggle,
> our interest in our old work is greater than ever, and just
> because of this we shall not attempt it again until the leverage
> of political power is in our hands. Now our work can always
> be retarded or undone without any reference to us, and it is
> no use to work like that.' So helpers are withdrawn and
> funds are withdrawn, not as is often said, because women

have turned from unselfish to selfish aims,[22] but because social workers, more than any other class, have the chance to know the strong and the weak points both of the law and its administration.

Nor does Miss Matheson expect that enfranchisement would suddenly overcome long-standing social problems:

Social workers do not live on mountain tops of misty ideal! They are men and women of the world, trained in a hard school of practical experience that forbids them to build a castle in the air on the hope that a future vote that shall be a panacea for social ills. They know that the vote is but a means to an end, a link in the chain of events that may make an end a reality, but all the more ardently do they desire to forge that link. The women's vote does not mean to them a sudden social regeneration, but it does mean an alteration in the balance of Parliamentary Programmes, a knowledge that Parliament has time first for those matters that have votes behind them, and that it would be found unwise to postpone many matters that, under present circumstances, enjoy several years of 'academic discussion'. Pure milk, infant care, the terrible social evil in these and other matters, Parliament should help if it cannot cure, and the women who are face to face with these dangers and difficulties are insistent that they should have their power of helpfulness reinforced, their experience utilised, and that they too shall be able 'to call Parliament to account' if it forgets or mishandles the problems that are to women their own.

Patterns of involvement

This last point of Miss Matheson's brings out an aspect of the development of social work and the women's movement that was frequently argued. Not only men, but women held that there were spheres of public life which they were particularly suited to, so that opening of the doors to women in a particular profession often meant marking off part of the work as particularly appropriate to women. This has been shown to be the case in the inspectorates, almoning, probation and moral welfare work. This was paralleled in medicine with the situation that many of the early appointments of women doctors were in hospitals (or hospital departments) dealing with women and children or local authorities in work with women and children.[23] In education, women teachers were almost wholly responsible for teaching in public elementary schools and for all teaching in secondary schools for girls. In higher education, however, there were[24]

> no great prizes for women. Since there is little or no endowment for research or post-graduate study, women have not as yet done much independent work in art or science and those who have done so being numerically insignificant, they are seldom successful in competition for appointments to higher teaching.

The International Congress of Women, 1899, acknowledged the immense amount of unpaid voluntary work in public service which women were beginning to contribute as members of Boards of Guardians, School Boards, parish and district councils, in the management of hospitals and other public institutions and the administration of charities. However it was clear that, although such work required a 'trained intelligence', the guides to judgment and 'knowledge tested by experience', such work was still the voluntary activity of leisured women and with the particular emphasis derived from their sex.[25] Whilst paid work was possible for the single women there were difficulties about married women working, even if welfare work was considered to be largely a woman's sphere. Mrs Barbara Fenwick, an ardent suffragist, spoke forcefully at the Congress on this topic:[26]

> But we are forced to realise that the woman however highly cultivated and trained is constituted in nature a creature of infinitely more delicate nervous organisation than a man, and that it is impossible for her to bear the nerve strain of housewife and of breadwinner. Such a strain would speedily spell nervous exhaustion, and inevitably misery in domestic life. As I have said no man would attempt to do so much and it must not be expected from a woman.

Thus, the battle for emancipation by no means inevitably implied radical changes in family roles, given that there was the firm expectation that domestic management was the women's task. Violet Markham had had to return to domestic management on the death of her mother and arising from her reflections on her childhood

with many servants to perform all the menial tasks she commented
(Markham, 1953, p. 33):

> Women in large measure fail to recognise how much their
> future as independent beings turns on finding some solution
> of the problem of domestic help. For if all alike, whatever their
> individual capacities and gifts, are forced unaided to grind
> their corn and make their own oil—tasks that never fall to
> man—neither in art, literature nor the professions can they
> hope to find time to attain excellence.

6   Overview 1860–1914

Main trends

If we seek to clarify the take-off stage for modern social work leading up to the First World War a number of conclusions arise from the detailed analysis so far. First, the greatest part of social work effort was in the voluntary field, much of this involving visiting similar in kind to that established early in the nineteenth century. For the majority of those involved in this work, there was an acceptance of the basic structure of society until the 1880s, when the late nineteenth century thought explosion began to spread through the educated part of society. Second, the demographic structure of society with its many single women provided the reservoir of people to undertake the visiting. Education, then nursing had gradually become acceptable professions for the single women on a paid basis. The institutionalisation of the teacher role and nurse role with formal training provided avenues of paid employment for the single woman who had to work to maintain herself but it took a long time for these posts to become regarded as suitable for ladies. In social work there was no such clear unitary role, and the availability of women with independent means hampered the development of paid work which has always been an important part in the development of a sphere of professional work. Third, there was the creation of new forms of social help, and the embryonic roles of child-care officer, probation officer and almoner which differed from the organising secretary role of Charity Organisation Society secretary and settlement warden. The fact that the theatres of war were so diverse in character obscured the fact that these workers were all soldiers. However, the development of paid work in the Charity Organisation Society, the settlements, hospitals, courts and inspectorates did give the impetus towards establishing social work as a career. But it was not until the 1890s and the first decade of this century that this gathered momentum. In the establishment of the Hospital Almoners Association and the Institute of Hospital Almoners in 1903 and 1907 and the Association of Probation Officers in 1913 was sown the seed of further searching for professional identity. Fourth, the pattern of charismatic leadership by great individuals gradually gave way to the pattern of formal organisation. It is important to recall that the majority of the social work organisations were created with and by men, and that the contribution of women was dependent upon the encouragement and support, spiritual and financial, of husbands, fathers and friends. Fifth, the development of organisation and paid social work led to increasing concern with establishing principles of social work practice which could be transmitted to the next generation of social workers through training schemes.

All these factors were overlaid by the attempt to establish social welfare work as an appropriate activity for a woman. Every new employment for women was a blow struck in the struggle for emancipation, so that social work was a small part of a much larger clash to establish women as full participating members of the community. Yet from the opposite standpoint every successful engagement in emancipation buttressed the social workers' efforts to help the poor and needy. Even within the broad social work sphere, however, it has been shown that the part women played was constrained by hiving off areas of activity particularly suitable for women. Thus, in the inspectorate it was a concern with children; in the settlements, however, separate settlements for men and women developed; in probation it was a concern with young children, older girls and women.

Social work as a career for women

Social work as a career for women only offered limited opportunities for women before the First World War. For a summary of thinking about social work as a career for women Cecile Matheson gives an excellent review in a paper in the *Journal of Education*, September 1908, entitled 'Training for Social Work, New University Course in Birmingham'. Miss Matheson comments of the general situation: 'Of late years philanthropic work has undergone a wholesome change. The sentimental dilettantism of the rich and the narrow activity of the underpaid and undereducated district worker are alike out of date.' Then, of the overall opportunities for women she says:

> As a girl passes out of school or college, her future career becomes yearly a more complicated question with parents and teachers. There is a far larger choice of professions for the average all round girl than existed twenty years ago.

D

Significantly, in view of the demographic pattern, there is a discussion of the motivating factors towards social work

> If we are wise, we consider other aspects of a profession besides its pecuniary value. Women need to have a human interest in their work, an interest that shall appeal to heart and imagination as well as to intellect and business capacity, also the middle aged worker who is without home ties of her own tends to grow weary of life and to seek to crush maternal emotions that seem to exist but to give her pain. . . .[1] It is probably the innate craving for human interest that leads so many to take up teaching and nursing. Failing an opening in one of these, a large number try to get what is vaguely known as secretarial work. One is apt to hear that these somewhat obvious professions are overcrowded; but it seems to be unknown to the majority of people that there is a small but increasing group of posts for educated workers which often have to wait unfilled for many months for lack of suitable candidates.

Miss Matheson admits that the 'prospects are not brilliant' and that although the openings offer a 'fair maintenance' there are 'no big prizes as in the teaching profession'. Nevertheless,

> there is work rich in human interest and work which gives scope for the exercise of every intellectual faculty. I refer to the group of employments that might fitly be called the 'social service' with its central salaried posts in various philanthropic undertakings.

Professional identity and the ideal of service

The fragmented elements in social work, as yet without any clear professional identity even though a foothold in the universities had been won, were not to cohere until a further sixty years had elapsed. At this stage, however, it is already clear that the picture of social work as solely women's work is an over-simplification. Men were responsible for many of the creative initiations, dominated committees and provided finance and support. Those who were liberal and progressive in outlook protected their protégées against the weighty resistance of fearful men in many spheres. There was also the immense importance of the class structure that made the Charity Organisation Society a microcosm of the nation with the influential upper-class committee and honorary secretary and the lower-class paid male visitors or agents. It is this rigidity of the class structure which, perhaps above all else, held back the development of any other point of view than that of social service as being for the respectable poor, and it is only in the probation service that state recognition breached this concept.

Women's advancement in the professions with the ideal of service to the community, led to a common feeling allied to breadth of vision and interests. To some extent this crossed class barriers, as witnessed to by the active involvement of women such as Eleanor Rathbone and Miss Matheson in the Union of Women's Workers and a concern over the industrial working conditions of women. There was, too, an ability to see the wrongs in society but to be understanding of the individuals within the system. An exceptionally clear statement comes from Dr Elizabeth Blackwell[2] in writing to Mme Bodichon in the 1880s. Dr Blackwell, the first woman admitted to the British Medical Register (in 1859) and with many welfare interests, writes from Hastings:[3]

Dearest Barbara,
I am very glad that such an excellent Guardian as our own friend Catherine Stott is elected. Little by little good women will step into the places that so much need them.
I am going to London on Monday to attend a very important meeting of our Repeal (L.W.A.) Society—and on Friday I shall go up for the organising meeting of the 'Small Farm and Holidays Society' in which I take much interest. Mr Albert Gray has sent me tickets. I believe the Duke of Westminster will preside. Although this is a movement apparently initiated by aristocratic landholders, yet as their circulars appear to me to be entirely just, I do feel sincere interest in helping them out of the false monopolising position in which so many past circumstances have conspired to place them.
So many things press upon all who are able and willing to work that I am compelled to choose just what my limited strength will allow me to do. I cannot now work in a whirl or a hurry, and I thankfully come back from London to be refreshed be sea and sky.

Although not written by a social worker, the attitudes characterise many of the best facets of social work as it developed during the later part of the nineteenth century. The desire to understand rather than condemn and to serve responsibly rather than to seek self-aggrandisement for women are the epitome of the best traditions of women in social work. It is one of the most startling facts of the late nineteenth century and the years before the First World War that the efforts of women—those of conservative views as well as those with progressive attitudes—had had a revolutionary effect. B. Kirkman Gray, writing in 1908, observed this with acute insight:[4]

> Almost all the men—in this instance as in some Acts of Parliament man must imply woman, for the exertions of women have had much to do with the humane treatment of the poor—almost all the men who have been responsible for the various modifications introduced have adhered or thought they adhered to the old individualist position, and yet the changes taken in their total effect have resulted in what is little less than a revolution.

Marx, Engels and Veblen—theoretical views

Before leaving this phase in the development in social work with its slow transition from voluntary to paid work, and the evolution of formal organisations it is necessary to mention two theories which deal with women's position in nineteenth-century industrial society. The first is the communist analysis of women's status in capitalist societies and the second is the analysis of T. Veblen, which more cogently than any other analysis relates women's economic status and their philanthropic activities. If the communist argument is accepted the only way to improve the position of women is to remove the capitalist system of production which produces prostitution and condemns women to a servile status: 'It is self evident that the abolition of the present system of production must bring with it the abolition of the community of women springing from that system, i.e. of prostitution, both public and private.'[5]

Engels's *Origins of Family, Private Property and State* broadens the argument:[6]

> What applies to women in the factory applies to her in all professions right up to medicine and law. The modern individual family is based on the open or disguised enslavement of the woman; and modern society is a mass composed of individual families as its molecules.

Engels maintained that 'the first principle for the emancipation of women is the reintroduction of the entire female sex into public industry. . . .'[7] With the disappearance of economic dependency and with equality before the law Engels considered that men would become 'really monogamous' rather than 'women becoming poly-androus'. Again Engels predicts that the emancipation of women 'becomes possible only when women are enabled to take part in production on a large scale and when domestic duties require their attention only to a minor degree.'[8]

Thus the battle for emancipation must be fought on two fronts— attaining full female suffrage and the extension of women's labour. J. S. Mill had concentrated on the former front but had not excluded the latter, although he had argued for the removal of legal impedi-ments to women's entry to employment rather than active pro-motion.[9] It is interesting that this aspect of the Marxian thesis received no attention in social work circles (Eleanor Rathbone rejected Marxism after reading *Das Kapital*; even Beatrice Webb came only slowly to an appreciation of the communist analysis of society). The dominant political ideology, in so far as it was ex-pressed, was progressive conservative or liberal rather than socialist. In welfare fields government intervention was well entrenched in the Poor Law, health and education services. The power of indi-vidualistic economic theories inhibited the growth of direct inter-vention in economic life. It was difficult for the women of liberal-minded families to espouse economic philosophies which would reject the very pattern of industrial and commercial life which gave them the power to undertake philanthropic work. It is this linking of philanthropy and economic life which is analysed by Veblen in his *Theory of the Leisure Class*.[10]

Veblen argued that the[11]

non-invidious part of the religious life—the sense of the communion with environment, or with the generic life process— as well as the impulse of charity or of sociability, act in a pervasive way to shape men's habits of thought for the economic purpose. But the action of this class of proclivities is somewhat vague; and their effects are difficult to trace in detail. So much seems clear, however, as that the action of this class of motives or aptitudes tends in a direction contrary to the underlying principles of the leisure class as already formulated. The basis of that institution, as well as of the anthropo-morphic cults associated with it in the cultural development, is the

habit of invidious comparison; and this habit is incongruous
with the exercise of the aptitudes now in question. The
substantial canons of the leisure class scheme of life are a
conspicuous waste of time and substance and a withdrawal
from the industrial process; while the particular attitudes here
in question assert themselves, on the economic side, in a
deprecation of waste and of a futile manner of life, and in an
impulse to participation in or identification with the life
process, whether it be on the economic side or in any other
of its phases or aspects.

Women were recognised by Veblen to be the largest group exempted
from pecuniary stress and thus could be expected specially to be
subject to the non-invidious temperament rather than men. They
worked out their temperament in a 'multitude of organisations the
purpose of which is some work of social ameliorations'.[12]
    Veblen goes on to outline the 'quasi-religious' or 'pseudo-
religious' organisations which were a result of this impulse:[13]

Such for instance are the agitation for temperance and similar
social reforms, for prison reform, for the spread of education,
for the suppression of vice, and for the avoidance of war by
arbitration, disarmament, or other means; such are in some
measure, university settlements, neighbourhood guilds, the
various organisations typified by the Young Men's Christian
Association and the Young People's Society for Christian
Endeavour, sewing circles, social clubs, art clubs, and even
commercial clubs; such are also in some slight measure the
pecuniary foundations of semi-public establishments for
charity, education or amusement; whether they are endowed
by wealthy individuals or by contributions collected by persons
of smaller means—insofar as these establishments are not of a
religious character.

Although men and women could both join in expressions of charity
and sociability Veblen reinforces the theory that women participate
more actively and more persistently than men, 'except, of course
in the case of such works as require a large expenditure of means.
The dependent pecuniary position of women disables them for
work requiring a large expenditure.'[14] He particularly emphasises
the association of priests and clergy with women: 'This is as the
theory would have it. In other economic relations, also, the clergy

stands in a somewhat equivocal position between the class of women and that of the men engaged in economic pursuits.'[15] In addition, in so far as women were inhibited from industrially useful work, they would assert any impulse to workmanship in other directions than business.

Veblen's argument most fully accounts for the philanthropic work of the nineteenth century, and the involvement of women in it. We have the picture of a large class of the population not involved in economic activities, fighting to give expression to pent-up religious and social feelings. As with the communist analysis, the implication is that only the removal of women from the leisured class would alter the situation. The perpetuation of domestic roles in economic life as shown by the employment of women in teaching, nursing, and social work was also a consequence of long established family roles and of the impulse of many men to keep women in a servile status.

Part II

Emergent profession
1914–39

7   The First World War

Impact on social work

The First World War was important in the development of social
work not because of any single development that took place or the
creation of new social work agencies but because of a series of events
and changes that altered the social and economic climate within
which social work was to develop. War created new opportunities
for service from women and many became involved in Red Cross
and hospital work, often with the aim of getting to the Front
(Markham, 1953).[1] This fact, together with the social distress at
home resulting from the war, meant that there was an excess of
demand over the supply for trained workers which stimulated
government concern and public awareness (Macadam, 1925, pp.
36–7). The impact of these trends in almoning can be gauged from
the fact that during 1915–16 it was possible to interview only five
applicants for training and the annual report of the Hospital
Almoner's Council discuss the situation in the following manner:[2]

> In view of the likelihood of an increasing demand, the council
> much regrets the diminution of the number of candidates who
> have come forward for training. It is not doubted that women
> who would not be taking up a training for a career in life
> have merely postponed it in order to devote themselves
> temporarily to work in connection with the war, and this
> council would be the first to honour them for doing it. At the
> same time it is the council's duty to be able to provide really
> efficient almoners at that most critical period of the close
> of the war, when social and economic conditions must be
> in the forefront of all reconstructive work.

At the beginning of the war the pressing problem was unemployment and the relief of hardship as breadwinners went to the Front.
Although this phase lasted only a few months, the contribution of
existing social agencies was vital. In Birmingham, for instance, in
the settlement district there was much distress following the outbreak

of war and the Charity Organisation Society coped with many applicants; not only had many heads of homes gone to war but War Office pay arrived irregularly and trade was in a state of flux. Of 310 cases dealt with during the first three weeks of the war, 145 were wives or parents of soldiers and 165 were unemployment cases. Later this work passed to Citizens Committees as they were established. Also the National Union of Women's Suffrage Societies had set aside its propaganda work and its members gave much help to relief societies in Birmingham at the start of the war. The settlement acted as a focus for meetings of groups of women and for activities such as toy making.[3]

Nationally, the initial response to the war crisis was the establishment of a National Relief Fund. The Local Government Board had been slow to act, so the Prince of Wales appealed to the nation for funds to meet the emergency, and six million pounds was raised. Miss Markham was made a member of the committee of the National Relief Fund but it was gradually realised that wartime social difficulties should be a statutory, not a voluntary responsibility and out of the National Relief Fund grew the Central Committee on Women's Employment, the most long-lived of all the war committees—for it survived till the summer of 1940 (Markham, 1953, pp. 144–9).

Munitions work

Increasing employment of women in the munitions factories gave a special impetus to social work training.[4] The welfare department of the Ministry of Munitions could not find enough trained workers and enlisted the help of the university social training schools to provide intensive short courses, while the Ministry gave grants to students.[5] Whilst Miss Macadam welcomed these developments she was less happy about all the courses which sprang up at that time: 'Training for social work began to be fashionable and training schemes, good, bad and indifferent, came into being.'[6] To deal with this situation an unofficial Joint Social Studies Committee was formed in London which later organised a conference on social training, held at the Home Office in June 1917. A second conference was also held at the Home Office dealing with training for welfare work in factories and in 1918, as a result of these meetings, the Joint University Council for Social Studies was formed to co-ordinate and develop the work of social studies departments in the universities. The first chairman was Sir William Ashby of Birmingham University and the first secretary was Mr St George Heath the warden of Toynbee Hall.

However, the welfare work with women undertaken in the munitions factories was limited in scope; the concept of welfare was very general and the women supervisors and lady superintendents dealt with a wide range of practical matters, including the design of caps and uniform, protective overalls and gloves, the availability of hot water and first aid.[7] Although a sympathetic approach was essential, no theoretical development or knowledge resulted from this new work. Even though the necessity for such work might seem obvious it often met with resistance from men:[8]

Lady superintendents have experienced very different receptions at different factories. Sometimes, a man about to employ women for the first time, has, of his own accord, begun by appointing a competent woman to engage his labour, and to care for the comfort of the women and girls, but not infrequently a lady superintendent encounters a certain amount of suspicion, if not of actual opposition. She has to move with infinite caution at first. There is a traditional distrust of women in the business world; men fear they cannot keep their tongues or their fingers from interfering with other people's work.

Training and opportunities for paid social work

During the war the divergence of the paths of general social work and casework became clearer, as well as the relation of paid to voluntary work. Miss Matheson in an article on 'Opportunities for Social Work and Training'[9] writes that,

gradually men and women have awakened to the knowledge that good-will is not in itself a sufficient guide to intelligent helpfulness and that he who would help his neighbour must first himself acquire the tools of his craft . . . .. These perceptions have produced numerous expedients for dealing with social disorders, hosts of societies, and multitudes of workers. In many cases these workers have only scanty leisure after fulfilling other duties and hence the custom has increased of having one or more experts at the helm of every enterprise who shall guide, organise and co-ordinate the voluntary effort. These experts are expected, as a rule to be responsible for the business

side of the undertaking; but they often act as unofficial
teachers, or rather, referees, to their helpers and committees.
The demand for paid workers, together with the growing
desire among leisured people to equip themselves for the duties
of their citizenship has led to the development of various
schemes of social training.

Miss Matheson goes on to describe the opportunities given by the
Labour Exchange and Insurance Commission and to a much lesser
extent by the Boards of Guardians (as assistant relieving officers).
Writing a year earlier, Miss Matheson gave details of the posts
which former students at the Birmingham Settlement had held:
six worked as care committee organisers under the London County
Council; five were in the Labour Exchanges; one was in the Insurance Department; five were organising secretaries for branches
of the Charity Organisation Society, and others were organisers
for various voluntary organisations.[10] Thus it is possible to distinguish here the conception of the social worker as a paid administrator and organiser of volunteers with a supportive and consultative
role. In the statutory insurance and employment services the worker
was primarily a humane administrator.

In her 1916 article Miss Matheson includes a discussion of other
openings for trained workers, grouping together different types of
religious rescue work, and then having a separate grouping for the
posts that 'require special technical training, such as inspectorships,
posts as almoners, school nurses, superintendents of schools for
mothers, etc.' There is no mention of the probation service. It is
important to place the developments in almoning and probation
in context as it is a temptation to overemphasise their influence on
social work at this time as the result of hindsight. We have already
seen that the majority of workers undergoing social training were
women but that the numbers involved were extremely small—hardly
the foundation of a profession of social work, with almoning only
a small part of the picture. Pay was relatively low with salaries for
club organisers, secretaries to relief societies, welfare supervisors
in factories, and LCC school care organisers ranging between
£100 and £150 per annum, and Miss Matheson advised trained
students never to accept less than £100 as an initial salary. She
commented about the general situation:

The work is almost always exacting the hours long and
uncertain, and salaries taken as a whole are low. Added to

this, the strain on the emotional powers is apt to be even greater than the strain on the physical powers. . . . Social work is a profession that demands wholehearted devotion that can only be given by those who take it up with love of their fellows as the first and strongest incentive. Of no profession is it more true that the true worker is born not made; if only in telling workers will remember that, being born, they need discipline and knowledge.

Even for those wishing to train, opportunities were limited for less well-off people. To counteract this a few bursaries were available at the universities; Birmingham, for instance, offered three bursaries of £10 per annum and settlements at Glasgow and Liverpool and London offered some free places for students of limited money. Increasing fees had occurred for almoners undergoing training and training fees were to remain an inhibiting factor in social work until after the Second World War.

Almoning

Almoning which represented, together with probation, the prototype of the social caseworker by contrast with the social work administrators and organisers, was itself undergoing changes during the war. There was a reduction in the number of male civilian patients. With state help available for the dependents of soldiers there was a decrease in the number of cases in which material help was required. The staffing difficulties of the hospitals led to a restriction of out-patient departments' work to dealing with the most serious cases and the 'complicated and varied organisations called into existence by the war of necessity add greatly to the labours of the Almoners Department'.[11] The range of the almoner's work was extending—to ante-natal, post-natal, temperance and home hygiene work—and because of the diminishing need to concentrate on preventing abuse it was becoming clear that 'the larger part of the almoner's energies must be focused on more constructive work'.[12]

Two representatives of the council set out on a propaganda tour in the provinces during the winter of 1916–17, to give information about the work and training. As a result of the visits to Liverpool Miss Cummins later addressed the annual meeting of the Women's Employment Bureau of the National Union of Women Workers at which the possibility of establishing training at provincial universities was discussed.[13] This work stimulated interest in the work and the council received 'a considerable number of enquiries from Women's Colleges, Appointments Boards, Women's Work Organisations . . .'. Salaries for almoners increased in some London hospitals and this was a mark of recognition. However, in 1917 only nine women received the council's certificate on completing training.

During the war almoning continued to be seen as an occupation solely for women, with the gradual development of an enlarged role which accented constructive work with individuals and the liaising, communicating function as a mobiliser of resources from an expanding range of functional statutory services. The division of roles between the sexes which affected the development of almoning remained important in the medical profession, in which during the war the most important extension of their work was in women's and children's hospitals and in local authority work with women and children.[14]

Probation

In probation there was a steady extension of the appointment of court workers during the war, although there were still many voluntary missionaries who formed the greater part of the service. It was mainly in dealing with juveniles and in the London area that the fastest progress was made. As first with the Charity Organisation Society and then almoning, we see the same picture of development in probation, with London as the initial growth point with a gradual spread to the rest of the country. The Home Office Circular of 22 August 1917 was welcomed by the NAPO and its executive committee resolved in 1918 that the probation system was working efficiently in parts and its was hoped that early steps would be taken to enforce the working of the Probation Act throughout the country.[15] At the same meeting the executive committee passed a resolution that it had always been the view of the National Association of Probation Officers that a fixed salary was imperative in the interests of officers and probation work. At the same time, the association was involved with securing the appointment of two members of the association (a lady and a gentleman) on the committee being formed dealing with probation matters. In its early growth, just before and during the war, the National Association of Probation Officers was keenly aware that to provide a good service, a sound organisation and extension throughout the country was needed, with adequate salaries which would be uniform throughout the country.

With the accent on juveniles in the early years it was to be expected that women would contribute to and have a voice in the association. Mrs Carey was one of those giving a paper at the 1915 annual general meeting, and at the 1916 annual general meeting she seconded Mr Fitzsimmons's motion drawing the Home Secretary's attention to the evil effects of improper film exhibitions and the 'disastrous effects thereon upon children of school age'.[16] Similarly, she seconded a motion strongly urging the Home Secretary 'that all women who are charged with solicitation and found to be suffering from venereal disease be detained in an Isolation Institution until cured'. Other matters of concern during this period were the presence of gaming machines in sweet shops and the need to suppress publication in the press of names of juveniles. On a lighter note, during the war period the lists of members attending the annual general meeting was divided according to sex; however, in 1919 the practice was adopted of mixing the sexes in a single list: 'In addition to Magistrates and other invited visitors the following ladies and gentlemen attended.'

Moral welfare and housing management

Moral welfare workers were also troubled by the position of women and girls during the war and Miss Higson's work from 1913 in Portsea, Liverpool, with young girls and women who were prostitutes or living with sailors, proved valuable.[17] She went to France in 1915 to investigate the needs of French girls as a result of the great increase in prostitution and illegitimacy, and helped in the establishment of a mother and baby home in Le Havre and in reviewing institutional conditions. Also, in October 1915, a private conference was held in London with the title 'The Theory and Practice of Moral Welfare Work'. The aim was to try to create a new attitude to the fallen and to focus on the need for training for rescue work; eventually this initiative led to the establishment of the Josephine Butler Memorial College. A further concern of the church was the spiritual needs of munitions workers and in the winter of 1917 a gigantic mission among thousands of munitions workers at Gretna took place. The awareness of the need to rationalise and rethink the church's moral welfare work was epitomised in the first Conference of Organising Secretaries, held in Liverpool in 1917, and the creation of an Advisory Board for Spiritual and Moral Welfare Work with Lady Davidson as its first chairman. In 1918

Miss Higson was appointed as the full-time organising secretary to the Advisory Board which was particularly concerned to recruit more moral welfare workers.

Octavia Hill had died in 1912, but the periodic meetings which she had arranged were continued by Miss Harriet Yorke. In 1916 the Association of Women Housing Workers was formed, its title changing to the Association of Women House Property Managers in 1917. The Ministry of Munitions appointed the first trained women housing managers in the same year for work in emergency housing areas (Macadam, 1925, p. 147).

Mental hygiene and American links

Conspicuous by its absence in this description of developments during the First World War is any extension of theory or fundamental discussion of techniques. Whether we look at the work of the Charity Organisation Society, settlements, almoning or probation there is little sense that social workers were progressing in their understanding of the relationship of the individual to the environment and the part that social workers played in helping people with problems. There was, it is true, a development of the understanding of poverty and its social causation following Booth's and Rowntree's investigations, and the growth in the complexity of statutory social services added to the field of expertise which social workers held in linking those in need with appropriate aid. Also the values of responsible service which had been developed and cultivated in the pre-war phase of social work were maintained. But a missing piece of the jigsaw was the clumsiness of our psychological knowledge which would help in the fundamental problem for social work of teasing out the inter-relationship of environmental and personality factors in an individual's life history.

The mental hygiene movement had advanced much more quickly in America than in this country. Although the British Child Study Association had been formed in 1893,[18] it was not until 1913 that Burt was appointed to the London Inspectorate to investigate children with special difficulties; however, his work during the war and afterwards was to exercise a strong influence in the whole educational field, not only in relation to difficult children. In America development in the hospital field and in work with delinquents was further advanced by the outbreak of war. Dr A. Meyer's work at Manhattan State Hospital, Dr Pitman's work at Massachusetts

General Hospital and the work at the Boston Psychopathic Hospital —all involving social service in the hospital setting directed to mentally ill patients and their after-care—had advanced considerably in the decade before the start of the First World War. In the field of delinquency W. Healey was the undisputed leader and his Chicago Juvenile Psychopathic Institute was established in 1909 after he had put forward the idea of a programme of research to a conference at Hull House in the previous year. His work strongly influenced social workers and his book *The Individual Delinquent*, published in 1915, was read by Mary Richmond with great interest; her own book *Social Diagnosis* was published in 1917. Also in 1917 the Judge Baker Clinic was founded with a training programme which included students from the Simmons and Smith College Schools of Social Work. Smith College offered the first full training in psychiatric social work in 1918. The whole field of mental hygiene was encouraged by the establishment of the National Committee for Mental Hygiene in 1909 with Dr T. W. Salmon as its medical director.

Other indications of America's broader interest in psychiatry and—despite much concern with the welfare of children and adults in need—of this country's more cautious approach were the banning of Havelock Ellis's *Studies in the Psychology of Sex*, which was the first systematic study in English of the ideas of Breuer and Freud, and the fact that the first translation of Freud's *Interpretation of Dreams* was published in America.

The war developed interest in psychiatry and Dr Salmon visited Europe in 1917 to study the effect of 'war neuroses'. The problem of soldiers suffering from psychological traumata as the result of shell shock and other war experiences had led to the establishment in this country of training in understanding the psychoneuroses in special centres because this knowledge had not yet been incorporated in medical training programmes. It was the experience of many specialists in trying to treat wartime neuroses, that apart from the particular instigating circumstances and symptoms there was nothing essentially different from the patterns of stress and breakdown which might occur in civilian life; often wartime patients had exhibited nervous symptoms before the war. Following Dr Salmon's visit to Europe the Division of Psychiatry, Neurology and Psychology was established in the Army Medical Corps and an elaborate training and hospital programme organised.

In the late nineteenth century British social work experience had had a strong impact in the USA, but then the Americans had developed a theoretical base faster than in England. For example, Octavia Hill's influence had been strong in the USA where her essays were published by the Boston Associated Charities. A further direct influence on Mary Richmond was Charles Loch's visit to her at the Baltimore Charity Organisation Society in 1896, during which he showed her an English case record which had impressed her by its progression 'from definite principles towards definite conclusion'.[19] Yet the quickening development of social work in America did not go unquestioned. Its status as a profession was attacked in 1915 by Abraham Flexner, who in a paper entitled 'Is Social Work a Profession?' pointed out that 'Social Work is the mediator whose concern it is to summon the expert'.[20] This feature of social work— as an intermediary between social services and citizens—has been held to involve special skills, equally as important as skills in psychological diagnosis, but it is clear that such an interpretation was not so immediately attractive to many social workers at the time and did not seem to hold the same promise of scientific progress as other approaches.

Thus it was that Mary Richmond's emphasis on social evidence as a basis for a differential casework, and the developments in psychiatry, established the possibility of a scientific social work and a realistic search for knowledge on which a social work profession might be based. As yet in this country social work was being undertaken in a variety of institutions and agency settings with little vision of a unity of tested methods of working in relation to a core of professional values. It is important that the first theoretical formulation of any depth was by a woman who had been prominent in establishing training schemes for social workers. In the field of psychiatry as with physical medicine men were the driving force with women as their ancillary workers in the social field. This reinforces the pattern that we have already seen in other forms of social work—of women tending to occupy the lower positions in the professional hierarchy in social work organisations, with training the field in which women in social work have been able to achieve a degree of leadership and influence.

The work of women in the war had been the turning point of the campaign for women's suffrage and under the Representation of the People Act, which received the Royal Assent on 6 February 1918, women householders over thirty years of age were enfranchised; other groups of women enfranchised were wives of householders, occupiers of property of £5 or more in value and graduates of British universities. Constance Rover in her study of politics and the suffrage movement appraised the change in the climate of opinion produced by the war (Rover, 1967, p. 205): 'The obvious effect was that women's contribution to the war effort was seen and appreciated and that women, instead of being subjected to frequent criticism in the press and by public figures, were generally praised.' Gaining the vote in 1918 gave a basis for future improvements in the position of women. In the following decades effort was concentrated on women's entry to particular professions, and to some extent there was a loss of unity in the women's movements.

8   Women's social position and career prospects 1918-39

Limited emancipation for women

A number of events occurred in the first two or three years after the war of significance for the twin fields of social work and the emancipation of women. The battle for emancipation reached a significant stage when Countess Markievicz was elected as an MP in 1918 and Viscountess Astor became the first woman to take her seat in the House of Commons in 1919. 1919 was also the year when the Sex Disqualifications (Removal) Act opened all public offices, the professions and higher appointments in the Civil Service to women. In 1920 Oxford University admitted women to degrees and membership of the university and in the same year the first women magistrates were appointed (169 in England, 42 in Scotland and 21 in Wales). Later in 1928 the full franchise was achieved for women. These events have a double importance in that they demonstrate positive achievements in removing women's handicaps to full participation in community and professional life but also show clearly how painfully slow the battle was; they were pinpricks in the real structure of power in the male world.

Before the war, although the number of working women had increased, this increase had still been confined to domestic employment and the lower professions. For instance, in the twenty-year period 1881-1901 the total of occupied women had increased from almost three and a half million to over four million. Yet the proportions of employed women in domestic work and manufacturing had remained at 44 per cent and 40 per cent respectively. The number of women employed in professional groups had increased

Table 8.1   Number of occupied women, 1881 and 1901

	Nursing and subordinate medical services	Teaching
1881	38,000	123,000
1901	68,000	172,000

102

57 per cent in that period but this was mainly in the teaching profession and nursing and subordinate medical services (see Table 8.1).

Even in 1911, women only formed 6 per cent of those occupied in the higher professions. All this bears out the picture given of the pre-war development of social work, that although philanthropy as a voluntary activity was a significant feature of social welfare in this country, paid professional work was insignificant as a career for any but a small minority of women because of the lack of identification of a clear area of professional expertise and the related problems of establishing training. The availability of a reservoir of women from the upper classes fostered an era of glorious amateurism but hindered the identification of an activity or competence for which training of a high quality was necessary. Thus it is that under the category of Social Welfare and Related Workers in the 1921 Census, the first Census to include this category in the list of classified occupations, the number was given as 3,085, 1,863 being women and 1,222 men. It must be remembered that this category was drawn much more widely than the limited range of social workers usually dealt with in accounts of the development of social work. It included: inspector, official or secretary of NSPCC or RSPCA; inspector, official or secretary of social and physical improvement, and temperance societies; play centre worker, temperance lecturer, welfare supervisor. Nevertheless, it is clear that men were already heavily involved in welfare work and formed about 40 per cent of the workers, a higher proportion than in nursing and teaching at that time. However, we have seen in the pre-war period that the distribution of men and women in different spheres of social work was variable, often depending on the sexual composition of the clientele and the sexual taboos restricting the contact of men with women or girls and of women with men and older boys.

Employment problems

Career prospects for women between the wars suffered from the same social difficulties that beset the whole country with difficulties in employment. There was a higher ratio of women to men with the wartime loss of men contributing to sharpen this feature of the sex structure for our population. The proportion of occupied female population over the age of fifteen remained approximately one-third, but the proportion of single women fell slightly between

1921 and 1931 from 53·5 per cent to 50 per cent. In the period leading up to the Second World War the same trend continued. The trend to smaller families gathered strength during the inter-war period, with families marrying in the 1925–9 period having an average of just over two children compared with the five to six children of mid-Victorian parents.

In general this was a period when women won the right of entry to many of the male professional strongholds and diversified their range of occupations. Dr Ivy Williams was the first woman called to the English Bar in 1922 and the following year Mrs Crofts became the first woman to be admitted as a member of the Law Society. In 1924 Miss Ethel Watts was the first woman to pass the final examinations of the Institute of Chartered Accountants. In the Civil Service Miss Enid Russel-Smith, Miss Alix Kilroy and Miss Mary Smeeton were the first women to pass into the administrative grade of the Civil Service by examination on equal terms to men. By 1931 the number of women in professional and technical occupations was 394,000 (men 404,000) but there was the same predominance of women in teaching and nursing which largely accounted for this total. During the 1920s entry was gained to many professions and the position of women was strengthened in the 1930s. Yet with all this effort there were severe limits, because by 1951 the proportion of women in the higher professions had only increased to 8 per cent compared to 6 per cent forty years earlier.

How things seemed in the early post-war period is graphically set out in an undated (circa 1920) manuscript of a speech by Miss Pauline Strachey at a conference on unemployment amongst women.[1] Miss Strachey asserted:

It was thus I learnt that in this country occupations were divided into men's work and women's work. When I investigated further I found that interesting agreeable and well paid occupations were classified . . . as men's work, and ill paid work was classified as women's work. When I investigated further still I found that in some of the men's occupations there were certain processes that were uninteresting disagreeable and ill paid and that these processes were classified as women's work, while similarly I found that in some of the women's occupations there were processes that were interesting agreeable and well paid and that these processes were classified as men's work. You will say that I am exaggerating. I am. But only a tiny bit. It is true as regards by far the greater part of these islands. Men's work can only be undertaken by people who have come through a certain training and women are forbidden to enter such training.

Miss Strachey goes on to assess the contribution of women to the war:

> My society during the war took a considerable share in the replacing of men by women: among other jobs it fell to our lot to select the first women to be employed in government munitions work—the supervisors to be trained to train others. We were enthusiasts on the subject ourselves. We knew we should find women who would be quick to the new learning. What we did find surprised even us—hundreds and thousands of women conscious of a strong natural bent towards mechanics and eager to use their gifts. And so in every occupation. It was a real revelation—not so much of unknown capacities as of the widespread suffering which the repression of those capacities was causing.

The difficult employment situation after the war and the unemployment problems during the 1930s were an important factor in slowing down the progress of women. In the immediate period following the war the world's employment situation worsened (not only was this due to the economic situation but also to the fact that many women gave up their jobs to men returning from the war). How this affected women in municipal authorities was commented on by Miss Strachey. The workers affected included

> amongst others such as clerks, matrons, and librarians, the great class of teachers and the comparatively small but important class of health workers. I cannot say that the axe has yet fallen here but its shadow is making itself unpleasantly felt in several ways—in a marked tendency towards reduction of salaries, in the omission to fill posts that become vacant and in the omission to make fresh appointments where increased work appears to demand them.

In an overall assessment of the situation Miss Strachey was of the opinion:

> We have gone back now to nearly where we were before the war, nearly but not quite. . . . In the comparatively short time

since we have had our votes we have made considerable
headway. Barriers are going down: the legal professions have
been thrown open, the higher division of HM Civil Service
will be open in 1924; in many other directions we have advanced
but it is not until we are admitted to the skilled trades that
relief will be felt on an adequate scale. There must be no
rest till then. The unsound economic position is at the root
of all their troubles. Equally with men they must be free to
enter what occupations they choose according to the work
they do. Equally with men they must be paid according to
the work they do.

The situation did not improve as rapidly as had been expected,
and in the *Women's Year Book* for 1923–4 a depressing picture is
painted of the effects of economic slump on the employment of
women.[2] Experienced teachers were out of work and many of those
leaving college had no jobs. The last remnants of the women who
had been temporary civil servants were being demobilised:[3]

> Teaching cuts still operate. Health Visitors, Sanitary Inspectors,
> and Infant Welfare Workers' appointments are less frequent,
> and social work is hampered in every diréction by lack of
> funds. The slump in salaries referred to above is even more
> pronounced than in June 1922. Health Visitors posts are
> advertised at scandalous salaries . . . .

As did Pauline Strachey, the handbook emphasised the importance
of the recognition of women's right to enter the professions:[4]

> the pioneer work that a small number [of women] have been
> able to do is distinctly cheering. . . . In Law, Accountancy,
> the Actuarial Profession, Estate Agency, Auctioneering and
> Surveying and Veterinary surgery, the few pioneers who were
> able to avail themselves of the situation lost no time in
> embarking upon technical training and in 1922 these women
> began to emerge fully qualified members of their profession.

A further problem, however, had been the growing tendency among
public authorities against the employment of married women either
as teachers or in other departments of public work.
    Some of the key women in social work and social service were
members of the editorial advisory committee of the *Women's
Year Book*—Elizabeth Macadam, Eleanor Rathbone, Mary Stocks

(chairman), Barbara Wootton and Chrystal MacMillan. Of these only Elizabeth Macadam remained firmly entrenched in the battle to extend the frontiers of social work, the others having moved away into broader fields of political and social life. This fact is described by Miss Clement Brown, looking back from the vantage point of 1933. She was conscious that many turned away from social work after the First World War, either going into politics or labour organisation, or into the fields of health, recreation, housing and education. Some turned away from the social work to 'other branches of the study of human beings to see whether further light could be thrown upon the solution of the problem of personality'.[5] But at this point they had been unified by a common aim—the extension of women's educational and occupational opportunities to a point of equality with men.

Some indication of the gradual loss of impetus in the general women's movement is given by the fact that in 1925 the *Women's Leader*, of which Elizabeth Macadam and Mary Stocks were co-editors, was in financial difficulties, and in 1925 Elizabeth Macadam had to write to Marjorie Lees in Oldham to ask for financial help to keep it going.

Low pay and poor prospects in social work

During the 1930s Ray Strachey investigated the opportunities for women and published a guide, *Careers and Openings for Women*, which contains much useful information about the employment situation.[6] He started from the premise that 'whatever society decides to do with the productive powers of women should at least be done with deliberate intention, and upon a basis of knowledge'.[7] In describing the existing prospects for girls over eighteen the following fields were listed: nursing, teaching, institutional management, social work, hospital almoner work, house property management, the professions. After explaining that social work was attractive to a large number of girls and that few openings were available under the age of twenty-one, Strachey continued:[8]

> No one can pretend that this is a career which leads to wealth, for the salaries and money rewards are often tiny, and the prospects at all times uncertain. But the men and women who do this work are not seeking for financial return. Some of them work for nothing, and the rest are content with a bare living. This career even more than Nursing or Teaching, is

undertaken in a vocational spirit, and for those who feel the impulse to devote themselves to it there are many varied possibilities. There is work in Clubs and Settlements and with Societies carrying on special social efforts, such as Housing Societies, Societies for the Blind, for the Unemployed, for Infants, for Mothers, for Invalid Children, for Country Holidays or Playgrounds, work with care committees, Police Court Missions and Rescue Homes. In addition there are jobs in the nature of research, surveys, investigations and the like and posts under the Charity Organisation Society. For most of these jobs a secretarial training is likely to be useful, and a Diploma in Social Science is a good preparation.

For university-trained girls hospital almoning and house property management were seen as the main careers with hope of expansion. The proportion of women graduates entering social work was not large and Strachey analysed the occupations of a random sample of 100 women graduates as shown in Table 8.2.[9]

Table 8.2 Occupations of women graduates, 1930s

	%
Teaching	58
Scientific Work	10
Social Work	8
Civil Servants	5
Secretaries	5
Other	14
	100

At this stage there was still a very broad view of social work as a field of employment and it had not yet begun to be confined to case-work organisations. The absence of any great prospects placed limits upon the type and number of recruits, its major competitor at the university level being the teaching profession and at non-university level nursing.[10]

Class and social work

Trained women, particularly those who had been to university, were middle- or upper-class. Some insight into this class factor and its permeation of the welfare system can be gained from considering comments from Cecile Matheson, Barbara Wootton and Mary Stocks, and an incident in the probation service in the 1930s. Miss Matheson provides a link with the past in a passage occurring in an article on settlement work in 1915. She writes:[11]

> All social agencies have their place in the upward struggle of a nation, but the Settlement has a peculiar influence that is denied to the non-residential centre. Its workers are not uniformed; they go about as ordinary human beings, but the neighbourhood is quick to recognise the mysterious power given by educational and inheritance of education, and to do it homage. It means a great deal when our women call us 'ladies', and in that word they express their sense of this power given to us by our happier growth. Because of this power they turn to us with a touching faith that we shall never be mean, or ungenerous or fail in knowledge or explanation. Because we live among them they regard us as of special treasure to be guarded and made much of. The newcomer is often afraid that pretty clothes, the motor of a friend coming to fetch her for a drive, or general evidence of well being, may seem heartless to those who have so little. On the contrary, she soon finds that pretty clothes are a pleasure to eyes wearied of the surrounding greyness, that the motor is looked upon as a kind of compliment to the neighbourhood, and that no one is beloved as the one with the cheerful smile. Their deference expressed itself in another way. 'Ladies' are not supposed to hear bad language, and we are surrounded by a touching chivalry that would protect us from all knowledge of evil. We think that it is perhaps a help to the women themselves that the approach of a 'Settlement Lady' is a signal for quarrels to cease and we feel this to be a great tribute to the Settlement. Of course all this deference is hard to bear until one realises that it is just one form of the respect of the young to the old, of the pupil to the teacher. We are practically, older souls and therefore people turn to us with confidence and trust, and believe that we will understand their troubles.

A few years later a different perspective is given by Barbara Wootton who, after graduating at Cambridge spent part of her time lecturing to social science students at Westfield College:[12]

The Social Science students of those days were very different from their modern counterparts. Few of them were training to become professional social workers; mostly they were young women of means and leisure who wished to engage in various charitable activities. Thanks largely to the influence of what was then the Charity Organisation Society (now imperfectly disguised as the Family Welfare Association), they had grasped that if you wanted to make a success of 'slumming', or to set the poor to rights, it is better to know something of the lives of the people into whose business you propose to interfere. So they came in their cars and their pearls and their elegant clothes to hear what I and others had to say, and I for my part dutifully tried to teach them what I had myself been taught.

Barbara Wootton's socialist convictions and distrust of traditional economic theory made her sceptical of social work when she later taught social work students at Bedford College towards the end of the Second World War.[13]

In the wider welfare field there was evidence of similar influence of class factors. It became customary for the women's view to be represented on a wide range of committees and boards and the inter-war period saw the evolution of the 'statutory woman'. Mary Stocks outlines how women such as Lady Violet Bonham Carter, Lady Emmet, Margery Fry, and Shena Simon became part of a small group of women used over and over again on government committees (Stocks, 1970, p. 103). Indeed, Mary Stocks joined this select band of women and as one of her activities served on the Unemployment Insurance Statutory Committee, becoming close friends with Violet Markham with whom she investigated service conditions of women during the Second World War.

A final example of the implications of class, and also the relations of men and women, concerns the probation service (Bochel, 1963). During the late 1920s the financial position of the National Association of Probation Officers was weak. At this time, Miss Gertrude Tuckwell, the first woman JP[14] was president and Lord Feversham was vice-president of the association. It was important that the social contacts should be exploited to the full and to aid this Miss Tuckwell and Lord Feversham exchanged positions in 1930. As an example of the canvassing that went on for the association a civic reception was organised at the Mansion House in 1930. Lord Feversham was promised a large sum of money in the same year by Mrs

William Carrington of New York. Through financial misfortune Mrs Carrington had to discontinue her grant, but for two years the Pilgrim Trust offered £1,000 annually. A small group of thirty influential persons including Lord Feversham, Miss Tuckwell and the Archbishop of York met at the home of Sir Herbert Samuel (formerly Home Secretary) and the outcome was a trust fund which established the Clarke Hall Fellowship and started an appeal which helped substantially with the finance of NAPO for twelve years.

These illustrations show to what extent social work and welfare were bound up with the oligarchic social business and government institutions of the nation. The paternalistic and maternalistic attitudes which derived from this natural social authority may appear suspect to present-day social workers, but only if we avoid asking questions about the sources of authority for present-day social work. It is arguable that for the authority of social position we have substituted the authority of social planners and professionalism. It is clear that many women were not unthinking victims of birth into privileged social situations, but acknowledged the problems which arose from this fact and attempted to use their position to produce a more balanced society.

9   Women in social work organisations 1918–39

General or specialised social work

It has been seen that before the First World War the Charity
Organisation Society dominated the social work scene under the
leadership—based on administrative skill and philosophical imagination—of C. S. Loch. The pattern of male secretaries continued
during the war and inter-war periods with the Rev. J. C. Pringle
(1914–19, 1925–36), H. L. Woolcombe (1919–23), M. W. Fox
Strangeways (acting secretary 1923–5) and B. G. Astbury (1936–56).
Although the Charity Organisation Society was not unenterprising,
in that it developed work on new housing estates and took part in
movements for legislation on hire purchase and the adoption of
children, there was a sense that it was not adapting itself to the new
situation of expanding statutory services. J. C. Pringle,[1] the dominant
force in the inter-war period, strongly upheld the traditional Charity
Organisation Society philosophy 'putting the Charity Organisation
Society at the centre and out of touch with political reality' (Rooff,
1972). In her study of the Charity Organisation Society, Madeline
Rooff emphasises that the Charity Organisation Society co-operated
happily with expanding statutory workers and acted as an auxiliary
family casework service, even judging that 'local charity organisations
came nearest to fulfilment in the society's history'. Yet during this
period 'there was an element of truth in the assertion that the period
was one of stagnation. The centre had lost its drive and an outworn
theory was perpetuated.' Because statutory services had many gaps
and inadequacies there was still much that the Charity Organisation
Society could do to help families as a whole, but no new coherent
philosophy was established. But even at the outbreak of the Second
World War the society had thirty district offices and it must have
been difficult for those working in the society to be firmly convinced
that radical rethinking was necessary.

It was just this necessity for a scientific theory that was slow in
developing in this country and which gave significance to the development in psychiatric social work. Had the Charity Organisation
Society been able to reformulate its methods and theory during this

period the history of social work could well have been more unitary. Yet in the period after the First World War social work was not characterised by a scientific approach. Miss Clement Brown in a study of eighty case records during the period comments:[2]

> One's first impression in pondering eighty case records is that there is no accepted discipline of social casework; that apart from certain administrative routines typical of different services, the whole process is largely determined by the immediate situation and the caseworker's common sense impressions and intuitive responses. The enthusiastic reader of Mary Richmond's *Social Diagnosis*, the student who comes expecting to find 'all the reason of science' clearly marshalled for the solution of human problems will come away sadly disillusioned.

It was true that Helen Bosanquet had as early as 1896 advocated something like the diagnostic procedure of medicine for social work but this was always seen as a relatively simple thing.[3] Attlee in his book *The Social Worker* in 1920 saw social work as a form of social activity particularly suited to women, but although he argued that the 'social worker required training like anybody else' his conception of the social worker was of a humane social welfare administrator having a dual role of helping individuals and of influencing social reform. Had he developed this view of social work at a more theoretical level and remained closer to the social work field, this might have provided a counterbalancing alternative or complement to the growth in psychological knowledge and skill which was to begin towards the end of the first decade after the war.

In a country where a wealth of broad welfare legislation was being created the linking, co-ordinating function of social work could have been developed as an essential part of knowledge and skill relevant to all administrative settings of social work. This never receded into the background as much as in America, but there is no doubt that under American influence, the quest for a scientific base moved in the direction of unravelling human personality. In essence there was an attempt to shift the focus from environmental influences to psychological ones. In spite of this shift the effort was diffuse in this country and this is one of the reasons for the slow development of social work as a profession in England. It is for this reason that for an understanding of social work in the inter-war

E

period we must still turn to an analysis of the functional specialisms and relate this to the position of women.

Almoning[4]

By 1919 there were about 50 trained almoners, increasing to about 74 in 1925 and 343 in 1939.[5] The institute had decided that there was no reason why men should not become almoners and from 1919 they were eligible for training, but there is no mention of a man becoming a student during the inter-war period (Miss Snelling mentions that a rumour of a male student did not 'electrify everybody until 1913'). Recruitment improved after the war and was helped by some VAD scholarships, but generally the training was only available to middle-class people who could pay the fees. The expansion remained to some extent centred in London and in 1925 Miss Macadam had expressed the wish that 'It is surely not unreasonable to hope that in the near future every hospital will have its own social service department'.[6] However, although Sir George Newsom, Chief Medical Officer of Health had given official recognition to the movement in his Memorandum entitled 'Recent Advances in Medical Education in England' (HMSO, 1923), the movement did not gain momentum as rapidly as in the USA.

The annual report of the Hospital Almoners Council (1918 and 1919) reaffirmed the interdependence of medicine and social work in the prevention of disease, but felt 'that to induce the Hospital authorities to accept this point of view has been uphill work'. In a significant passage the report continues:

> It cannot be supposed that the possibility of social service in
> hospitals is exhausted. Hitherto its limit has been casework
> for the good of the individual, and this must always remain the
> vital part; at the same time there are other issues. Casework
> alone, though it may be helpful and constructive to the
> individual, will not reach the root cause unless there be
> progressive understanding of the problems underlying it. In
> social research work there is still much ground to be covered.

Why, in view of the setting out with such aims and hopes, did almoners become disenchanted with the inter-war period? Miss Snelling calls the period 1920–40 'Depression and Stagnation', and in spite of the growth of almoning sees the mood of the two decades as 'negative, both in almoners' social work and in their training'.

One important reason was associated with the almoners' attitudes to collecting contributions from patients. Until after the war most hospital treatments had been free; the service was for poor people and in 1919 only patients with incomes up to 10*s*. or 12*s*. per week above rent were considered suitable for out-patient treatment. The almoner's concern with money had been in assessing means and eligibility, but not collecting money. Following the war financial difficulties forced voluntary hospitals to ask patients for contributions towards treatment or maintenance; almoners were to be expected to assess and collect the contributions. The association accepted this task as part of their work but insisted that scales of charges should be flexible. In time this task became a normal part of almoners' duties and was used as a justification for appointing almoners to voluntary hospitals because of their efficiency in raising revenue. At the time there does not appear to have been any strong resistance to acceptance of this function as part of the almoner's role. Miss Snelling regarded this as a professional calamity in that they

> put upon almoners for the next thirty years the burden of
> arguing defensively that they were social workers in the teeth
> of a public conviction that they were collectors of fees. Not
> only was this a public conviction; the hospital boards, the
> doctors and nurses, social workers outside the hospitals,
> and the universities came to see them as collectors first and
> social workers second.

Miss Beck considered that the

> gulf between the hospital authorities' idea of an almoner and
> the almoner's aspirations as a medical social worker had
> widened in some places until few could bridge it, and almoners
> who still considered that their vocation was medical social
> work might find it impossible to undertake simultaneously
> both the work for which they had been appointed and the work
> for which they had been trained.

Thus between the wars the running battle which almoners had fought with the male-dominated hospital administrators and doctors for acceptance continued unabated. They felt that their true social work functions were misunderstood and above this often had to cope with inefficient administration of the general running of hospitals (Beck, 1948). There was too, apart from London and the largest provincial cities, the problem of isolation; there was often no other trained social worker in the district to give support. Miss Beck was concerned about students and implied that sometimes in difficult circumstances these fell because not all the second generation of almoners could be expected to 'possess the immense force of personality and conviction of the original hand-picked and closely knit group of pioneers'. The women accepted for training were expected to have 'had a liberal education (of a University student or its equivalent), and be women with a wide outlook and broad sympathies, possessing a genuine interest in the social problem of the day'.[7] Great emphasis was placed on the need for tact and intelligence in dealing with the patients and the hospital authorities and one wonders whether 'tact' with its connotations of non-directiveness and passivity was always the best approach. The earlier title of 'ladies' and 'candidates' for those taking almoner training had given way by the earlier 1920s to 'students',[8] but we have seen that because of the fees the majority of applicants had to be middle-class women.[9] It is possible to argue—and Miss Snelling implies as much—that almoners sold their social work souls to the devil; their willingness to comply with this seems at least in part to be due to deferential attitudes of almoners and an unwillingness to depart from a middle-class behavioural code which would not embrace anger. In giving acceptance the almoners had to be compliant and put faith in expressions of the worthwhileness of their efforts from medical authorities without the certainty that this would result in action.

The almoners did make attempts to win over the men and broaden the representation on its committees. In 1925 the vice-presidents of the institute were Thomas Eden Esq., MD; Sir Frederick Milner, Bart.; Mrs Scharlieb, CBE, MD; and the Hon. Sir Arthur Stanley. The executive consisted of:

Miss Cummins	Miss Richmond
Mrs Eden	Miss Ronaldson
Miss Edminson	Mr James Thomas
A. Charles Grey,	Mrs Major Stevenson
Esq., MD (chairman)	(Women's Employment
Miss McGraw	Bureau Joint
Rev. J. C. Pringle[10]	Council)

The following year a number of new vice-presidents were added to the existing ones:

Sir John Rose Bradford	Sir Henry Hadow
(president of the	Sir George Makins
Royal College of	Sir Berkley Moynihan
Physicians;	Sir John Robertson
Lady Bradford	Sir St Clair Thompson
was president)	Sir Thomas Barlow

In the same year new members of the institute were: Dr Elizabeth Bolton, Dr Birly, Dr Fairbairn, Ida Cannon (of the Social Service Department, Massachusetts General Hospital), Miss Macadam (Hon. Sec., Joint University Council), Professor Tillyard (Birmingham University) and Professor Carr-Saunders (Liverpool University).

A further important effort to proselytise was made at the local level by the establishment of advisory committees at Leeds in 1924 and later at Liverpool, Birmingham and Newcastle, all of which had training committees by 1930. These committees closely associated with the universities had the function of developing training and selecting students. In 1934 the Liverpool advisory committee consisted of the following:

Chairman	Miss Keeling, MEB, MA
Vice chairman	W. Rutter, Esq.
Hon. sec.	Miss L. G. Price, AIHA

Executive committee

Miss G. I. Black, BSc(Econ)	Miss Williams, AIHA
Professor A. M. Carr-Saunders, MA	C. A. McRoberts, Esq.
Miss Glenn, AIHA	C. O. Stallybrass, Esq., MD
Miss Roxburgh, MA, AIHA	J. P. Steel, Esq., MD

and representatives from the general, women's and children's hospitals on Merseyside

The Leeds advisory committee of the same period had, in addition to university and almoner members, medical representatives from Leeds General Infirmary and the Leeds Public Health Authority. Nevertheless this had not prevented one member of the IHA Council resigning in 1933 after many years of membership because he thought that the institute was 'out of touch with the modern hospital movement and so they had no hope of getting social service departments developed within those hospitals' (Snelling, 1970). He thought that they should get the key figures from hospital boards on to the council and stop re-electing the same members.[11]

If the attempts to establish a widespread service in the 1920s and to overcome the resistance already described were only partially successful, there was positive development in internal organisation at the end of the decade with the establishment of a system of subcommittees—propaganda, provincial, report and hospital training.[12] In 1931 a general training sub-committee was established. The development of the advisory committees had strengthened development in the regions. But did the evolution of training for almoners—a pivotal issue in professional progress—establish a focus on theory related to skill in practice? If this had been possible there would have been less cause for the misunderstandings of doctors and others about the nature of medical social work repeatedly commented on by almoners. In 1919 the almoning training had extended to two years: four months general family casework, three terms at the London School of Economics, and eleven months' hospital work; this pattern remained almost unchanged during the inter-war period, and this meant that there was no direct teaching on methods of social work, this being done in the apprenticeship model during practical work. The JUC's earlier concern with industrial welfare widened to a general concern with courses of social work and turned more particularly to almoning in 1925. In 1925 the institute lowered its age of entry to the final year of training in response to JUC pressure, so that students completing social science courses could embark immediately on their practical training. Thus the minimum age for qualification became twenty-two and it was also agreed that younger students should normally complete a two years' certificate course as a prerequisite for the final year, giving a total of three years in all; graduates or older students would be allowed to omit the social studies two years or take a reduced social studies course. Social studies students were still mainly women and their social studies courses had as yet still not gained full academic responsibility. Miss Macadam, secretary of the JUC, had been co-opted to the council in 1925 after attending a meeting of the institute to propose that the JUC and the institute should draw up a joint report on the work and training of hospital almoners. This was done and the result was the JUC report 'Training for Hospital Social Work', 1926. Unfortunately, the possibility of developing social work theory was seriously handicapped when the institute's tutoring appointment, begun in 1913 with Miss Verral (later Mrs Thomas), fell into abeyance when she left the institute in 1925. This had held the germ of theoretical growth as Miss Verral had made arrangements for lectures at the London School of Economics and for reading time during the institute's qualifying year. For all the inhibitions to theoretical development, it is as well to recall that Miss Macadam felt in 1925 that training for hospital almoners was more systematically organised than training for most forms of social work and attributed this to the fact that they had their own professional association which awarded its own certificates. They were also able to attract some highly qualified women to training. In 1928, for instance, there were forty-five students in training, twelve at the London School of Economics, twenty-five at hospitals and twelve with the Charity Organisation Society. Nine of the students were graduates: four of Oxford University, one of Cambridge, two of London and two of Glasgow; while one student held the Oxford Diploma in Economics.[13] Not only did the fees of the institute make the profession mainly middle- and upper-class but also the limited access which women, especially working-class women, had to higher education. Nevertheless, at the onset of the Second World War, Miss E. M. Batten found the training offered by the institute lacking in method and in theoretical content and suggested that a tutor should be appointed to a preliminary training school.[14] Although the association and institute reacted positively, the war prevented exciting prospects from realisation.

Some aspects of the development of almoning are more easily looked at in relation to the growth of psychiatric social work and American influences, but it is appropriate to consider the development of almoning work in municipal hospitals at this point because it relates to a female profession not only infiltrating the male-dominated hospital world but also attempting to encroach the bastions of a patriarchal, paternalist local government system. Already before the war almoners had taken note of the 1911 Insurance Act and by the mid-1920s could try to take a more global view of the changes in the relation of voluntary and statutory social services. In 1926 it was recognised that[15] the

> first quarter of the twentieth century has shown an increase
> in social legislation which has affected the details of an
> Almoner's world in many ways. Gradually the state has taken
> over certain types of social work, which were carried through
> the experimental stages by voluntary work; while the same
> tendency is to be noted in much of the work done for children
> and young persons. The almoner co-operating with the

authorities with regard to the welfare of individual patients may have regrets for the passing of the old spirit of voluntary service, yet she finds that the scope and possibilities of her work are enormously increased by the operation of modern legislative enactments.

The passing of the Local Government Act 1929, with the passing of the control of Poor Law hospitals to the municipalities inspired the institute to draw up a memorandum emphasising the value of hospital social work and urging local authorities to make adequate provisions for it in their new schemes of administration. This memorandum was sent to all local authorities and medical officers of health in summer 1929. In this move is revealed the identical aim of the probation officers who had worked for a uniform court service throughout the country. If only local authorities could be convinced of the value, then it was feasible to see Miss Macadam's vision of a network pattern of hospital social service as no obsessional dream but a practical aim. Although Surrey County Council had appointed a trained almoner by the end of 1929, by 1935 only six other local authorities had formed almoning departments (including the London County Council). Extension of almoning departments in municipal hospitals might have progressed more quickly had it not been for the economic depression. The annual report of the institute for 1932 put the position more hopefully: 'Although Hospital Boards hesitate to establish a new department in these times of financial stringency, the movement grows; in spite of—or because of the present difficulties.'[16] Therefore most appointments were still to voluntary hospitals throughout the 1930s.[17]

Organisationally, the main structure was that of a single almoner manning a department or of a head almoner and an assistant. In 1930 there were sixty-eight hospitals with head almoners and sixty certified assistant almoners working in the same hospitals, plus five more almoners working in other London hospitals; only one of the sixty-eight head almoners was married.[18] In January 1935 there were 212 certificated almoners in posts at home and abroad, of whom only five were married. This was a single woman's profession, but with the increase in numbers of students in training (1931, 150; 1935, 122) it was not unnatural that eventually there would be wastage through marriage. In 1936 twenty-two almoners and students just qualified retired through marriage, so that even with the limited expansion between the wars in the late 1930s, it was not easy to meet the needs of new departments and of wastage.[19] Almoning provided a career, but one that was circumscribed in promotion opportunities and uncertain in conditions of work because of the widely varying standards of administration and clerical-administrative support within almoning departments. An opportunity to clarify the pay structure came when in 1937 the Bureau of Hospital Information asked the institute to draw up a scale of almoner's salaries for the information of hospital boards.[20] The institute looked at existing salaries and found the general level to be:

(a) single-handed Almoners according to type of hospital and length of experience required: £225–£300.
(b) Head Almoner with one assistant: from £250.
(c) Head Almoner with two or more assistants: from £350.
   Assistant Almoners:
(a) An assistant in first post after training: £200–£250.
(b) An assistant with experience: from £225, according to length of experience and size of hospital.

Nevertheless, at this time the salaries were at least equivalent to teaching and much better than nursing. The average normal salary for a certificated woman teacher in 1938 was £258 (Tropp, 1959), and even in 1946 the maximum for a staff nurse was £280 (Abel-Smith, 1961). To have taken the first step to national scales was important, because only a few years previously the institute had reiterated its policy[21]

to refrain from laying down any rules for the conduct of its associate members; so is the matter of conditions of work also left for mutual arrangement between the Almoner concerned and her hospital board. The Institute does, however, when the question arises, endeavour to stress the necessity for maintaining an adequate standard in the matter of salaries and holidays.

The comment continues with a reminder:

To anyone who realises the heavy responsibility and the need for initiative which the work entails and the standard of education and training which it requires it is plain that salaries should bear reference to these demands and that holidays be generous.

E*

This attitude to salaries—that it was slightly infra dig for the institute to taint itself with such matters—is again evidence of the cultural background of the almoners and also an element of political *naïveté*. It is as though the institute was—in spite of all its patient work—just awakening to the hard realities of a changing world. But also it is a measure of the resistance which almoners had to overcome and the sheer bad luck of the Depression years that Miss Beck found herself making the following assessment on the early development of almoning: 'After thirty years, almost every new appointment was still a pioneering venture.' Miss Snelling perhaps expressed the attitude of the late 1930s well in saying that by 'the late 'thirties the almoners were getting angry'. There may have been individual almoners who were keen protagonists for women's rights, but the records of the institute reveal no evidence of great concern with this matter. During the late 1920s the institute was represented on bodies such as the National Council of Women and the Central Council for Women and Girls, but the link does not seem to have been an active one. Similarly, although Mrs Stevenson represented the Women's Employment Bureau on the council, nothing of great moment seems to have emanated from this contact. This is also a mark of manners and breeding, which may be content with the patient furthering of a cause, rather than a spirited attacking outlook. In the event the failure to grow faster as a movement was only partly because of almoners' attitudes. They faced immense difficulties arising from inherent faith in the hospital systems and economic problems affecting both voluntary and statutory employers. Ultimately their cause was not helped by a failure to develop a theoretical basis to their work which was transmissible in a training course and which could be formulated clearly for other helping professions and the public.

Probation

As with almoners during the inter-war period, probation was marked by the gradual employment of probation officers by a statutory authority as well as voluntary bodies. The 1907 Probation Act had not made the appointment of probation officers obligatory and the 1922 Departmental Committee had found that 215 courts had failed to take steps to appoint a probation officer and that in many areas there were poor conditions of service and salaries.[22] When Miss Macadam looked at the situation in 1925 she found that there were about 800 probation officers, the great majority of whom were acting on behalf of religious and other voluntary societies.[23] Some, however, were appointed by the police courts and the Home Office itself appointed some officers in London dealing with juveniles[24] and a few dealing with adult offenders. Although there was a widespread recognition of the importance of the voluntary contribution to social work in the courts, the 1922 committee felt that there was a need for societies sponsoring court work to improve the education and training of their candidates, and saw the need to attract men and women of a higher education and better training. There was an ambivalence, characteristic of the period, leading to concern as to whether training would destroy the missionary spirit and whether in any case entrants to the service would be forthcoming of the right calibre. It was suggested that salaries for full-time men should be £200–£350 and for women £150–£250. A probation advisory committee was established following the report.

In 1925 the appointment of probation officers was made compulsory and the Secretary of State was empowered to regulate salaries and conditions of service, making each petty sessional division responsible for the supervision of probation officers. Training developments were slow, however, for the 1935 Departmental Committee had to make renewed pleas for training:[25]

> Emphasis has rightly been placed on the personality of the
> probation officer, but though in the past some probation officers
> have done excellent work without training, personality by
> itself is not enough. It must be reinforced by the knowledge
> and resources which the trained social worker possesses.

Following the report during the next year the Probation Training Board was established and a pattern of twelve weeks' training sponsored by the Home Office started. The Probation Training Board, with representation from appointing authorities and universities, was a mark of government recognition for social work training. Thus, throughout the period and, indeed, during the Second World War there was concern over the poor quality of probation workers. Most were of poor educational background, untrained, and those with training generally only possessed the Home Office twelve-week course. As the majority of probation officers were men, one had an overall picture of a poorly qualified male staff, who were nevertheless paid more than women throughout the 1920s and 1930s. The women were more often of a better educational background and likely to have had a social science qualification, yet this was not reflected in salary or status—as late as 1945 there was only one woman principal probation officer (Younghusband, 1947).

Already it has been shown how the role of the woman probation officer was principally with women, girls and younger boys, and between the wars one has further confirmation of the way in which women's work was determined by women's role in the family and society's attitudes to sexual roles. At the 1919 Annual Conference and annual general meeting of NAPO[26] there were twenty-five women present out of fifty-two attending, nine of them married and sixteen single. Mrs Holland read a paper on dealing with the married women and the child. After commenting that 'one of the most difficult problems of the present day is that of the married women and the child, and especially from the rescue point of view', she showed some ambivalence in being confined to dealing just with the women: 'I have often felt that I should like to take the man's part or do something to set things right on both sides. So we want to have a well balanced mind.' None the less, she emphasised the special contribution of the woman probation officer: 'I think it is time we women placed ourselves in such a position that we can help. The girls who come in for affiliation orders do need our help and we want to be ready.'

Following Mrs Holland's talk there was a discussion about mother and baby homes, affiliation payments and the effects of the war in removing the fathers of illegitimate children. Women probation officers had frequently been involved with the war pension committees and had often undertaken the collection of affiliation payments. In view of the discussions in almoning about the collection of contributions, it is noteworthy that one speaker (male) argued that receiving affiliation or separation allowances was not part of the probation officer's job. Mrs Holland had been slightly opposed to mother and baby homes but Mr Burnett put in a good word for them during the discussions illustrating not only attitudes to women but the limitations of thinking about social work at that time:

> Some of the homes are not what they ought to be but some of them do wonderful work . . . . But I do say this, let us give the workers at the home a word of encouragement, and they are not here to defend themselves. We shall get better

homes some day and I have got a deep regard for those
sweet women who are carrying on this difficult work. Let us
give them a word of encouragement . . . the only safety for the
child of immoral parents is to take the child away from the
mother, or to put her into some place where by religion
and other influences you can perhaps stir up some
maternal instinct.

Another speaker, Mr R. Banks KC, a magistrate at Great
Western Police Court, Battersea, was more direct in his sentimental
approach to women: 'I feel with regard to any Lady Probation
Officer that she is one you cannot be in the presence of five minutes
without knowing that she is walking in the footsteps of Christ.
(Hear, Hear).' Mr Banks was something of a wit and touched on a
theme often talked about but not often discussed in social work
literature, that of women's dress:

He would like to say something in connection with the ladies
and their work amongst girls. He wished that the ladies would
dress better (laughs and applause). There was no reason why
any should associate Godliness with the rag-bag. It could be
no attraction to those amongst whom they worked to appear
as if they had come out of the rag-bag.

In spite of this psychological acumen, Mr Banks would have sought
to remedy the situation by women probation officers wearing a
distinctive type of dress in visiting the girls at home. Another male
speaker, Mr Burnett, agreed with the tenor of Mr Banks' remarks
about women but pointed out that some often 'had not sufficient
money to buy better clothes. (Hear, Hear.)'

Mrs Mackintosh of Manchester developed the rescue theme
further in a paper on 'Probation and Missionary work among
Women and Girls'. She praised the police for putting women probation officers in touch with girls embarking on a life of prostitution
without charging them and gave reinforcement to ideas about
treatment:

For a very naughty child, where the home and environment
are bad, it is impossible to do anything unless she is taken
away. There might be some home where they can be kept until
they realise the other side of life. I stopped at the Borstal
institution on my way up to town, and it really is an
extraordinary place; one saw unlocked doors, happy girls,

working or enjoying wholesome play, everything absolutely unlike what it used to be.

Mrs Mackintosh then went on to stress the need for after-care whether the girl was at home, in a hostel or in a foster home.

The positive contribution that women could make with boys was stressed by Colonel Rich at the 1925 National Conference. He thought that in the work of looking after young people it was very, very important that they should have plenty of ladies in the work. They already had a lot, but the influence of some of those good ladies who worked amongst the lads was very great.[27]

That the differentiation in roles remained during the inter-war period is confirmed by the issuing of a Home Office circular on 31 July 1930 sent to justices and dealing with the serious objections to the use of men in the supervision of girls and women. This was considered by the 1936 Departmental Committee and the attitude reinforced.[28] Even apart from the risk arising from the relationships between a male probation officer and woman client it was thought that

a woman can deal with the case of another woman or girl
more effectively and with more freedom and less difficulty than
a man, and to place a woman or girl under the supervision
of a man is . . . neither to the advantage of the probationer
nor fair to the officer himself.

The point was driven home by the statement that the 'supervision of women presents special difficulties and in such cases an experienced woman officer is needed. Women probation officers are required for the supervision of children as well as women and girls placed on probation.' Other uses for women were in matrimonial cases where it could be helpful for a man and woman to co-operate, and in social investigations 'for which they are specially equipped by their knowledge of the details of home life, and for which they are employed in other branches of social work.'

Knowing that you were 'sweet', 'good' and 'walking in the foot-steps of Christ', indicated to women probation officers that they were appreciated and wanted. But it was small consolation to know that you were undertaking specially difficult work and getting paid less for it. An indication that the women were not happy with the situation is given by Miss Crossland, who at the 1925 National Conference spoke about her experience as a representative at a

Home Office meeting to discuss superannuation schemes. She said that,

> with regard to the previous Schemes her mind was in absolute chaos. She had spent the whole of the previous day at the Home Office as the only woman on the Committee. She was pleased to think that they had the advantage of a woman's membership, because she thought the women were lost sight of, whenever they were spoken of they were called female officers and she disliked it so much. (Hear, hear.)

Miss Crossland thought it unfair that women should pay the same for pensions as they were lower paid.

In the probation service one can see how the nature of the clientele determined the proportion of women as a result of certain taboos and cultural patterns. In 1910 and 1930 the breakdown of persons on probation in England and Wales was as shown in Table 9.1.[29]

Table 9.1   Persons on probation, England and Wales, 1910 and 1930

| | Under 16 | | 16–21 | | Over 21 | | |
	Male	Female	Male	Female	Male	Female	Total
1910	3,294	435	2,773	642	1,908	1,171	10,223
1930	7,069	486	5,010	892	3,126	1,406	17,989

It could be reasonably asked why the same factors did not operate with almoning since men and women are sick in hospital and men have diseases of sexual organs and other ailments which are embarrassing. The answer would seem to take two forms. First, nursing and auxiliary medical services have traditionally been female occupations, developing from family roles, and in America, by contrast to this country, many of the early almoners were recruited from the ranks of trained nurses. Second, already in hospitals there had developed a series of conventions for nurses and doctors in coping with contact with patients of the opposite sex, whether by the control of the contact situation, rigid procedures, denial of emotion and joking relationships.[30] In the probation service, the problems of women and girls are very frequently concerned with problems of sexual development, promiscuity and illegitimacy, and fears of accusation of sexual assault. Moreover, the interviews might not take place in a neutral office situation, but alone with the woman in her home. A further factor involved is the professional status of the men in the probation service. The early male agents in the Charity Organisation Society had been of lower middle-class or upper working-class origins. Similarly, the evidence of the inter-war period clearly suggests similar origins for the majority of male probation officers. Given this situation, and the lack of clear professional identity within the probation service, it follows that one could not have much trust in their ability to cope with potentially sexual situations in a professional way as one could in a doctor or psychiatrist.[31] Besides these negative arguments there was the recurrent theme, referred to in the 1936 Departmental Committee's report, that women can understand other women best. Whether put forward by women or men this argument in extreme forms has tended to be used to create arenas of female activity within dominantly male spheres, an uneasy compromise, or as an attempt to create an exclusive community of women.

Psychiatric social work[32]

There seems to be substantial agreement that the importance of the development of psychiatric social work in this country stems from the influence it brought from American social work—it was not an indigenous development like the Charity Organisation Society, almoning and probation—and that it was the carrier of psychological knowledge which might in the future underpin the scientific basis of social work practice.[33] Also, significantly in contrast to settlement work and Charity Organisation Society work which had always had a conceptual and practical concern with neighbourhoods, psychiatric social work developed the idea of technique in a functual organisational context not linked to specific neighbourhoods. At this preliminary stage we can note that this was a development of an auxiliary medical service which provides useful contrasts with almoning.[34]

The principal facts of this implantation can now be outlined.[35] Mrs St Lee Strachey, a woman magistrate, became interested in child guidance work and had discussions with the Commonwealth Fund of America before leaving England to see child guidance work in the USA in 1925. Burt's *Young Delinquent* was published in the same year, and Mrs St Lee Strachey was in touch with the movements in penal and mental welfare. She was impressed by the clinics she saw in Philadelphia and on her return called together representatives of the Central Association for Mental Welfare, the Howard League for Penal Reform, the Magistrates Association and the National Council for Mental Hygiene. Miss Scoville (executive assistant, Commonwealth Fund) was invited to England to look at the possibility of establishing a clinic here; she came in the summer of 1926 and reported favourably to committees, who would, however, only agree to the establishment of a clinic if it were used for training, preferably in association with a university. By October 1926 more than thirty people widely representative of interested groups sent a letter to the Commonwealth Fund asking for assistance in establishing a child guidance clinic for training, service and research. The letter had stressed that it was hoped that a clinic would help to correct the lack of 'psychiatric viewpoint in social work'. The fund reacted favourably and detailed proposals were made for a group of ten to visit the USA for three months and to finance five psychiatric social workers for a year of training in the USA. In this country a 'British Representative Committee of the Commonwealth Child Guidance Scheme' had been formed, with thirty-six members and Dame Evelyn Fox as secretary, and welcomed the proposals. Early in 1927 Miss Scoville came to England again and preliminary selection of observers and social workers to go to America was made, with more detailed schemes for the establishment of a child guidance clinic. The Commonwealth Fund's director came to England after Miss Scoville and approved the arrangements in progress. The five social workers to go to America were Katherine Butler (almoner), Catherine Craggs (Central Association for Mental Welfare), Elizabeth Horder (a locum probation officer), Noel Hunybun (assistant organiser in the school care service of the LCC), and Doris Robinson (a social worker at the Tavistock Clinic).[36] Also in 1927 the Child Guidance Council was established. Islington was selected as the home of the London Child Guidance Clinic and appointments were made the following year—director, assistant director, chief psychologist, and assistant psychologist and chief social worker, and these went to the USA in the autumn of 1928, for three to four months. The clinic opened in July 1929 under the auspices of the Child Guidance Council and the Commonwealth Fund, which provided finance for three years. Until September 1930 the clinic was administered by the Child Guidance Council, but then became an independent body governed by a committee which included medical and lay representatives and a medical board.

There was no affiliation with the university, but a joint training scheme for social workers was established with the Social Science Department at the London School of Economics. In 1930–4, 59 psychiatric social workers were trained, and during 1935–9, 106 workers were trained; of all these only 11 were men (Timms, 1964a). The Association of Psychiatric Social Workers was formed in 1930 with seventeen members.

In thinking of the impact which American developments were to have in this country, I have emphasised the contribution of women, but a fact not often mentioned is that the Commonwealth Fund, although founded by Mrs Stephen V. Harkness in 1918 with an initial gift of $10,000,000, was throughout this period under the direction of her son Edward S. Harkness as president (1918–40) and had a number of men as general directors, with the mental health programme associated with Barry C. Smith's appointment as general director in 1921.[37] The fund had never originally intended to venture on any scale in the health field because of the great amount of work already being done. However, although the programme launched late in 1921 was called the 'Program for the Prevention of Juvenile Delinquency' it was primarily a mental health programme. The foundation was different in scale from much of the charitable giving of the late nineteenth century in this country, but ultimately represents the same philanthropic frame of mind; those with large fortunes, whether derived from landed property, aristocratic lineage or, increasingly, industrial profits, were a major force in many social work developments and many experiments would have foundered but for money from the Carnegie and Gulbenkian foundations. But this particular development (because the terms of the fund were broadly drawn to allow any activity for 'the welfare of mankind') was controlled ultimately by a small group of powerful men at Harkness House.

In trying to account for later direction of social work in this country it is important to get an idea of what Mrs St Lee Strachey and later observers saw when they went to America. It is also important to realise that we only drew on one part of the Commonwealth Fund programme.[38] Dr Salmon (National Council for Mental Health) had approached the fund in 1920 and, on getting a sympathetic hearing, an advisory committee had been convened at Lakewood, New Jersey, which included J. Prentice Murphy, Dr Heally Augusta Bronner, Bernard Glueck and Dr Salmon. As a result of these discussions, four divisions were set up:

1   Bureau of Children's Guidance under the auspices of the New York School of Social Work.

2   Division of the National Committee on Prevention of Delinquency and on Mental Hygiene, with responsibility for the demonstration child guidance clinics.

3   National Committee on Visiting Teachers, affiliated with the Public Education Association of New York.

4   Joint Committee on Methods of Preventing Delinquency, which co-ordinated and interpreted the problems.

The four divisions were closely associated with twenty-five social work agencies, and the clinics were responsible for training many psychiatric social workers, many of whom became consultants in family agencies and other non-psychiatric settings. The first clinic was opened at St Louis in 1922 with a staff of one psychiatrist, one psychologist and three social workers, and the model of a team approach at the staff conferences was established. Edward D. Lynde made enormous claims for the clinics[39] and asserted that they had demonstrated the 'universal' value of casework to the average man; it was applicable to all classes and all kinds of need. At this time, through the 1920s, psychoanalysis was becoming more influential in America and some social work teachers, including Charlotte Towle, Porter Lee and Marian Kenworthy, espoused and taught Freudian psychiatric views.

How all this seemed to a practising English social worker is illustrated by the impressions of Olive Crosse, who went to America as a student for about a year from late September 1928, and delivered a paper to the council of the Charity Organisation Society on 28 October 1929, which was later published in the *Charity Organisation Quarterly*.[40] Miss Crosse divided her first eight months between the New York School of Social Work and the Child Guidance Institute, spending three mornings a week attending lectures and study classes (seminars) at the school and two days and two half-days in practical work at the institute. The school had been established by the New York Charity Organisation Society and differed from any that Miss Crosse had seen in England in that it was definitely practical in character, and specialised in teaching casework, child placing and other fields of social work.[41] The lectures were confined to post-graduate students or experienced social workers and included subjects such as interviewing, casework, mental testing and problems of recreation and community organisation. Because there was little state help, the main burden fell on bodies such as the Charity Organisation Society, and Catholic and Jewish charities. Miss Crosse made a comment that very effectively contrasts the British and American social work scene at that time. In spite of the voluntary sponsorship of social work services, although there 'are some voluntary workers, particularly in Boston . . . on the whole the professional worker is more largely accepted and the general trend of the Society is away from our tradition of voluntaryism'. The mental hygiene movement was gradually penetrating into the field of family casework by means of psychiatric consultants attached to district charity Organisation Society offices and by teaching at the summer school of the New York Institute of Social Work.

Miss Crosse gave her individual impressions. What of the observer group financed by the Commonwealth Fund? A report by them in 1928 was signed by Ralph H. Crowley, Letitia Fairfield (divisional medical officer to the LCC), Bernard Hart, T. M. Morton (principal organiser of children's care work, LCC), Janet Salmon, Charles E. Spearman, and St Clair Townsend.[42] Dr Fairfield and Miss Morton also reported to the LCC special services sub-committee and their report was published in 1929.[43] There was general agreement about the value of child guidance clinics and that it was essential to have highly trained and qualified staff. This is of particular interest because although Dr Fairfield in her LCC report quotes Dr Shrubsall's definition of child guidance—'In essence it consists in the application of the established principles of scientific diagnosis and treatment to mental as well as physical, deficiencies and disorders'—she also refers to the results of the Commonwealth Fund clinics equivocally:

It was interesting to find that men of the highest eminence in the work of psychiatry and mental disease . . . regarded the 'Child Guidance Movement' as of the first importance and worthy of the attention of the best brains. As to the results obtained one felt that with few exceptions they justified the efforts expended. Statistical analysis of results is here exceptionally difficult, and after going over the figures from all the Commonwealth Demonstration Clinics with their statistician Miss A. A. Clarke, it seemed hopeless to extricate anything that would give a fair test of the work done. The best proof of its value is the very widespread desire for more clinics, the demand being greatly in excess of the present supply of trained workers.

Miss Morton, in her section of the LCC report, was more positive and quoted the 1929 Report of the Commonwealth Fund which gave the results of 196 cases selected at random from cases at the Bureau of Children's Guidance, New York as: Successful, 93; Partially successful, 61; Failure, 42.

It is clear that from the beginning the gulf between the ideal of a scientific discipline and the crude attitudes to evaluation and experimental method was wide.[44] The structure of the team and the methods were accepted on the basis of a male medical authority; the dominance of the psychiatrist in the team epitomised the broader male authority that blessed the new methods.[45] But this did not mean that generally the approach was dominated by a Freudian viewpoint. Dr Fairfield treats this aspect in a very balanced way:

> In view of the very lively dread of psychoanalysis in certain quarters, it may be said here that I did not find anything approaching analysis being carried on at any clinic. Most of the staffs were not Freudians, but behaviourists and even in the few cases where the psychiatrists belonged to the analytic school, they did not think the precedence suitable to clinic conditions. The general tendency is to interfere as little as possible directly with the child's mentality, but to influence for good preferably through the adults who are in a natural relation to authority to him, e.g. parents, priests and teachers, and through other environmental factors.

As already described, the movement became established and during the 1930s the work setting of psychiatric social workers developed as shown in Table 9.2 (Timms, 1964a).

Table 9.2   Work setting of psychiatric social workers, 1930s

	Hospital	Child guidance	Community care	Other
1933	18	18	—	(18)
1937	43	24	—	—

By 1939 there were eighteen child guidance clinics recognised by the Child Guidance Council, and by 1937 forty-four clinics. Most of the clinics were voluntary, although some local education authorities other than the LCC had established them; the voluntary clinics often had a difficult struggle to raise money as they were not as well known as established charities. As with almoners, the establishment of psychiatric social workers in hospitals was dependent on the initiative of individual hospitals.

The groups visiting the USA had been predominantly interested in child guidance clinics but they also looked at visiting teaching services, which had developed in America just before the First World War and provided a school social work service. The visiting teachers were either social workers with teaching experience or teachers with additional social work experience and were members of the school staff. The Commonwealth Fund observer group judged in their report that they did not think that visiting teachers on school staff would be acceptable here:

> We are of the opinion that the emphasis laid on the social
> training and experience of the Visiting Teacher and the
> amount of time they devote to social work, would be likely
> to make their advice to professional teachers unacceptable in
> this country and to create difficulties in the schools.

The rigid structure of much of our school system and the recommendations of the 1928 signatories—echoed by Dr Fairfield and Miss Morton in their report to the LCC Sub-Committee—perpetuated the ambivalence of schools to social work which has continued to the present day. The school care system in London, developed at the beginning of the century by Miss Morton (who had been a Charity Organisation Society worker) when the LCC established school care committees in 1907, were a paradigm of earlier charitable forms of organisations, with organiser, structuring the services of volunteers and giving them guidance and support.[46] The volunteers would visit families, help to ensure that children attended clinics, received medical attention when necessary and help with employment. The volunteers, with a general protective helping role, were women. The other main stream of welfare work in relation to schools, as described earlier, was concerned with school attendance officers established with the 1870 Education Act; these were in the main men. Miss Macadam argued that[47]

> the intricate work of home advice and visiting is much less
> suited to men than women visitors yet the majority of attendance
> officers were men. In 1870 it may have needed a stalwart male to
> penetrate slum quarters, when bricks were freely thrown about
> and to coerce recalcitrant parents into sending children

to school. Today the school has become a social centre; it concerns itself with the social environment of the child and the attendance officer of the seventies must ultimately be replaced by the trained school welfare worker of the twentieth century.

In implication that worker should have been a woman. It is significant that, within the child guidance teams, the woman psychiatric social worker was the home visitor who dealt with the mother, whilst the psychologist and psychiatrist dealt with the child, and that the emphasis on women's suitability for home visiting because of her domestication led to a long-term neglect of the father both in diagnosis and treatment. Thus the failure of the school and health systems to perceive the ingredients of a service which was neither purely health or education, led to psychiatric social work being relegated to a peripheral institutional role in the educational system and to fight the same battle that the almoners were undertaking in the hospital system. Had a comprehensive social work service been initiated with the impact of American child guidance experience the story of social work might have been very different.

It might also have been different if training for psychiatric social work had been permanently related to a basic training in hospital social work. Miss Snelling (1970) relates that in the period 1924–9 almoners had become increasingly aware that the psychological aspects of social work needed to be included in almoning training. During the period of the establishment of psychiatric social work training, almoners sought to establish greater study of psychology, with related practical placements during the basic almoning, and also that almoning should become a basic training for hospital social work, with training in psychiatric social work as a specialised advanced training. Through a series of accidents and mistimings, efforts in this direction were abortive, although a small number of individual almoners went on to take the Mental Health Course in the early 1930s, but as an entry to a different branch of social work. Had the institute been able to reach its objectives the new psychological knowledge and methods might have given a greater stimulus to stronger theoretical training in social work methods; also it might have led to an unmistakably advanced social work course at the London School of Economics.

There are further points to take account of when considering the institutional development of psychiatric social work. The first is the tendency of the child guidance worker to focus on problems of delinquency prevention and maladjustment, whereas the original conception was to deal with a variety of children with the whole range of behaviour problems.[48] This affected the development of subnormality services adversely. Dame Evelyn Fox,[49] who had been secretary of the group making an approach to the Commonwealth Fund, delivered to a conference on mental welfare on 23 November 1934 a paper entitled, 'Modern Developments in Work for Mental Defectives. A Historical Survey'. After reviewing developments since the appointment of the Royal Commission in 1904, she welcomed the

> very marked awakening of interest amongst educated and thoughtful men and women in the newer aspects of mental health work, notably in the prevention of mental disorder and as a natural and logical corollary, in the importance of work for children. That interest should focus on this problem is infinitely desirable; they have a wide constructive value for natural health which work for defectives cannot claim to have. But this should not blind people to the fact that Mental Health cannot ignore the problem of mental defect any more than that of mental disease, since the social effects of both are so far reaching. It is a most disquieting feature of the present time that the centre of interest has swung so completely over to mental disorder that mental defect has become the Cinderella of mental hygiene.

The glamour of psychiatry, which was seductive and brought psychiatric social workers into a special relationship with male psychiatrists, may have been a strong contributory factor to those workers being gradually considered not simply an additional specialism in social work but as an élite social work profession—*primus inter pares*—by virtue of their additional psychological knowledge. The Commonwealth observer group had asserted that in co-operating with social workers in agencies outside the child guidance clinic

> care must be taken at the onset that the social worker of the organisation is the right type of person to carry out the direction and advice of the experts, and that the degree of responsibility she takes with regard to her cases should be in proportion to the experience she acquires in child guidance methods.

The pamphlet 'Psychiatric Social Work and the Family'[50] had argued for the essential similarity between the problems with which psychiatric social workers and other social workers had to deal, but added: 'The difference lies in the degree of difficulty rather than its nature.'[51] Because of the impossibility of making mental health services universally available, social workers had to 'carry a large share of what they recognise as problems of mental health', and therefore needed to be aware of mental health insights. The early groups of psychiatric social workers were, therefore, carriers of rare knowledge and insight which were therefore assumed to be equivalent to scientific techniques in social work. It was not realised that although there was a need for psychological knowledge, it only stood in the same relation to social work method as knowledge derived from other disciplines such as sociology, ethics, economics and administration. The emphasis on the inner life could also lead to a lack of balance in looking at the interaction of personality and environment. In the same paper we find the statements that 'financial dependence is only a symptom. The disease is a deeper seated dependence which is emotional.' It is not surprising that the paper shows perplexity at the problem of unemployment, and expresses it in language that could well have been translated into Charity Organisation terms:[52]

> At a time when a large section of the community are owing to the state of the world's finance, unable to have a job that gives them any sense of pulling their weight, it is specially hard to see how to put such ideas into practice—the Brynmawr experiment shows how hard—but this seems to be no excuse for slackening our thoughts on these lines, even with cases of chronic financial dependency.

Nevertheless it is clear that, although psychiatric social workers emphasised the importance of personality, it is a mistake to assume on the basis of selected writings that they were ignorant of environmental influences or underestimated their importance. During the inter-war years they were sympathetic to social reform and often active in pursuing it alongside other social workers. Sociologists who are critical of the developing role of psychiatric social work have often lacked historical judgment and displayed political *naïveté* in expecting this fledgling professional group to cure massive social problems.

House property management

After the Second World War, house property management ceased to be thought of as social work, but during the inter-war period it was still thought of as in the mainstream of social work. The campaign at the end of the First World War to provide homes 'fit for heroes' showed a concern for housing policy which during the next two decades was illustrated by the building of model estates, large slum clearance programmes, and rent restriction. The Association of Women House Property Managers submitted evidence to the Ministry of Health in 1919–20 on slum areas and on the operation of the Rent Restrictions Act. A good picture of general housing problems facing the country in the 1920s is given in A. Sayles's *The Houses of the Workers* (1924), in which the unsatisfactory conditions of much of the poorest housing was attributed to incompetent management by owners or junior clerks who dealt with tenants. It was thought that

> an essential condition of success in dealing with any slum areas on these lines is the appointment of a trained and skilled manager—preferably a woman. The work involves an enormous amount of personal attention to detail, tact, discretion, common sense and sympathy. The manager has to enter into intimate questions of sleeping arrangements, when it is a question of avoiding or remedying overcrowding, and will need persuasive powers of the highest order if satisfactory results in cleanliness and care of the houses and fittings are to be achieved: constant changes of tenancy are not satisfactory results.

Growth in municipal housing led to the employment of women house property managers by local authorities, the first being appointed in 1927. The municipal managers formed their own organisation and in 1928 an Octavia Hill Club was formed by Miss Jeffery. In 1932 the workers involved in all these bodies formed the Society of Women's Housing Estate Managers (changing its name to Society of Women Housing Managers (Incorporated) in 1937). A Women's House Property Managers Certificate of the Chartered Surveyor's Institution was initiated in 1933.[53]

There was much emphasis on the difficult tenants but municipal housing departments varied in their methods of organising the work (Alford, 1959):

> While some authorities employed trained managers to collect rents on the all purpose or functional method derived from Octavia Hill others organised the rent collectors on more

commercial lines and employed special welfare officers to deal
with difficult families. But whichever method was employed,
the 'problem family' was given a considerable amount of
attention.

In the housing management field we can see the clear organisational
tension between structures aimed at the needs of the majority of
coping tenants and those aimed to devote more resources to tenants
with special difficulties.

During the Second World War, municipal housing managers were
involved with billeting, rehousing after bombing and in the management of requisitioned property. In the post-war period housing
management became less concerned with individual difficulties and
the job content covered the control of waiting lists, letting of pro-
perties, rent collecting, accounts records, differential rates and
rebate schemes, the care of estates and the operation of the law of
landlord and tenant. The traditional Octavia Hill approach diminished in influence, and led to the difficulties in co-ordination between
housing departments and social work agencies such as children's
departments and family service units. These problems were discussed
in the Seebohm Report, which considered that it might be necessary
for social workers to be seconded from a social services department
to help with the welfare work.[54] Men working as housing managers
in local authorities had organised their own association, the Institute
of Housing. In 1948 the Society of Women's Housing Managers
omitted 'Women' from the title and men became eligible for training
and membership. These two associations formed the basis of a new
association, the Institute of Housing Managers, in 1965.

The scale of housing developments since the 1920s had led to a
concern with broad policies and administration, which made it
increasingly difficult to focus on the special needs of individual
families. Social work was only a small part of the broader functioning of housing departments, and housing management had moved
out of the field of social work.

Moral welfare

Following the First World War, moral welfare work blossomed
with the establishment of the Josephine Butler Memorial House in
1920 with Miss Higson as its first warden, and the related strengthening and widening of the scope of activities throughout the country.
The training work at the Memorial House was based in Liverpool,

with strong support from the Bishop of Liverpool and close links with the university. Some women of high calibre were attracted to the college in the inter-war years, and of the eighty-eight women trained in 1920–8, five had BAs and four had MAs.[55] The women went into a variety of residential and outdoor posts, some working as probation officers or children's workers, and others as organising secretaries or on the staff of training or mother and baby homes. An early worker, Miss C. Butterfield, recalled the time when she started work in a letter to the *Josephine Butler College News* in 1971:

> Grace Philpot and I left J B in 1927 and she came with me as part-time assistant to Tottenham. We were engaged by a C of E Committee, and the Local Authority officers were at first inclined to look a little askance at us; but we persisted and persevered and Grace Philpot who had made a speciality of work with children, soon ingratiated herself with the Director of Education. And we began to co-operate with the Tavistock Clinic and many Head Teachers.
>
> 1930 found us recognised by the LEA as the agency dealing with disturbed children but financial support only went as far as travelling expenses, including meals. I can remember the Chief Attendance Officer being properly shocked when one of us presented our accounts for escorting a boy to Dover as 1/6d. for lunch. 'Good Gracious,' he exclaimed, 'we cannot have that, you'll have the rest of us starving' and changed it to 2/6d. which he still considered frugal. Those were the days.
>
> Achieving co-operation with the Maternity and Child Welfare Services was a tougher proposition, but ultimately it was achieved. In those days the Sunday opening of Cinemas began and the Local Council was called upon to vote for the Charities which should benefit from the proportion of money received. I think it was largely as a recognition of the help we were able to give the Maternity and Child Welfare that we proudly found ourselves at the top of the list.
>
> These are very small examples of the thin end of the wedge which workers in our day strove to bring home to the public conscience, and which we like to think led to the support of present day workers by the state.

Miss Butterfield's letter admirably demonstrates the pioneering atmosphere of the inter-war period. The educational work undertaken by Miss Higson, first as warden at Josephine Butler Memorial House

1920–8, and then from 1929 as the first lecturer in moral welfare for the Archbishop's Advisory Board, had this quality too. She lectured throughout the country, to men as well as women, on the causes of prostitution and encouraged the educational work of the moral welfare movement as well as improvements in the care of unmarried mothers and their babies. Her concern with men and boys was forcibly expressed: 'At the very beginning of my work as Central Organiser I had rebelled against the idea that this was "women's work for women".' (Higson, 1955, p. 71.) Throughout the inter-war years Miss Higson worked with the White Cross League and also the Association for Moral and Social Hygiene towards the extension of this side of the moral welfare movement, culminating with the appointment in 1938 of the Rev. G. L. Russell for an experimental period of three years for work among men and boys. Work with both sexes was unified in 1939 by the amalgamation of the White Cross League with the Church of England Moral and Welfare Council. Yet social work within the moral welfare movement remained almost completely women's work; in 1970 only three male former students of Josephine Butler College were holding social work posts, and it proved almost impossible to break through the traditional image of moral welfare work as a field for women.

Miss Higson retired in 1942, by which time moral welfare workers had helped with work in Citizens' Advice Bureaux, problems in reception areas, work near military camps and educational work in the women's services. Her own work built on and enlarged the tradition of nineteenth-century pioneer women and assessed by the Bishop of Chichester as follows:

> In her fine career of service she not only showed outstanding religious faith and a wonderful love for others; she also displayed great powers of leadership, great gifts of human sympathy, great practical insight and a remarkable power of sincere persuasive speech. She never failed to urge the importance of co-operation, not only with other churches but also with the local authorities and statutory workers.

Settlements

In 1920 Attlee wrote: 'Settlements for women are now as numerous as those for men, although the movement started a little later; and several men's settlements have subsequently felt the necessity of the co-operation of women and have started a woman's home' (Attlee,

1920, p. 208). He thought that the women's settlements were better supplied with whole-time workers, as the men tended to follow their whole-time occupations during the day. The women could be particularly useful in visiting work during the day-time and in undertaking all work with women and children. The secretarial work was also largely done by women. Attlee considered that settlement life was a pleasanter alternative for some young women than a possibly lonely life in lodgings.

The social conditions of the 1920s and 1930s gave opportunities for new work and also presented special problems. At Manchester University Settlement unemployment led to the setting up of day clubs for unemployed men and boys. Classes for young mothers were established and a camping hut was used for week-ends and longer holidays for children. New housing estates in Manchester led to the initiation of an information bureau and an involvement in the start of community centres in the late 1920s. Of particular interest were surveys about health and housing. However, the difficult financial position almost led to the collapse of the settlement operations in the early 1920s.[56] Although relief work was carried out in the 1920s to cope with poverty in the neighbourhood, this part of the settlement work was dropped as soon as possible. As in many organisations, it was more difficult to keep the settlement alive and responsive to changing social conditions than in the early pioneering days, and the activities seemed more directly oriented to welfare than education.[57]

The ideals of settlements were nurtured and kept alive, and links with the social studies courses maintained. Expansion of statutory services, such as housing and maternity and child welfare, gave a new emphasis to co-ordinating work in a neighbourhood and to survey work to examine needs and gaps in existing services. An example of this was the Survey of Social Services in North Kensington and Lambeth, undertaken by Miss E. Ross during the period 1936–8.[58] Miss Ross had been a resident at Lady Margaret Hall Settlement from 1930 to 1934, and had received help from the National Council of Social Service, Political and Economic Planning and civil authorities in planning the study. The report talked of the settlement purposes in the following terms:

> In all kinds of ways a residential settlement can be a power
> house for neighbourhood activities. The presence of a number of
> people living together, wholeheartedly concerned with the
> spiritual, mental, social, and physical needs of a district and its

people—prepared to learn by friendship and service how their neighbourhoods live and think, bears fruit in a number of ways. A body of neighbourhood knowledge is built up, making the settlement a natural centre for information, whilst its close touch with local developments leads it to take a share in initiating new experiments . . . . A settlement is a place for free discussion, it has no political colour, and can sometimes witness all the more effectively to the urgent need for better conditions which the day by day work of its residents and workers discover. Linked in this case with an Oxford college, it acts as a 'bridge' between people of different backgrounds; and provides not only an outlet for service but also an opportunity for new understanding.

The activities at one of the settlements in the district comprised: care committee and after-care work, children's country holiday fund, recreational clubs for all ages, a children's library, discussion and dramatic groups. Many other activities and meetings were also held there.

Only a few areas were fortunate enough to have settlements and, although their co-ordinating activities were valuable, they did not form the basis of a national pattern of organisation. The statutory community centre movement developed neighbourhood work on a non-residential basis. It incorporated elements of the residential settlement, thus diminishing the need to think of the appropriateness of an extension of the residential principle on a wider scale. The tendencies of the casework organisations, by comparison, were very much against living in the area in which you worked. It was, in retrospect, one of the most important functions of the settlements to keep alive the concept and practice of work within a limited neighbourhood.

Women inspectors

Throughout the inter-war period women's progress in the Civil Service was as a whole unspectacular. At the time of the Tomlin Commission, 1930–1, there were only twenty women in the whole administrative class, about 2 per cent of the total (Kelsall, 1955). The House of Commons Resolution of 5 August 1921 had allowed women over twenty-two to apply for posts in the administrative class if they had served for a year in a department or in one of the women's services; this arrangement was to last for three years, after which women were eligible to compete in open competition.[59] However, over the period 1923–39 inclusive, out of the 490 competitive appointments only thirty-three or 7 per cent were given to women. Both Kelsall and Martindale show that before the Second World War there was still much resistance in many government departments to the employment of women, especially at the very highest levels; it was not until 1939 that Dame Evelyn Sharp was appointed to Assistant Secretary in the Ministry of Health after which she became Principal Assistant Secretary in 1943. Kelsall asked why women fared so badly in gaining appointments. He found that by 1938 women had improved their chances of selection by open competition and that they gained home administrative appointments roughly in proportion to their numbers. Therefore the main reason seemed to be increasingly the small number of women competing for administrative class posts. He attributed this to the marriage bar (not removed until 1946), that women were not willing to risk preparation for an uncertain career (many posts were still closed to them—overseas and defence posts, for example), that they felt a prejudice existed against their sex, that equal pay had not been honoured, and that many university women felt a responsibility to go into teaching. This, then, was the climate of the higher Civil Service into which women inspectors were gradually fitting.

The Ministry of Health took over the functions of the Local Government Board in 1919. We have seen that the Local Government Board was male-dominated and that it had been hard to gain a place for women. The women inspectors who inspected Poor Law infirmaries and the work of the committees concerned with the boarding-out of Poor Law children were transferred to the new department; Miss Wamsley, who had been an inspector since 1913, was made superintending inspector. Women doctors concerned with maternity and child welfare were also employed by the Ministry of Health and a few women inspectors were appointed to assist them in 1919. In 1925 the two staffs of inspectors were amalgamated and placed under the woman senior medical officer for general supervision. Miss Wamsley was appointed Assistant General Inspector until her retirement in 1931, after which the post was not filled by a woman (Martindale, 1938). The women inspectors assisted the medical officers in inspecting the work of the local authorities under the Maternity and Child Welfare Act and also in the inspection of Poor Law establishments. These posts were executive class and good nursing was considered a qualification for them (Evans, 1934). A woman was also one of three inspectors dealing with the welfare of the blind. There were also a small number of appointments on the Board of Control, where in the late 1930s four women inspectors were involved in visiting mental patients.

Within the Home Office women factory inspectors increasingly proved their worth and after the First World War the segregation of men's and women's areas of work was almost completely abolished and a single system of administration and seniority, regardless of sex, was established by the late 1920s. Women advanced to the grades of deputy chief inspector and superintending inspector, with many women in full charge of districts.[60] In addition to the factory inspectorate there were a small number of posts in the children's branch of the Home Office (formed in 1923) relating to the inspection of reformatory and industrial schools, and children's homes approved by the Home Office. When the probation branch was established in 1936 a woman was one of the probation inspectors, and in 1935 Lilian Barker was appointed as assistant commissioner in the prison commission.[61]

In the welfare areas the imprint of women was still limited both by their small numbers and the range of work which they were involved in. That the Home Office was a much more hospitable environment for growth is illustrated by the fact that in 1949 the inspectoral posts in the Ministry of Health were one chief welfare officer (Miss Geraldine Aves), three welfare officers and four temporary welfare officers; all of these were women. In the Home Office children's branch there were thirty-eight inspectors of whom eighteen were women. At the higher levels, Miss Rosling was one of four assistant secretaries, there were two women out of six principals and three out of four assistant principals.[62]

F

What can we then conclude about social work during this second, extended, phase after the first phase associated with the Charity Organisation Society? Generalisations are difficult because of the diversity of the fields, but certain features mark this phase as transitional blending the old and the new. In the same way—and perhaps as a consequence—as the period 1918–39 involved the steadily increasing intervention of government agencies who assumed increasing responsibility for housing, insurance, health, education and child welfare functions, but in an *ad hoc* and piecemeal way, with the Poor Law still remaining as the symbol of a passing society; so developments in social work training mirrored the ambivalence of English society towards activities it had previously associated with middle- and upper-class charity. At the same time as more paid workers were being appointed as probation officers, almoners and psychiatric social workers, there were still far more voluntary workers to be found active in our large cities. Attlee's hope that the days were past 'when people without any qualification than a good heart and the means of obtaining money plunged straight into social work without any consideration of what was being done by others or what effect they were going to have' (1920, p. 145), was not to be realised in the inter-war period. Even amongst paid workers the majority were untrained, and those who were fully trained, with a social science qualification as well as a social work training in almoning, probation or psychiatric social work, were principally women mainly working in London and the south.[1]

Training patterns and problems of recruitment

Because there was inadequate co-ordination between the Ministry of Health and the Home Office, there was no clear-cut responsibility to take a broad view of social work training. Legislation such as the Probation of Offenders Act 1907, the Children's Act 1908, the Children and Young Person Act 1933 and the Mental Treatment Act 1930 gave added impetus to the employment of social workers in courts, hospitals and local authorities, and this remained the position until the end of the Second World War. Neither, within the individual central government departments, was there much understanding of social work or a firm commitment to see that supply should meet the demand for social workers. The universities were insufficiently committed to extending social work training with their own funds and the scale was too small to stimulate any impetus toward a system of schools of social work or of training colleges as happened in education. The different branches of social work tended to develop along separatist lines with a number of professional organisations.

This confused picture of social work training—the majority untrained, and the trained divided between the main patterns of social science diploma, certificate of the Institute of Almoners, the London School of Economics mental health courses or the three-month Home Office probation training, or a combination of both— continued through the Second World War. In contrast to America, there was no dramatic shift to devalue voluntary work in contrast to paid professional work. The training courses provided for workers intending to go into voluntary and statutory agencies as either paid or voluntary workers.[2] For instance at the LSE from 1930 to 1933, of 103 students obtaining salaried posts thirty-eight obtained posts as hospital almoners, ten obtained posts as club leaders, sixteen obtained posts as employment managers, and thirteen obtained posts as HM factory inspectors. Of sixty students receiving the Mental Health Certificate in 1931–4, one-third took up employment as psychiatric social workers in child guidance clinics and about one-fifth with adults suffering from mental disorder in general and in mental hospitals. The rest returned to or took up family case-work, work with delinquents or with defectives, and research. The majority of students were still women. At Liverpool University, for example, on 1 November 1933 there were seventeen first-year students (three of whom were men) and nineteen second-year students (one of whom was a man) (Salomon, 1937). But in thinking of the general pattern it is important to realise that there were more men probation officers than women probation officers, almoners and psychiatric social workers put together.

We have seen that the field of social work provided an opportunity for women to open up a new profession but that their power to do this was heavily dependent upon male acceptance and patronage, particularly in the medical profession. The enfranchisement of women meant that in social work, as in many professions, women concentrated their attention on their particular profession or on other social and international affairs. Within social work it proved hard to get rid of preconceptions of what was women's and men's work, and women's contribution was determined by their domestic role and sexual taboos. In the 1939 National Council of Social Service Report of the Advisory Committee on Recruitment and Training for Social Work[3] the supply and demand situation was described as follows:[4]

> there are few branches of social work in which more or less serious difficulty does not arise in obtaining an adequate supply of competent workers, whether salaried or otherwise. . . . While economic and other factors affecting the problems of supply vary to some extent as between women's and men's social work, there is no doubt that in women's services as well as in men's, there is a real shortage of suitable candidates for responsible posts.

One of the major problems was how to communicate what social work was about to government departments and to the general public. The variety of posts and diffuseness of the field militated against an easy understanding of common elements in social work. In 1920 Attlee had listed the following posts as open to women experienced in social work (Attlee, 1920, p. 124):

Sanitary inspectors
Factory inspectors
Inspectors under the Midwives Act
Infant life protection inspectors
Poor Law inspectors
Education inspectors
Health visitors
National Insurance inspectors
Organisers of Care Committees (London)
Secretaries under the Labour Exchange Act for Juvenile
    Advisory Committees
Managers of Labour Exchanges (women's side)
Secretaries under the Choice of Employment Act
Probation Officers
Housing Inspectors
Relieving officers

Women and professional development

How far did social work move towards a profession during the inter-war years and what part did women play in this? Definitions of professions vary, but if we take four important elements and look at them in turn, this should bring us closer to an understanding of the changes occurring in this period. The four aspects are: the existence of a body of knowledge; an identifiable field of practice; existence of a professional organisation controlling entry to the profession; and training of appropriate level and length.

Social work knowledge

We have seen that the largest single change in knowledge was the impact of psychology which gradually began to permeate the consciousness and practice of social workers in the late 1920s and early 1930s. This was no accident, for, strange as it may seem on looking back, some people were becoming disenchanted with simplistic ideas of social organisation and wished to bring the inter-action of individual with environment into the foreground. Casework allied with a psychological approach was to be the means of doing this.[5] As an indication of the feeling change involved, Miss Clement Brown said in 1933:

> Criminologists, industrial psychologists, psychopathologists,
> are all telling us that the individual's misbehaviours, social
> failure, industrial failure and mental illness are due not only to
> his constitution but to his lack of certain fundamental
> satisfactions in his life. That the lack of love, appreciation,
> and independent achievement leads directly or indirectly to
> certain distortions of adaptation; a withdrawal into phantasy;
> an undoing of the past; and over insurance against the future.

How one director of a British school viewed casework is trenchantly set out by Nora Milnes of Edinburgh University School of Social Studies in a paper she read to the International Conference on Social Work in 1928.[6] Miss Milnes argues that casework is more than the casepaper and that because it was associated with the Charity Organisation Society method of working 'only favoured by a minority of social workers in this country', it had become associated with all the sins that the Charity Organisation Society were accused of. Rather than take the defensive Miss Milnes moves into the attack:

Casework, then is not merely a method or a means although, as has already been said, to the majority of social workers this is in truth all it implies. Were this so, then there would be little to discuss. But it is because casework indicates definite and definable principles that the subject will remain of permanent importance, so long as human beings remain as they are today; with sympathy and a desire to help individuals where luck seems out. And in mentioning individuals we begin to approach the root of the whole question; for casework is the outer sign of an inner faith—a faith which rests upon a belief in the individual and with the capacity of the individual to carve out his own life. . . .

Casework then, becomes the antithesis of mass or socialistic measures, and the defender of casework finds that his plan will not rest merely on negating socialism but in proving that there is still much to be said for what can be described as individualism.

Miss Milnes' statement is important because it represents an approach to social work still influential after forty years—an ethical principle embraced in technical procedures. It is this lack of distinction between a value orientation and a technique which has continually befogged social work debates. In passing we may also note that Miss Milnes assumes that casework is characteristic of voluntary social work rather than statutory work.[7] There is the thought that 'statutory' is equivalent to 'bureaucratic' procedures and lack of attention to individual needs. In looking at the attitudes of Miss Clement Brown and Miss Milnes it is fair to say that the integration of psychological knowledge into social work on their period was a valuable complementary addition to the knowledge based on economics, government and a study of social welfare organisations. It had made a particular appeal to the sensitivity of key women social workers of the time and in general did not lead them to make extravagant claims. The mental health course at LSE was eclectic in its approach[8] and the crusading spirit was on behalf of an overall mental hygiene influence, not for a particular psychological school such as psychoanalysis. The effect was gradual and has been examined by Miss Clement Brown in what was probably the first research study in this country into casework methods based on examination of case records.[9] Eighty cases were examined, forty of which were closed in 1924–7 and forty closed in 1934–5. The cases were taken from the records of hospital almoners, the Charity Organisation Society, probation offices and school care committee workers. The outstanding differences in the second series of records was the greater range of facts commented on and an increase in the degree of interpretation which the social worker made (i.e. about the meaning of observations, the relationships between facts, or a summing up of the situation as a whole). There was an increase (though lesser) in the use of an embryonic diagnostic method:

> Perhaps the most that can be said from a preliminary survey of these records is that the social worker in 1934 is making use of a greater range and variety of resources, and that he is doing this with considerably more self-criticism and conscious analysis.

A further difference in the later period relates to co-ordination, a subject of debate in social work to the present day:

> It seems evident that social workers are becoming more aware of the need for a close linking up of all the organisations dealing with special aspects of individual problems. The latter series of records contain reports of conferences between various agencies concerned with one family, a type of consultation of which there is no illustration in the earlier records.

Another aspect of the later series is that these records gave evidence of concern about the relationship of the social worker with the individual:

> It is therefore particularly interesting to find that the later records show an appreciably greater concern with this very fact of the relationship between the individual and the social worker, and that the inter-play of attitudes between those who seek for help and those who offer it is for the first time becoming itself subject to critical analysis.

We may fairly conclude that the changes recounted by Miss Clement Brown and in the section dealing with psychiatric social work represented an important addition to the knowledge which social workers could draw on in their day-to-day dealings with clients and one which could be passed on in training. The knowledge content that an added awareness of psychology gave to social workers was a necessary ingredient in the ability to understand social situations and to move beyond admonitions for the social worker to be tactful and sympathetic.

Fields of practice

When the presence or otherwise of a clear field of practice is examined one meets a state of almost total confusion. First, there was the voluntary/statutory schism for, whilst the depreciation of the volunteer never developed as in America, there was great concern lest the advance of statutory social-work services would stifle vocation and lead to an unwholesome rigidity and impersonality in services. This was as much a philosophical viewpoint as one about social services. In a world where increasing statutory responsibility and authority had become a feature of industrial urban countries, there were fears that the material welfare disbursed by the state would sap individual and community life. B. G. Astbury stated the position at the Third International Conference on Social Work, 1936:[10]

> In Great Britain the idea of state provision has grown steadily since 1906, and as a natural consequence, the community has concentrated thought and energy upon working out, under the several departments of the National Government, or of the local authorities, the enormous administrative machinery required. There are many signs that the community is rapidly discovering that, in the process, it has lost no small amount of the personal touch, individual treatment and neighbourly interest which are essential to success.

Astbury seemed to accept the inevitability of the growth of statutory services and posed the dilemma of family casework in trying to 'define the future function of the Voluntary Casework Agency'. Although he accepted the necessity and value of voluntary statutory co-operation, he was troubled by the possible consequences of family casework being relegated

> to the position of a mere handmaid to the state official. . . .
> We must here and now take stock of the present position and
> try to formulate a policy; the basis of which must be
> team-work if our movement is to survive.

J. C. Pringle, in a paper 'Community Effects to be sought in the Process of Performing Primary Human Duties',[11] touched on

similar themes, expressing a degree of acceptance of the new broad
state services, but with reservations:

> Our surmise is that in all that 'realms of nature' with which
> social service is concerned, the prestige accorded in the
> ministries, severally in different localities, to the Church of
> England, Free Church, or Roman Catholic Missions, the
> Church Organisation Societies, the Settlements, the Working
> Men's or Lad's Clubs, in friendly alliance with the ubiquitous
> teachers and doctors, has passed today to the Ministry of
> Health, or Old Age Pensions; Inspectors; Employment
> Exchange Managers; Unemployed Assistant Board Officers. . . .
> The failure so far of the Probation Officer to win much of a
> share in it something of a mystery. The Police have as much
> or as little of it as they care to earn. The with-holding of
> any of it from the relieving officer, who has done quite as
> much as to earn it as anybody, suggests that Fashion
> distributes prestige with the heartless unscrupulousness
> attributed to the guide Fortune, but observed in the Film staff.

Pringle did not bring any evidence that the statutory services were
inefficient or impersonal but objected to the fashionable whims that
laid less importance on community action as expressed in a variety
of voluntary organisations.

Family casework, then had no clearly defined field in the 1930s,
and unlike almoning and psychiatric social work, was not attempting
to become established within statutory services. Almoning and
psychiatric social work had established a recognisable foothold in
the health field but had an enormously difficult task in gaining
acceptance and patently failed in demonstrating to other professions
that 'social casework' was a common element in many fields of
practice. The hopes expressed by Ferens Rajnis at the 1928 Second
International Conference on Social Work in Paris that generic social
casework was[12] 'rapidly moving toward the creation of a new
discipline bringing into a new synthesis the philosophy, knowledge
and method which up to date has been extracted with such wearisome
care from the various special sciences' were premature as was his
assertion that the

> creation of such a new practical science will be the greatest
> contribution of modern social casework, not only to all
> kindred social endeavours but to the general task of

F*

rehumanising a society which is in itself maladjusted because of the existence in the midst of so many suppressed, dismembered, and stultified personalities.

Probation as well as almoning and psychiatric social work had a defined area of operations buttressed more firmly within the court system than were the almoners and psychiatric social workers in the hospitals and local authorities. This was because the probation service was established by statute and probation officers worked to statutory rules and regulations, whereas psychiatric social workers and almoners were not required or regulated by statute; the lack of a statutory requirement for hospitals to provide a social work service had the drawback of hampering the widespread establishment of a uniform service, but gave also a certain amount of freedom from regulations. In all these developments social work sailed between the Scylla of an excessively generalised agency (e.g. Charity Organisation Society) and the Charybdis of over-specialised or defined fields of practice, making it very difficult to pinpoint the larger field of social work and its boundaries.

There was the further difficulty of identifying 'social work' with one method of working in social work, i.e. social casework. Those who had experienced the individual approach in training, with its American influence, could substitute social work and social casework for each other quite easily. In the other direction was the existence of the secretary/organiser/administrator tradition, in the inspectorate, school care committees and settlements, and many workers in these settings could substitute 'social service' for 'social work'.

Professional organisation

The consequence of these problems of definition is clearly illustrated in the halting attempts towards a profession of social work taken in the 1920s and 1930s. Nora Milnes (see Snelling, 1970) and Miss Amy Sayles[13] had tried to organise social workers into a body after the First World War but had not met with success. In 1936 the British Federation of Social Workers had been formed and continued through until after the Second World War as the only representative body of social workers. Constituent bodies were:

Association of Children's Care Committee Organisers
Association of Children's Moral Welfare Workers
Association of Family Caseworkers
Association of Occupational Therapists

Association of Psychiatric Social Workers
Royal College of Nursing (Public Health Section)
Association of Tuberculosis Care Committee Secretaries
Society of Women Housing Managers
Women Public Health Officers Association
Moral Welfare Workers Association
Association of Mental Health Workers
National Association of Probation Officers

The first chairman of the BFSW was Mr H. E. Norman, a probation officer, but the council was predominantly female. In 1942, for instance, the only two male members of the council were Mr Astbury of the Association of Family Caseworkers and Mr Stavely of the National Association of Probation Officers. The federation had poor finances, relying a great deal on unpaid work. Because of the variety of affiliated organisations the first affiliated bodies 'could not always agree on which other association should be included, or whether the common bond should be comparable training or common interest in social problems' (Waldron, 1959). Because of the lack of money the Carnegie Trust was approached and financed a paid secretary for three years. The organisation still met with financial difficulties and the office and secretary were given up, with the federation maintaining only a weak existence. The psychiatric social workers were very active, seeing the federation as an opportunity to promote a mental hygiene approach.[14] One of the most active workers in the federation was Miss Bernice McFie, later chairman of the BFSW 1948–51.

Training

Developments in training have been discussed and we have seen that apart from training for almoning and psychiatric social work the basic training in the universities was the social science diploma. A. Salomon (1937) gives the most comprehensive account of the training programmes for social work in this country in the 1930s. It is ironic that because the LSE mental health course was a specialised rather than general social casework training, there is no evidence to suggest that the methods introduced there were firmly incorporated in other training centres; thus the new psychological knowledge, blended with a social casework approach, had to be transmitted by a highly trained group of able women moving into other fields of practice, or by social workers with other experience or training taking the mental health course. It may have been a move in the wrong direction to establish a specialised mental health course rather than a new type of general social work course but the fact that this step was made is indicative of the lack of clarity and congruence in the ideas which individuals and organisations had about social work. Problems in training reflected the variety and confusion of organisations involved in social work.

Similarly, it was impossible because of the fragmented state of social work to conceive of controlling entry to the profession. The most that was achieved was in the professional association of almoners and psychiatric social workers which only admitted trained workers to full membership. In none of the avenues of social work practice did social workers control entry and have the power to prevent employers from appointing untrained workers. Both almoners and psychiatric social workers, although a small proportion of all social workers, formed a quasi-professional élite of middle- and upper-class women, insisting on high intellectual and moral standards, the greater number of them still single, and with a broad social purpose realised in a particular form of social work. Probation officers with the preponderance of men officers had driven quickly for the establishment of a universal service and decent salaries, but we have seen that the creation of a national network of court social workers did not carry automatically the establishment of a high level of training.

The National Council of Social Service had recognised the difficulties of social work in this country and stated at the beginning of the report of the Advisory Committee to Standing Conference on Recruitment and Training for Social Workers (1939) that:[15]

> In surveying the problems connected with the recruitment, training and appointment of social workers, there must be a clear recognition that the term social work connotes a great variety of occupations, each with its own characteristic function and method and that the problems of recruitment, of training and of conditions of service show a corresponding variety of special features.

It was seen that this was confusing to young men and women at universities and as a solution to this problem the establishment of a new central agency was suggested, with the function of surveying problems of recruitment and training, acting as a clearing house for information and publishing literature, and surveying existing

facilities and the need for extension. Other factors than the infor-
mational ones were discussed and there was general agreement that
the 'recruitment of competent men and women for professional
social work is further hindered by the inequity of prospects and
relatively unfavourable conditions of service which prevail'. Besides
the problem of low salaries for some social workers, absence 'of
adequate and recognised professional standards, such as in the Civil
Service and other professions are secured by stringent training
requirements and by competitive entrance examinations', deterred
men and women from taking up social work because it operated
against the growth of a recognised status. It was to be a quarter of
a century before the main recommendations of the committee were
to be achieved. However, it is important to realise that the diagnosis
of the problem had already received clear expression before the
Second World War.

Five women

The main trends in social work between the wars have been described
with particular emphasis on women's influence. Although individual
women have been mentioned, it is valuable to follow through
briefly a small group of women during the inter-war period and note
the directions they followed.

Eleanor Rathbone

Eleanor Rathbone had been heavily engaged in Soldiers', Sailors'
and Airmen's Families Association relief work during the war and
the National Union of Women's Suffrage Societies with which she
was associated itself concentrated its efforts into war work. Eleanor's
direct work with families in distress led her to formulate her ideas
about family allowances which were expounded in the *Economic
Journal* in March 1917. In 1924 *The Disinherited Family* was published, and although she remained concerned with this issue her
main efforts were directed to political life in Liverpool and international affairs. Eleanor Rathbone had had experience in the
Charity Organisation Society and later in war relief work which had
influenced her strongly in her overall thinking about social problems.
This approach, so evident in the lives of many of the early social
workers, was the realisation of a process which these developing
social casework services came to more slowly. Margaret Rich, who

delivered a paper to the 1936 International Conference on Social Work,[16] understood this when she commented:

> If existing institutions tend to contribute to the maladjustment of large numbers of individual members of society; they are too expensive both from the economic and human standpoint to be tolerated by society as a whole. An essential and still only partially developed function of social casework is this articulation of the data growing out of its experience that may be useful in wider areas of social planning.

Violet Markham

Violet Markham, of the same generation as Eleanor Rathbone but with settlement and unemployment experience, had come to the decision by 1918 to embrace suffragist aims and principles in spite of her 'affection and regard for many of my anti-suffrage friends'. She had come to accept that 'without this reform, social and political life would rest on a basis chronically lopsided and unfairly weighted against one sex'. She did not expect women to 'regenerate the world' and had been unhappy about the violent action of the suffragettes. Nevertheless, she espoused the cause and stood as a Liberal candidate at the 1918 election. She was defeated and between the wars was active in public life in Chesterfield, being elected to the town council in 1925 and taking office as mayor two years later. In 1934 she was invited to become a member of the Unemployment Assistance Board, the forerunner of the National Assistance Board, and became active in international labour organisations. Both Violet Markham and Eleanor Rathbone were women of fine intellectual quality who decided not to seek a career in social work but to throw their main efforts into the establishment and operation of broad social services. Their background of experience in social work provided them with philosophical and practical attitudes towards the establishment and administration of social services.

Elizabeth Macadam

Eleanor Rathbone played a key role in the establishment of the Social Science Department at Liverpool University, and was associated with Elizabeth Macadam through the Settlement. Miss Macadam moved to the Social Science Department from the Settlement and throughout this period was one of the main protagonists on behalf of social work and social work training. Her secretaryship of the Joint University Council gave her an influential role in discussions on training and contact with the whole field of social work training and new developments. She was also firmly entrenched in the campaign for women's rights. Her main contribution was not in the detailed analysis of social work process, but in the establishment of social work as a valid profession within the welfare field. Her *Equipment of the Social Worker* (1925) and *The New Philanthropy* (1934) are corner-stones for an understanding of developments between the wars. The former book, though in some ways covering similar ground to Attlee's, has both a greater feeling and more intimate knowledge for the field of social work. It was the first weighty survey of the state of social work representing the new professional tradition, and one whose plea for research into social work methods was strong, and has been voiced ever since. Perhaps more than the 1939 NCSS Committee Miss Macadam attributed the low status and pattern of recruitment to low salaries (1925, p. 206):

> Another result of low salaries offered for social work is that, like some kinds of teaching, it tends to be mainly recruited by women. It is undeniable that a better type of woman can be secured where a low salary is offered. This tends to drive men out altogether. Some branches of social work from their nature may be regarded as women's preserves, but for the majority, men and women are equally required.

As we have seen, the size of the organisations involved generally did not provide a career structure to attract well qualified men. This point was made in *The New Philanthropy* (1934, p. 296):

> Salaries are so low in comparison to other professions that a man who aspires to a wife and a family, however well qualified by both inclination and ability, must usually look elsewhere for a career. It is more possible for women, at least where they have no dependants, to run risks in undertaking work which has a special attraction for them. Hence in the departments of social science the majority of the students are university women of very good calibre, with pass or honours degrees.

The New Philanthropy was the name which Miss Macadam gave to the system of combined statutory and voluntary social services developed in the preceding forty years, which was 'quite unrivalled elsewhere'. At the heart of the staffing problems was seen to be the state's acceptance of state responsibility for 'one social service after another' without assuming responsibility for maintaining 'the high standard for training and selection which had been established' (1934, p. 292). Neither the Royal Commission on the Civil Service, 1931, or the Departmental Committee on the Recruitment, Training and Promotion of Local Government Officials had made special recommendations relating to social-service staff, even though the JUC had submitted evidence about the importance of special qualifications and training for social service personnel. That Miss Macadam's views, and those of other social workers, were gradually piercing the armour of informed opinion is illustrated by the Political and Economic Planning report, 'British Social Services, 1937'. In a discussion of staffing and recruitment the report states:

> In view of the importance of home contacts in some of the constructive community services and of the home visitation involved in the administration of the social assistance services, there is plainly a real need for a comprehensive course of training in Social Casework to be undertaken by all who wish to engage in this career. The health visitors' course and the recently adopted training course for probation officers are good examples well worthy of attention in this connection. Some of the voluntary social services which have become so large-scale in character as to have a considerable professional personnel also provide excellent qualifying courses and examinations. Thus the supply of women house property managers and hospital almoners (serving with voluntary and public authorities) is maintained at a very high professional standard as a result of examination requirements which now obtain and the qualifying courses which prepare for them.

Sibyl Clement Brown

Miss Sibyl Clement Brown belonged to a newer generation of social worker, was a carrier of the mental hygiene movement from America, and an ardent thinker about the development of social work. Apart from her writing during the period we are fortunate to have a recent account of her impressions.[17] A graduate of Bedford College, Miss Clement Brown went to Birmingham for her social studies training. This was still based on the general social studies curriculum, but after contact with the juvenile court and reading Healy's *Individual Delinquent* (loaned to her by Mrs Barrow Cadbury, JP), she went to

America for three years with a Rockefeller grant, travelling widely and seeing child guidance projects and work with delinquents in Los Angeles, Massachusetts and New York, and completing a thesis on the topic of leadership among adolescent delinquent girls. As did the later observers and students, Miss Clement Brown 'found amazing contrast between education for social work in the two countries'. Gordon Hamilton's teaching on social casework, later to be embodied in her textbook *Theory and Practice of Social Work* (1940) was at the 'heart of the training'.

The opportunity to link the developments in America to British social work came when Professor Carr-Saunders, who had visited the Los Angeles Child Guidance Clinic in 1926, wrote to Miss Clement Brown about the embryonic child guidance movement in this country and stressed the importance of 'the psychiatric point of view in all fields of social administration'. On returning to this country, Miss Clement Brown had three years of clinical experience at Guy's Hospital, the East London Child Guidance Clinic and also at the London Child Guidance Clinic and Training Centre. She then became tutor to the first course of training for psychiatric social work, the Mental Health Course at LSE from 1930 to 1946.

Miss Clement Brown's theoretical contribution is important because of its influence on students passing through the mental health course, her educational work through writing and lectures, and because it shows a group of broader issues of social service organisations—never in this country did psychiatric social work become so detached from environmental considerations as in some American schools. In her third lecture in Birmingham in 1933, 'Mental Hygiene and the Social Worker of the Future', Miss Clement Brown asserted that, 'one development of the future will be a universal service of this kind, in every country', echoing Miss Macadam's hopes for almoning. With regard to the organisation of social agencies she summarised what most studies were agreed on:

(1) The need for careful personality study before any kind of individual or social treatment is attempted
(2) The need for combination of different experts in the study of personality and behaviour
(3) The necessity of combining research with service if either is to profit by the other.

In a prophetic statement Miss Clement Brown continued:

Now if in social work we are to shift our attention from

symptoms to needs, it seems to me that we shall tend more and more to centralise our agencies, public or private, into neighbourhood centres, as indeed we already have done to some extent in our settlements—as has been recommended in the Elberfeld system of Germany—and that, radiating out as it were from these centres as a clearing house, will come organisations dealing with special aspects of treatment.

Miss Clement Brown, like Miss Macadam in *The New Philanthropy*, recognised the need for a coherent pattern of social service for schools and urged the importance of experiments of the visiting teacher or school counsellor type. Towards the end of her lecture she examined the conditions for the development of social work:

> Unless social work is going to be swept on one side as an unproductive profession—perhaps even this criterion of progress is something we should include in the vistas of the future—it has got to be prepared to exercise both articulate analysis and skilled intuition in making a selection from cases as a general practitioner makes a selection of patients for the specialist. . . . The effective use of such specialists will depend upon our understanding of their function, and how they can dovetail into our own work. I can see no way of meeting this problem unless general social workers set themselves to get the knowledge which will help them recognise serious symptoms of personality distortion when they see them.

As tends to happen in any profession, particularly an emergent one, the gap between the thinking of the articulate élite and the mass of social workers was wide and accounts for the emphasis of educational work within the child guidance movement—how wide the gap was becomes apparent after the Second World War. At the close of this period Miss Clement Brown, characteristically lucid, sums up the relationship of social work and mental health:[18]

> The kind of social work we have come to describe as 'psychiatric' represents, to my mind, a stage of development in social casework as a whole, rather than a distinct profession. The stage of development did not come into being because certain individuals filled with curiosity travelled to the United States and returned with stories of a strange new cult which they were anxious to introduce to their less fortunate colleagues at home. It was an inevitable outcome of changing

knowledge, ideas and attitudes towards the problem of
human beings.

Miss Clement Brown's clarity of mind and vision of social work,
were to continue to influence social work to the present day, both
in the development of the child-care service, and through her
influence (with Margaret Ashdown) on students such as Mrs K.
McDougall and Mrs C. Winnicott.

Eileen Younghusband

A figure who does not feature prominently in the literature on
committees of the time but who was later to have an immense
influence on social work, in this country and internationally, was
Eileen Younghusband. Born in 1902, daughter of Sir Francis
Younghusband, she was educated privately and at London University. She was a social worker in south and east London from 1924
to 1929, lectured at the London School of Economics from 1929 to
1939 and was made a JP in 1933. It was important that she developed
in a period when a new stream of thinking was flowing into social
work, because we have seen how tied it is possible to become to the
dominant philosophical and social systems of our childhood and
early adult life. Looking back, Dame Eileen saw the 1920s and 1930s
as essentially an 'uncreative era' compared with the pre-war period.
But in terms of establishment of broader social services and the
evolution of ideas this was certainly not the case.[19] The failure was
in the speed with which social work was institutionalised. A number
of factors accounted for this: what Dame Eileen has called 'the
invisibility of the function', i.e. the problem of defining social work
within the field of social welfare;[20] the economic depression; and
the continuing difficulty of overcoming resistance to the male-
dominated universities, the hospitals and in local government.

Part III

Social work 1939–71: an expanding mixed profession

Social Workers, like cats, are traditionally feminine. The feminine gender is therefore used in this report, since the masculine would in some places strike strangely on the ear; though in others the feminine must be held to cover both sexes. Social Work in this country is still regarded as a woman's occupation. The war has artificially accentuated this, but in the permanent pattern it is to be hoped that men will be employed not only as at present as personnel managers, probation officers, youth leaders, settlement and community centre workers and as secretaries of Councils of Social Services, but that they will also enter certain casework fields. There is a deplorable tendency to think that, though a woman social worker needs training, a man has acquired all he needs to know through some all-sufficing experience of life which is a substitute for and not an enhancement of training. But now women have made their way in the other professions alongside men, while men are needed as much as women in some forms of social work.

> E. Younghusband,
> *Report on the Employment and*
> *Training of Social Workers*, 1947, p. 5.

11   The Second World War

War and welfare

It is always a matter of speculation whether trends and events crystallised in wartime would have occurred within a peacetime framework.[1] It is nearly always the case that many developments in wartime which seem important in retrospect are attributed to the war situation almost as a spin-off justifying war effort; in contrast we very rarely point to events in peacetime and say that they were caused by peace. In fact, all one can do is locate a number of specific changes and relate them to the previously developing pattern. When examining the position of women in social work during the First World War a number of effects were apparent: with men abroad in the forces women did work previously considered mainly men's work, with the consequent enhancement of status and increasing acceptance of the employment of women in a wider range of jobs; government interest in welfare was extended—the war threw up particular welfare problems and the government was concerned that people with welfare functions should be trained; the effects of war on the mental functioning of soldiers increased interest in psychiatric problems and knowledge; then there were particular effects which differed according to the function of the welfare agency—such as the effects on the clientele group of almoners or probation officers. Permeating all these effects is the tendency for greater government intervention in all aspects of civilian life including welfare: war can act as a catalyst affecting the growth and forms of welfare.

For the fullest account of social problems in the Second World War, the study by R. M. Titmuss[2] is the standard reference work. The war had the effects referred to above: by 1943 four-and-a-half million men were in the armed forces, civil defence and other services, two and three-quarter million more women than in 1939 were employed in industry, the forces and civil defence, and probably another one million were serving full time or part time in nurseries, canteens, hostels, clubs and rest centres. The threat of air attack, with the resulting evacuation, caused serious dislocation and disruption of normal life. Billeting of children in reception areas caused

167

problems and with children remaining in their own families there was less supervision and contact with their mothers. There was an increase in delinquency and much evidence of disturbed behaviour in children separated from their normal environment and their families. Thus the war intensified certain forms of social pathology and called forth or extended specific patterns of service, such as hostels for disturbed children, fostering, residential nursery and day nursery care, and also advisory services.

Elizabeth Macadam judged that the Second World War had had a mixed effect on social work as many social workers were called up for unskilled occupations. She further comments (1945, p. 28):

> Some hospital almoners became unemployed as hospitals emptied their wards. Evacuation and billeting were mostly undertaken by untrained volunteers. However there were developments in psychiatric social work where psychiatric social workers did valuable work with servicemen and with disturbed children in hostels.

Although we will look at these changes in more detail, it is relevant to mention here that the war led to the appointment of social workers to central government ministries (the Ministry of Labour, Ministry of Health, the War Services and War Ministries). For example, the Ministry of Health added social workers to the evacuation services for the first time in June 1940, and by August 1941 officers were serving including a chief officer and some regional appointments.[3]

Almoning

The impact on different branches of social work varied. In almoning at first there was the initial distressing redundancy of some hospital almoners as hospitals emptied wards. But this was only a temporary measure and by the late autumn of 1939 many of those dismissed were reinstated. As the war developed, and with it the emergency medical services, the demand for almoners increased and the Ministry of Health issued a memorandum to all hospitals in the Emergency Scheme advising the appointment of almoners.[4] It was clear that the evacuation had a big impact and that a major reason for the appointment of almoners was the increased administrative work as a result of dealing with population movements from one area to another; in these circumstances dealing with admissions was an important and onerous administrative task. Some almoners, as did many other social workers, transferred to other welfare jobs and helped at rest and feeding centres, at shelters, and in reception areas. However, by the end of 1940 most of these had returned to hospital work. Three 'almoners of standing' were appointed as temporary welfare inspectors of the Ministry of Health under Mr Willink, the commissioner for the homeless of London.[5] Miss Florence Horsburgh, MD, addressed the 1940 annual general meeting of the almoners on the wartime health services and the part of the almoner in them.

Expansion was steady and by 1945 there were 650 almoners in posts, nearly double the number at the start of the war. In one year (1941) sixty-five new almoning posts had been created, thirty-seven in hospitals under a statutory authority and twenty-eight in voluntary hospitals.[6] Yet it had been shown by research undertaken by Miss H. Rees that a number of hospitals were employing almoners to collect forms and statistics rather than to do medical social work for the patients.[7]

As thinking developed during the war about the future of health services, almoners participated in these explorations and reacted to the plans as they emerged. In 1942, the year of the Beveridge Report, the Institute of Hospital Almoners was asked for views on the future of new health services and sent a memorandum to the Ministry of Health and the Royal College of Physicians, re-emphasising the importance of the almoner seeing the patient in his family and social context.[8] The following year the interim report of the Social and Preventive Medicine Committee of the Royal College of Physicians discussed the almoners' functions and the structure of almoners' departments, suggesting that almoners were required in hospitals, health centres, regional organisations and in teaching hospitals.[9] In spite of strong friends in the medical profession (Sir Farquhar Buzzard had been president of the Institute of Hospital Almoners from 1933 to his death in 1945; Professor Moncrief was chairman of the executive in 1945; as mentioned above, Willink had had experience of using almoners during the war), the 1944 White Paper on the National Health Service contained no mention of almoning. It was welcomed by the IHA and Willink, the Minister of Health, addressed the 1944 annual general meeting. Over 400 people were present and heard him assure almoners that, although they were not mentioned in the White Paper, he was fully alive to the importance of their work, considering them essential to the success of the health service.[10] In spite of this reasoning approach, Willink had greater problems on his hands than almoners and probably regarded the service as a minor detail when compared in scale and complexity with the other problems of structuring a national health service.

In terms of professional development, plans were laid for the amalgamation of the institute and council and in October 1945 the Certificate for the Incorporation of the Institute of Almoners was obtained.[11] This allowed a single voice for almoners to be heard. Also towards the end of the war, the Hospital Almoners Council was invited to submit its views on salaries to a government committee examining the salaries and wages of hospital staffs. With other health workers, a Professional Staffs Committee was formed to discuss with employing bodies the question of national scales, which were eventually decided in 1946. On the training side the institute's course had been strengthened by the appointment of Miss A. B. Read as a tutor late in 1939. It had been decided to continue with a full programme of training and it became necessary to appoint an assistant tutor in July 1944. Miss Read had established a pattern of class teaching and co-ordination of the overall training programmes, the need for which had been implied by Miss Batten's 1939 address; it had not been possible, because of the onset of war, to introduce the preliminary training scheme proposed in 1939. In the later part of the war, this changing approach bore fruit and the training began to take on a more modern professional appearance (Snelling, 1970):

> Committees discuss the writing and handling of reports on students' practical work; how to ensure that reports reflect progress in handling relationships in social work: how to ensure that there are interim discussions between supervisors and students so that time is left for further progress before the goodbyes. The students come forward in 1943 with their own proposals, detailed and constructive, for improvements in social science and the almoners course.

All these particular changes indicated a developing professional consciousness but one which, notwithstanding the wartime expansion of almoning, was still constricted, with only a limited acceptance from the medical profession.

Psychiatric social work

In psychiatric social work, much smaller in scale than almoning, most of the pre-war work had been in the hospital field where there was the same problem of the male medical hierarchy which needed educating. Each hospital had its own ideas of how to use psychiatric social workers with consequent difficulty in establishing a firm role within the hospital system. As had occurred with almoning, the main development had been in London and the South.[12] After the fiasco of the false predictions of mass mental illness at the start of the war, a number of important developments took place, but there was no enormous expansion of training from 1940 to 1944, a period during which ninety-two psychiatric social workers were trained. Naturally the war prevented expansion in the numbers of men being trained as psychiatric social workers, a trend which was to establish itself again following the war.

The major wartime developments were in community care, particularly work in hostels for disturbed children, and in work with service men and women. These developments were fostered through government stimulation under the aegis of the Mental Health Emergency Committee (to become the Provisional National Council for Mental Health in 1942). Within the community the employment of psychiatric social workers was mainly related to evacuation problems and they advised foster parents, selected children for admission to hostels, supervised the care of children in particular hostels, decided on when children would be suitable for rebilleting and in finding sympathetic billets (Titmuss, 1950, p. 381). Thirty-two psychiatric social workers had been appointed by local authorities by the end of 1942, although the costs were met in full by the central government. In relation to the total evacuation and hostel programme the impact was limited, but Timms stresses the importance of this work as leading 'directly to experiments in community care as it is envisaged today'.[13] Timms also recounts a project at St Andrew's Hospital, Northampton, which in December 1941 led to a request that the regional workers of the Mental Health Emergency Committee should help with ATS and WAAF cases in the hospital by a psychiatric social worker visiting regularly to see selected cases and to arrange home visits and after-care. The success of this experiment led to the appointment of psychiatric social workers to each of the twelve civil defence regions and eventually eighteen psychiatric social workers were appointed with a staff of forty-five other social workers; this service dealt with 10,000 cases during the period up to 1946. In 1942 it was estimated that about one quarter of psychiatric social workers were in wartime employment,[14] but in contrast to the almoners the specific wartime contribution was maintained throughout the war. However, in spreading its wings into new fields during the war, the psychiatric social work was continuing a trend already established in the 1930s, when psychiatric social workers had already begun to infiltrate probation work, family casework, children's services of all kinds and Borstal institutions.

The soul-searching that gripped the nation's social thinking from the earliest days in the war was exemplified by a meeting at Burlington House on 30 May 1942—arranged by the Association of Psychiatric Social Workers and to which psychiatrists were invited—which examined the future of psychiatric social work. Professor Aubrey Lewis, Professor of Psychiatry at the Maudsley Hospital, and Miss Sibyl Clement Brown both gave addresses. Professor Lewis accepted that psychiatric social workers were 'a variety of the species "medical social worker". In other words she is a social worker specialising in the health field.'[15] Yet he was adamant that her ultimate allegiance was to the medical group: 'I cannot see how she can prudently or without detriment to efficiency divorce herself from the medical group of which the clinic or hospital is the centre and the psychiatrist the leader.' The issue was—and still is—should the psychiatric social worker be relegated to a subservient, auxiliary role, female planets to the male psychiatrist's star. Professor Lewis felt it necessary to warn psychiatric social workers against 'too great a dependence on extreme individual approaches such as that characteristic of Freudian psycho-analysis, or traditional consulting room medicine'.

He wanted psychiatric social work to 'have some principles of its own' and to develop 'not according to paper plans but according to demonstrated need which can be measured in economic loss through preventable mental ill health or thought of in terms of preventable human misery'. With a vision never fully realised, because socialised medicine is still in its infancy, he envisaged for the future a great increase in social and preventive health services of which psychiatric social work would be a part:

> With a well adjusted and regional distribution of medical services, the psychiatric social worker would no longer have the narrow attachment to her hospital or clinic; but would very likely be attached to a sector or district, circulating as the psychiatrists and other specialists would; between hospital, health centre, industrial clinic, rehabilitation centre and the patient's house.

Although Professor Lewis's insights were acute and delivered with urbanity and wit there is more than a touch of the middle-aged father lecturing his daughter about to begin her career in the tone of his remarks. His paper had followed Miss Clement Brown's, but her address—characteristically not mentioned in her own account of the Burlington House Conference[16]—may to some extent be regarded as a reply. In part she accepted the strictures of Professor Lewis: 'For many years the stress in both our training and our work was laid upon the circumstances of the individual rather than upon personal attitudes and relationships.'[17]

Miss Clement Brown emphasised that the pressure for the introduction of psychiatric social work in the 1920s had come from those having to deal with the social complications of difficult individuals such as the Howard League for Penal Reform, the Magistrates Association, the Central Association for Mental Welfare and the National Council for Mental Hygiene; she would therefore 'like to place the accent of our embarrassingly awkward title on the word *social* rather than *psychiatric*'. Consequently as a matter of logic and conviction, she saw as the essence of social work 'that its function shifts with social change and that its disciplines must be constantly developing'. In looking back over the gains of the previous thirteen years, Miss Clement Brown thought that the greatest of these was

perhaps the realisation that the process of bringing about any sort of growth in individuals, and harmonising of human relationships is the highest sort of art, learned only through disciplined experience, through a constant stirring of the imagination, and not just through the simple application of knowledge.

In looking to the future Miss Clement Brown used a family metaphor in a statement that catches the excitement, seriousness and vision of those days: 'Few adolescent professions can have looked forward to such exacting years for the test of their value.' In much of their approach Professor Lewis and Miss Clement Brown were bonded by a similar vision of the future. The major gulf between them was how much independence should be accorded to this precocious daughter profession, whether she would identify with her peer social workers or with her paternal male medical colleagues.

Probation

In the probation service the declaration of war had the immediate effect of preventing the enactment of the Criminal Justice Bill 1938, which had embodied many of the suggestions of the Departmental Committee, 1936. However, in spite of the frustrations of this attempt to amend and consolidate the legislation relating to the probation system, and although the war put new difficulties in the way of the probation service, there was nevertheless continued development along the lines proposed in the 1936 report (Bochel, 1963). The Bill had contained provisions particularly related to women. It had gone beyond the 1925 Act by specifying that a sufficient number of probation officers should be appointed to each area to ensure that one man and one woman could be assigned to each petty sessional division;[18] this would have ensured the appointment of women in all divisions. The head of the probation branch had said in 1937 that they were 'growing tired of the explanation that there was no work for a woman member to do'.[19] The Bill went on to confirm what seems to have been the traditional view of women's work in the probation service. In Clause 4(2) it stated that 'where a woman or girl is placed under the supervision of a probation officer the probation officer shall be a woman'. However, there were still probation areas without women probation officers; in 1943 there were still 300 courts without the services of a woman officer compared with under 100 courts in 1950 (Bochel, 1963, p. 340).

Because of the high proportion of men in the probation service, enlistment had a considerable effect. Although probation was a reserved occupation for all men over thirty-five (later this was extended to men over thirty) a quarter of full-time male officers went into the forces. Nevertheless, the number of full-time officers increased from 509 in 1939 to 750 in 1945. The shortage of male officers at the start of the war led to the employment of women to supervise boys up to the age of fourteen, as well as women and girls, so that men could be used for the supervision of adult men.[20] Central government staff were also called up for war service and Mr Reynolds, head of the probation branch, was transferred to war work until 1943, his place being taken temporarily by Miss Rosling. Miss Rosling had been a probation officer before becoming an inspector and Mr Harris, Assistant Under-Secretary at the Home Office commented: 'Her success in administration is shown by her recent promotion to the ranks of acting principal in the Home

Office.'[21] Two other women, Mrs Hadley and Miss Williams (headmistress at Burford House Approved School) joined the probation branch inspectorate as a result of wartime staffing difficulties.

The August 1941 issue of *Probation* contains addresses given to the twenty-eighth national conference of NAPO and is particularly concerned with the effects of war work. Extension of women's work has already been mentioned, and they, like men, were involved with the problems of evacuation and problems of transferring supervision. To avoid overloading the service in evacuation areas only the most difficult cases were transferred to local supervision, notification of the change of residence sufficing for the majority. Other problems experienced during the war were the closure of a number of homes and hostels and the slowness in the development of approved lodgings. As in the First World War, there were financial difficulties on the part of wives whose husbands had gone to the services and 'for months after September 1939 and even today probation officers throughout the country were besieged with wives whose problems included such urgent matters as arrears of rent and threat of ejection, threat of the loss of personal possessions by failure to maintain payments under hire purchase agreements, inability to continue insurance premiums and other financial obligations and many others of a similar nature.'[22] Because of the separation of husbands and wives there was a considerable emphasis on matrimonial work involving much liaison with forces personnel.

Throughout the war NAPO pressed for adequate salaries, strengthening of the national probation structure, and satisfactory conditions of service. The chairman's address to the 1941 conference, delivered by Mr G. E. Gorland, stressed that good service conditions were necessary in 'the maintenance of personal service to the people who come to the court. . . . Personal service cannot be of the best if we are handicapped by bad equipment and by lack of reasonable facilities.'[23] He also put great store by co-operation with other services and social workers:[24]

Another important thing is that the Association as a whole must work for a closer co-operation with other social organisations. . . . We look forward and see the tremendous responsibilities that will rest upon the shoulders of probation officers and of the Association and of all the social services. The more we can co-operate, the more we understand each other, the more we work with each other, the infinitely stronger we shall be.

Like the psychiatric social workers, the probation officers were working towards an uncertain future and trying to clarify their objectives. The wholesale re-examination of the social services and the strength of the inspectorate made them anxious about their place in the post-war structure of social services[25]—so much so that in the summer of 1944, Miss Gertrude Tuckwell and Miss Margery Fry and a group of London magistrates met to discuss their unease about the probation service. A memorandum was prepared and it was intended that Miss Tuckwell and Miss Fry should make a confidential approach to the Parliamentary Under-Secretary (Bochel, 1963, pp. 346ff.). Before the approach was made, the Home Secretary announced the appointment of a new body, the Advisory Council on the Treatment of Offenders, of which Miss Fry and the permanent under-secretary were both to be members. The memorandum was sent to the chairman, Sir Norman Birkett, and the council received evidence from the Magistrates Association and NAPO when considering the future of the probation service. Although no official public action resulted, the relationship between NAPO and the Home Office improved during 1945. In its future dealings with the Home Office, NAPO was strengthened by adapting a new constitution in 1945 and by a stronger financial position. On making application to the Home Office, NAPO was officially recognised as a negotiating body in relation to the remuneration of probation officers.

It is clear from the exposition of Titmuss and from the examination of different groups of social workers, that the war had disturbing social consequences and that this produced reaction by the government. Some developments started before the war were hindered, but the government realised that social workers could help people in distress and, in so far as it could see specific functions for them, was willing to give administrative and financial support. Wartime demands on social workers were superimposed on the existing problems of the different organisations and the embryonic vision of a better society caught the imagination of social workers who wished to share in its formation. Except in the probation service—which was however considerably depleted in the early years of the war—the main welfare burden fell on women and gave opportunities for work at a senior level. Only in the male-dominated probation service, however, was a war bonus paid (in keeping with other civil servants). From March 1941 probation officers earning up to £250 were awarded a bonus of £26 for men and £19 19s for women.[26]

The Caxton Hall Conference, 1942

It is perhaps not surprising that the majority of speakers at a BFSW Conference held at Caxton Hall in February 1941 dealing with 'Social Changes Due to the War and their Significance' should have been women. The idea for the conference came from a meeting with Mr H. E. Norman in January 1941, following a discussion with the Master of Balliol College about how the BFSW could help the Nuffield College Social Reconstruction Survey. Yet even before the war a group of social workers had started a research study group under the guidance of Dr Audrey Richards, the anthropologist, with a similar aim—to pool their field experience and to make known the sociological implications to government departments.[27] This was followed by a series of lectures on social psychology by Karl Mannheim, but the war held back the movement temporarily.

The conference is important because those present not only focused on the detailed problems arising out of the war and possible solutions, but examined the place of social work in society. Miss I. Forstner, a hospital almoner, dealt with this theme in some detail and some of her comments give an insight into the state of consciousness of social work at the time. She said:[28]

> I think it is true to say that before the war, most social workers concentrated too much on their day-to-day problems, in their own particular field. . . . We did not pause to look at the social picture as a whole and our own place in it. . . . More and more social workers are beginning to realise that these very problems on which they concentrate so conscientiously arise out of the prevailing conditions in the community; the needs arise out of these conditions and the social provisions exist to meet these needs either perfectly or imperfectly.

Following this Miss Forstner wondered whether social workers only had the function of implementing existing social provisions, and went on to analyse the functions of social workers in the following manner as:[29]

(1) To interpret the existing social services to those who have need of them.

G

(2) To attempt to see that these services are used to the best
advantage of the individual and the community.

A third function which I consider to be important, has been
sadly neglected. This function is to contribute to the planning
of new social services and the modification when necessary of
the existing ones. One of our weaknesses at the moment is that
we are not clear as to what we mean by 'a social worker', we
find it difficult to explain what it is we regard as our particular
skill. . . . This failure to crystallise our own ideas is due, I
think, to the concentration of the social worker on day to day
casework. In social work, as in other professions we have
tended to specialise. . . . It is only by a constant interchange
of experience and ideas between the various branches of the
profession that we can hope to become sufficiently informed, as
individuals or as a profession, to make any real contribution to
the planning of social services.

Other speakers echoed this kind of approach. Miss B. M. Watson
(Charity Organisation Society) maintained that it was[30]

above all essential to define clearly the functions of a social
worker and to interpret them to the various Government
Departments concerned. . . . Are we not too complacent. The
zest of the pioneers has given place to stagnation. We have
been too silent and have failed to educate one half of the
nation to how the other half still lives.

Miss D. M. Dyson (psychiatric social worker) suggested that the
social worker was 'primarily the interpreter'.[31] One of the reasons
for social work's lack of acceptance in the community was its lack
of articulateness. Miss Clement Brown commented that 'the fact
that in our present generation we have not been articulate about our
work' was 'further evidence of our failure as a profession'.[32] There
was another reason, supplied by Miss Cameron, warden of Lady
Margaret Hall Settlement, namely that 'In the past social work has
been looked upon with a good deal of suspicion by working class
organisations, who have accused us of patronage and inquisitive-
ness'.[33] This was related to the fact, regretted by Miss Clement
Brown, that entry to social work was generally dependent upon a
good level of parental income. However, Miss Clement Brown
thought that a significant effect of the war had been to put social
workers at the receiving end of welfare services—that they had

become clients of the social services themselves. The clients of the social services, and how to get closer to them, were prominent topics in some parts of the discussion. Miss Cosens (LCC Children's Care Organiser) was quite clear that 'the old idea that the Social Worker is mainly concerned with the relief of material need has passed away. The use of Social Workers in the reception areas is outstandingly concerned with problems of human relationships. . . .'[34]

Many speakers recognised the increase of state intervention and anticipated it continuing after the war. This was welcomed but there were some fears about the impact on the individual. Miss Clement Brown tried to dispel these anxieties whilst discussing

> the extraordinary separation which has been allowed to grow
> up between social workers undertaking individual service, or
> 'casework', and those whose function lies in planning and
> administration. In our discussion of this problem we tended
> to assume that casework was the practice of the 'voluntary' or
> private social services and that social workers employed by
> public authorities must always be regarded as administrators.
> This is of course untrue. Both types of work are sponsored by
> agencies, supported from public or private funds or by a
> combination of the two.[35]

She was reluctant to accept that statutory agencies would not support 'individualised' service of the casework type and was more optimistic than many of the willingness of public authorities to further experimental work of this kind.

Training and research received a good deal of attention, particularly the questions of the divorce of theory and practice and the place of the universities in social training. A number of speakers decried the lack of integration between academic studies and practical work, although Miss Black, from the Social Science Department at Liverpool, gave a spirited defence of the university and questioned whether the links between university and field were as 'slender as sometimes supposed'.[36] She said that some of her best students had come with scholarships from local education authorities, and wanted to encourage suitable older students to undertake training. Others were worried that insufficient attention had been given to developing case study material for class teaching or to developing research. Miss Clement Brown drew attention to the fact that the only English references in a recently published American book on social casework were on child psychology and local government (out of a bibliography of six pages); her keen wit followed this with the acute remark:[37]

> I am inclined to think that if we had something clear in our heads, some of us would write—though unfortunately the converse does not hold good. It is interesting that in this connection no one has mentioned the conditions under which we work, though these are hardly such as to promote thoughtful study.

On the subject of research Miss Clement Brown thought that social workers in this country needed

> a much closer relationship with centres of social research. Is it too much to hope that one day, we may have some freelance research workers to help us in the study of our own practice and to pass on our findings in a useful form to those responsible for planning?

During the inter-war period Elizabeth Macadam and writers within particular branches of social work had called for research, but to very little avail. This particular deficiency in social work was to be repeatedly discussed down to the present day, but without making many inroads into the problem.

At the end of the conference Miss Fry mentioned developments during the war which she thought had been shown to be of permanent value, such as the use of foster parent care instead of large reform schools, the general attitude of welcome for family allowances, the need for more provision for the elderly and for club leaders for young people. She was proud of the fact that no mention had been made of workers' own difficulties over salaries or conditions of work, something which she thought 'must be unique in a conference of professional social workers'.[38] Again she reflected the thoughts of many social workers in stressing the need for social workers to get their ideas across to the public (perhaps even more than to ministries). In addition to her remarks Mr Norman crystallised the meaning of the conference very significantly: 'The Conference should make us feel that we were all part of one large body of social workers, thinking with an international mind, speaking in international language, and doing international service.' There had been glimmerings of this feeling in the period before the war, yet the war did signify a *gestalt* switch, through which the identification of common elements in social work became a major task, to be paralleled by the striving towards professional unity in one organisation. It was as though the unity of nineteenth-century philanthropic ideals had been refracted through a prism revealing the variegated branches of social work as a spectrum of different colours, only during the Second World War to pass through a second prism which was to blend them in a common focus, though this was a quarter of a century away. This development of a common consciousness of the identity of social work was illustrated by the probation service's groping towards contact with other social organisations, and also by the joint meeting in 1944, between the almoners' and the psychiatric social workers' associations. At this meeting the desirability of a common basic training for the two fields was discussed, the need to develop a more scientific approach to social work and also the possibility of establishing a joint library (Snelling, 1970). Acceptance in the university, however, was still only grudging and illustrated by the fact that the mental health course at LSE was financed partly by the Commonwealth Fund up until 1944, with appointments to the course below scale, temporary and unestablished (Clement Brown, 1970).

Voluntary effort in wartime—women in action

Social work thrives on social pathology and upheaval and we have seen how in particular branches of social work there was expansion during the war and a critical self-examination. The personal difficulties thrown up by the war had shown that 'the gulf between administrative provision and the actual and effective implementation and use of such provision needed constant bridging; it was the job of the social worker to build the bridges' (Titmuss, 1950). Social workers had proved their usefulness and, from being virtually ignored by government departments, they rose in official esteem so that there resulted what Titmuss described as 'something approaching a famine of social workers'. It was in the tradition of British social work that voluntary organisations and volunteers should plug the gap. Unlike American social workers, British social workers had never passed through a phase when voluntary workers had been denigrated because of the professional aspirations of paid workers. Volunteers and paid workers had always co-existed and if psychiatric social workers and almoners did not use volunteers intensively in their work it was because of preoccupation with their own problems rather than a devaluation of voluntary effort. It is arguable that one of the greatest inhibiting factors on the development of professional social work in this country is the exaggerated official patronage at central and local government levels given to the virtue of voluntary effort.[39] This has led to inadequately staffed statutory social work services and patchy voluntary services. The poverty of our statutory social welfare provisions meant that a key part would be played by voluntary organisations and voluntary workers.

In 1943 the number of women engaged in women's ancillary services in the UK stood at 461,000, and in 1939 over 127,000 members of the Women's Voluntary Services were helping the movement from evacuation to reception areas.[40] WVS members were also heavily involved in staffing rest centres, in administering clothing schemes for evacuees and in running the Londoners' Meals Service. Trained social workers were also to some extent involved in these schemes, particularly the ones dealing with Londoners, but the principal burden fell on the WVS and other volunteers. The National Council of Social Services co-ordinated the Londoners' Meals Service with the WVS and was also responsible for floating two new organisations, the Citizens' Advice Bureau[41] and the Women's Group on Public Welfare.[42] The Citizens' Advice Bureaux were established to meet the needs of the citizen for information and advice over a wide range of welfare matters, particularly those dealing with evacuation, billeting, service questions, rationing and other wartime problems. A skeleton organisation had been planned before the war and on the first Monday after the declaration of war 200 CABS were opened, a number which had increased to over 1,000 by the end of 1942. In spite of the fact that official information centres opened later, the CABS continued to expand their work and were popular with the public. The Women's Group on Public Welfare came into existence in September 1939, one of a number of *ad hoc* groups supported by the NCSS, and by 1942 its membership was representative of thirty-nine national organisations, it had held forty full meetings and had established nine sub-committees. In April 1943 it was responsible for the publication of a study of evacuation conditions titled *Our Towns—A Close Up*. An indication of its other consultative work is the pressure it put on the Ministry of Health over the establishment of nurseries for two- to five-year-olds (Titmuss, 1950, p. 169).

As in the First World War, voluntary organisations coped with social problems in advance of the slower response of statutory agencies. When London was suffering under the bombing of 1940

Titmuss describes the reflex action of the voluntary organisations (1950, p. 261):

> It was the voluntary organisations—the Charity Organisation Society, the Society of Friends, the Settlement workers, the London Council of Social Services and many others—who helped to hold the line during this period while the official machine was beginning to take effective action.

In a variety of contexts Titmuss repeatedly describes the importance of voluntary effort—of ordinary people as well as members of organisations—in coping with the problems of war. The existing administration and organisation of the NCSS, the Charity Organisation Society, had proved invaluable as a base for coping with the problem of social distress and for starting new organisations. One voluntary organisation which owes its existence to the war and which did not have this base was the Pacifist Service Units, later to become the Family Service Units. Founded by a group of conscientious objectors, it had the object of giving practical service to poor families and the workers started in Liverpool. The organisation is important because it gave a new embodiment to the settlement ideal of bridging the class gap, and because it was a forerunner of many recent ideas to replace military service by alternative forms of community work. As women were exempt from military service, its male origins are understandable, but for men to embark on personal service of this kind which would generally be thought to have been within the compass of a woman's rule was an innovation, and perhaps in this small beginning we may detect the seed of a growing flexibility in attitudes towards men's and women's roles in social work.

Venereal disease

An aspect of the Second World War which had posed far greater problems during the First World War was that of venereal disease.[43] The dislocation caused by the war conditions, foreign troops, and casual relations caused by the war resulted in an increase in the total first infections for gonorrhea and syphilis from 48,814 in 1940 to 65,474 in 1943. Although the 1943 total was nearly the same as for 1934, the government had introduced compulsory medical inspection and treatment in November 1942 under Defence Regulation 33B. Failure to comply made a person liable to a maximum of three months' imprisonment or £100 fine. The 1916 Royal Commission on Venereal Diseases had advocated the treatment of VD on a voluntary and confidential basis, and the new regulation was opposed by many moral welfare workers as being contrary to the principles established by Josephine Butler. In the operation of Regulation 33B health visitors, almoners and other social workers and the police were used to track down suspected contacts by questioning landladies, publicans, dance hall officials, etc. Some social workers and doctors supported the regulation but others rejected it because it encouraged promiscuity and assumed that women were the main source of VD infection. As in the nineteenth century, the unfair operation of the regulation was obvious—the majority of those being reported being women. Moral welfare workers abhorred the regulation and had a full programme of principles and practical measures to deal with VD in a positive preventive manner. However, it was not until well after the end of the war that the regulation was rescinded. The history of the regulation during the war illustrated very clearly how easily governments can resort to punitive and basically inhumane measures (there was no redress for a person not infected) if faced with a social problem, particularly as the government during the war seems sometimes to have been insensitive to the needs of mothers and children, and late in reacting to them.[44]

Child welfare, women and social work

All existing social workers and organisations were drawn into dealing with the many problems caused by the war. Their clients were all affected in one way or another by absent fathers, evacuation, homelessness and the many difficulties of practical survival. Evacuation and billeting, however, with the resulting behaviour problems in children, brought the needs of children to the attention of the public at large and to the authorities. The increase in illegitimacy, the behavioural problems of children in wartime, and the conditions in many children's homes left much to be desired. General conditions were revealed by a survey by the Women's Group on Public Welfare. More specific criticisms of the quality of public care were voiced by Lady Allen of Hurtwood in her letter to *The Times* in July 1945 and her subsequent pamphlet.[45] The diffused administrative responsibility for deprived children was seen as a major culprit, causing particular deficiencies, and following *The Times* correspondence a committee of enquiry was appointed to investigate the care of deprived children in England and Wales in March 1945.[46] All three of the major departments concerned with the welfare of children—the Home Office (Morrison), the Ministry of Health (Willink) and the Department of Education (R. H. Butler)— appointed the committee under the chairmanship of Miss Myra Curtis. The list of appointees included two women MPs, a woman councillor and five other women apart from Miss Curtis; Miss Clement Brown was a member of the committee. There were eight men on the committee including one MP, two doctors and a head of a voluntary organisation. Thus the committee was the first to have such an evenly balanced membership and a female chairman, the direct result of its function to examine the care of children, which fell naturally within women's province.[47] Miss Rosling, who had done so well in the probation department, and Mr G. T. Milne of the Ministry of Health were joint secretaries to the committee. The committee worked prodigiously and its significance was great in a number of ways. It was the first enquiry in this country directed towards the welfare of all groups of deprived children, irrespective of class or income or particular problem. Second, it provided the possibility of breaking through the functional organisation of statutory social services which had developed during this century. It is noticeable that voluntary organisations very frequently are aimed at particular groups in need, such as the aged, children, the handicapped and the mentally ill, whereas the development of insurance, health, education and housing services to cover broad areas of social welfare is always in danger of blindness to groups of people whose needs have to be met by a variety of services. Third, because child welfare did not lie easily under education or health services it was at least a possibility of the establishment of an agency with a primary function of social work. The full terms of reference were:

> to be a committee to inquire into existing methods of providing for children who from loss of parents or from any cause whatever are deprived of a normal home life with their own parents or relatives; and to consider what further measures should be taken to ensure that these children are brought up under conditions best calculated to compensate them for the lack of parental care.

These terms of reference posed a problem which very clearly fell within the psycho-social sphere which social work was trying to

G*

identify as its own. This is evident by the wide range of welfare bodies who were witnesses to the committee, including the British Federation of Social Workers who were represented by Miss D. Keeling, Miss G. Kennedy, Miss R. Duncan, Mrs L. Turner, Mrs K. McDougall and Miss Bliss. Here at last, one might say, was a happy confluence, an area of work which seemed especially appropriate for women and about which there was sufficient public concern for the establishment of a firmly based service. The reports of the committee were not published until 1946 and will be dealt with in Chapter 13.

Having examined the wartime developments in some detail, it is pertinent to recall that, apart from the probation service, the vast majority of trained workers were still middle- or upper-class women from families of substantial means with a leaven of students aided from voluntary services, local education scholarships, or university bursaries. This fact gives immense significance to the 1944 Education Act which gave the possibility of the democratisation of social work by drawing on a wider range of the community for its personnel. Without the changes brought about by the Education Act 1944, it is doubtful whether the image of social work would have altered to the same extent and whether in many fields of practice men would have been attracted in any numbers. We have already found that it is exceedingly difficult to make generalisations about social work, and that one of the major variations between its different branches was the prevalence of women or men. The story of social work during the post-war period was to be very much involved with variations of this kind. During the war, however, the reliance of social work upon the services of the single woman was a unifying link with the past and they had to cope with the stresses and discipline of the unmarried state. Emphasis upon vocation, for so long an excuse for not paying salaries appropriate to qualifications, would never have been acceptable in a generally male-dominated profession. British reticence prevented the open acknowledgment of this connection but it received acknowledgment in a short article by B. Eva Billiams in 1942 entitled 'On Knowing Oneself',[48] which is reminiscent of some of the writing of Miss Matheson at an earlier period. She writes:

Modern life does not, of course, provide opportunities for happy marriage for all women, but many can find a very satisfactory life in occupations which were closed to them a few years ago. There will, however, remain a few, and these often very fine people, to whom no very satisfactory way of sublimation is open or are too 'highly sexed' to find such a way. For them chastity will be hard, but none the less desirable if they are to find happiness. But here again, in order to achieve happiness a knowledge of oneself and one's motives is essential. The social worker who says to himself: 'I love managing other people's lives', and then avoiding anything that would hurt the personality of another, uses this urge of hers for the improvement of social conditions, is the kind of person whose work is usually successful in regard to herself and to others. She works with less strain because she does not expect other people to be grateful to her; she is getting all the reward she needs through the work itself. Many women will not recognise or admit their sexual needs, and urges: they are afraid of them, and so pretend they do not exist. They are often irritable, nervy and bad tempered; and very trying to live with, for they are dissatisfied with life and wasting their emotional energy. Never was self knowledge, and the wisdom that goes with it so necessary as it is now, in a time when honesty and truth are so little valued.

The selflessness of many women's motivation for social work had led to a situation in which they had been used unthinkingly in a man's world to meet many social needs. The strength of their urge for service was played upon, in spite of evidence over the best part of a century of their efficiency and organising ability as well as their capacity of sympathetic response to suffering and their imaginative grasp of human problems.[49] Whilst social work was linked in the public mind with being a woman's profession there were limits to its growth, and a dependence upon sympathetic men in responsible positions. The Second World War—like the First World War—had shown the high qualities of understanding and administration that women could bring to demanding and new situations. In the next few years it was to be seen how lasting the new-found government esteem was to be.

12   The demographic background after 1945

Marriage, family and work

It was only after the Second World War that the proportion of married women working rose beyond the proportion of a century earlier. This was a trend which continued between 1951 and 1961. Whereas the total male population of fifteen years old and over increased by 6 per cent and the occupied proportion increased by 4 per cent, the equivalent increases for the female population were 4 per cent and 12 per cent (see Table 12.1).[1]

Table 12.1   Occupied women, 1951 and 1961

	Total female population 15 and over '000s'	Occupied female population 15 and over '000s'
1951	17,999	6,272
1961	18,706	7,045
% increase 1951–61	4	12

This led to an increase in the proportion of women in the occupied population from 31 per cent in 1951 to 33 per cent in 1961. There was also an increase in the proportion of economically active women in the same period from 40 per cent to 52 per cent. Marriage became more popular and the proportion of single women was 38·9 per cent in 1961 compared with 50 per cent in 1931. From 1931, too, there had been an increasing trend to earlier marriage and we had become a nation of small families by the time of the 1951 Census. In employment there was a growth of part-time work by married women between the two censuses, with almost 40 per cent of married women part-timers in 1961 compared with almost 25 per cent in 1951.

The trend, which had been continuous although gradual, in the entry of women to the professions was maintained and not only did women continue to spread into a greater variety of occupations between 1951 and 1961 compared with 1931 to 1951, but they made a slightly more pronounced entry into the higher professions. Of the 261,060 doctors, dentists, accountants, solicitors and architects in 1961, women formed 9·6 per cent (25,150). Yet because of the increase in male professional and technical workers the proportion of women in all professional and technical jobs fell from 42 per cent in 1951 to 37 per cent in 1961.[2]

These developments implied that any profession relying heavily on women's labour would either have to adapt itself to the new demographic situation, or to arrange conditions of work to suit married women, and attract more men into the profession if it were not to run into staffing difficulties caused by the high loss from the profession because of the early age of marriage. In the decade 1940–9 it has been shown that women students on Birmingham University social studies courses were marrying earlier than in former decades (Table 12.2).[3]

Table 12.2   Women social studies students, 1909–49, age of marriage

Decade of leaving course	Total women in sample	Married		Average age of marriage
		No.	%	
1909–19	36	8	22	34·1
1920–9	37	15	41	26·9
1930–9	69	34	49	28·7
1940–9	96	37	39*	23·7

* This lower proportion is because recently qualified students had not yet married.

Naturally, the smaller size of families meant that there would be an opportune time for married women returning to work but this would only be possible if the conditions were right. Thus, whilst the marriage bar for women in non-industrial occupations such as the civil service, the teaching profession, the police and other bodies, had been removed at the end of the Second World War, there could still remain serious obstacles to married women working.

Trends in the balance of men and women in social welfare

How did social work fit into this pattern? Table 12.3 gives the numbers of social welfare and related workers at the four censuses, 1921, 1931, 1951 and 1961.

Table 12.3   Social welfare and related workers, 1921–61

	Men No.	%	Women No.	%	Total
1921	1,222	40	1,863	60	3,085
1931	3,859	53	3,389	47	7,248
1951	9,418	43	12,733	57	22,151
1961	19,990	52	18,100	48	38,090

G. Routh has converted the earlier figures to percentage increases to demonstrate the more than proportionate increase in the numbers of social welfare workers (Table 12.4).[4]

Table 12.4   Social welfare and related workers, rate of increase

	% increase 1921–31	1931–51	1921–51
Male social welfare workers	500	200	1,000
Female social welfare workers	200	350	700
Lower professions	108	145	156
All occupational classes	108	107	116

The growth in the 1950s, although proportionately not greater than earlier periods, was absolutely of much more significance. Caution should be used in attaching too great a significance to these figures, because the definition social welfare and related workers includes a large number of occupations not considered in this study.[5] Nevertheless, it is interesting to note these broader changes and to emphasise that there has been a large increase in both men and women welfare workers. Even though in 1951 the proportion of men to women had fallen since the inter-war years, one of the reasons being the effects of the war, there had still been a large increase in men taking up this work. By 1961 the number of workers in this category had nearly doubled and men outnumbered the women. This situation shows how dangerous it is to deal in percentages alone, for although men were evenly balanced with women, the profession was still heavily dependent upon women's labour.

This dependence upon women's labour and the effects of earlier marriage are shown in Table 12.5 which gives the marital status of female social welfare workers in 1951 and 1961. The proportion of

Table 12.5 Female social welfare workers, marital status 1951–61

Female social welfare workers	Single		Married		Widowed and divorced		Total
	No.	%	No.	%	No.	%	
1951	7,424	58	3,851	30	1,458	12	12,733
1961	9,010	50	6,680	37	2,410	13	18,100

married women had increased from 30 per cent to 37 per cent but was not very far from doubling itself in absolute terms; approximately one-sixth of the total welfare workers in 1961 were married women compared with one-fourteenth in 1951. The impact of this phenomenon was a shock to social work, as it was to the rest of society and particularly the teaching and nursing professions. It is a feature which must be borne in mind when examining any particular developments during the post-war period.

Social welfare, teaching and nursing

Another important fact bearing on our understanding of the period after the Second World War is that the large increases in social work still left it a very small profession in relation to teaching and nursing (Table 12.6). A clear implication of this situation is that, given the

Table 12.6 Teachers, nurses and social welfare workers, 1951–61

	Teachers			Nurses			Social welfare and related workers		
	Total	Female	%	Total	Female	%	Total	Female	%
1951	301,679	182,489	61	149,323	130,179	87	22,231	12,733	57
1961	444,900	261,660	59	291,290	262,740	90	38,090	18,100	48

existence of training opportunities, a small percentage shift in the motivation of women to enter social work rather than teaching or nursing could make a marked contribution towards social work manpower. However, nursing and teaching, more heavily dependent on female labour, have their own problems and if qualified manpower is scarce one would only want to attract more women into social work if the supply of grammar school leavers is expanding. Fortunately, recent predictions from the Department of Education and Science[6] show that in the latter part of the period the number of girls with 'O' and 'A' levels was increasing and anticipated to increase substantially during the next decade (see Table 12.7).

Table 12.7   'O' and 'A' level passes

	1000s							
	5 or more 'O' levels				2 or more 'A' levels			
	Girls		Boys		Girls		Boys	
	No. %of age group		No. %of age group		No. %of age group		No. %of age group	
Actual 1961	47·2	14·9	50·7	15·6	15·0	4·9	25·8	8·1
Actual 1968	66·8	19·9	72·3	20·4	30·0	8·8	44·8	12·4
Projected 1971	78·6	24·2	84·4	24·8	38·2	11·7	53·1	15·5
Projected 1981	136·7	33·9	147·7	35·0	75·1	18·7	96·8	23·0

The projections were substantially greater than those of the Robbins Report which had estimated fewer 'O' and 'A' level successes than were actually achieved in 1968. It was also found that the number of 'A' level passes was increasing through further education studies, particularly for girls.

In terms of planning recruitment to social welfare services we may ask was social work getting its fair share of young women during the 1950s? One method of analysis which shows up a very different picture from a simple statement of the ratios of men and women is to see what proportion of total female professional and technical workers were formed by nursing, teaching and social welfare workers, and then to relate this to the changing proportions between these three professions. The first relationship is shown in Table 12.8. Whilst the proportion of women in the three professions rose to three-quarters of all female professional and technical workers, the proportion of women social welfare workers actually declined during the decade. Thus, far from improving its position as a potential career for women, social work was falling behind in obtaining its share of available qualified young women. During 1951–61 those men and women employed as social welfare and related workers had increased as a proportion of all professional and technical workers from 1·8 per cent to 2 per cent. This was due to the increase in the number of men coming into the profession. If a

Table 12.8 Female workers in teaching, nursing and social welfare, 1951–61

	1951 No.	1951 %	1961 No.	1961 %
Female teachers	182,489	56	261,660	48
Female nurses	130,179	40	262,740	48
Female social welfare and related workers	12,733	4	18,100	3
(a) Total	325,401	100	542,500	99
(b) All female professional and technical workers	523,057		707,320	
(a) as % of (b)		62		76

similar analysis is carried out to that for women covering the teaching, nursing and social welfare professions, one sees that the proportion of all men in the three professions compared to all male professional and technical workers fell slightly from 21 per cent to 20 per cent, but within this total for the three professions the proportion of men in teaching and nursing fell slightly whilst that for social welfare increased (Table 12.9).

In spite of this increase it remained true that social welfare did not make its mark and did not produce a large-scale shift in trying to

Table 12.9 Male workers in teaching, nursing and social welfare, 1951–61

	1951 No.	1951 %	1961 No.	1961 %
Male teachers	119,270	80	183,240	79
Male nurses	19,144	13	28,550	12
Male social welfare and related workers	9,418	6	19,990	9
(a) Total	147,832	99	231,780	100
(b) All male professional and technical workers	714,197		1,174,770	
(a) as % of (b)		21		20

attract more able manpower. This was clearly shown by the report on *The First Employment of University Graduates 1961–2.*[7] Of 7,445 men graduating (first degree) in arts or social studies in 1961–2, only fifteen (0·2 per cent) went on to training for social work (compared with 17·9 per cent for teacher training). Out of 3,792 women graduating in arts or social studies in 1961–2, 110 (2·9 per cent) went on to train for social work (compared with 34·5 per cent for teacher training).

During the 1960s the number of men entering social work continued to increase and this was reflected in the statistics on the first employment of graduates completing their first degree 1968–9.[8] As in the earlier year, more women than men went on to further training. Of these who went on to further training in teaching or social work the position was as shown in Table 12.10. Compared

Table 12.10   Numbers of first-degree graduates entering further training

	Men		Women	
	No.	%	No.	%
Teaching	2,917	26	3,596	54
Social work	56	0·5	248	4
Total entering further training	11,253		6,632	
Total graduates	31,669		13,334	

with the 1961–2 position, of 13,738 men graduating (first degree) in arts or social studies, forty-nine (0·3 per cent) went on to social work training as compared with 1,799 (13·1 per cent) who went on to teacher training.[9] Of the 9,450 women graduating at the same time in arts and social studies, 230 (2·5 per cent) went on to train for social work compared with 29 per cent who went on to teacher training. In spite of the large increase in the number of graduates during the 1960s, which led to a decrease in the proportion of men and women entering teacher training and which had been heavily concentrated in social studies,[10] the proportion of male graduates going on to social work training had only increased marginally and the proportion of women graduates in arts and social studies going on to social work training had actually diminished.

The weight of this evidence confirms that large absolute increases in the numbers of social workers in the period after the war disguised the fact that social work was not benefiting sufficiently from the increasing reservoir of young men and women graduates who might be considered potential recruits. Considered as a whole, social welfare and social work had managed to attract more men and in total it appeared that there was an even balance between the sexes. Yet while it may be reckoned as a partial achievement that more men were attracted to social work, it must be recognised as a remarkable failure that social welfare was losing ground in the battle for women's labour.

13 Social work under the microscope 1945–51

The welfare state and the significance of child care service

The war had stimulated government interest in social work and the way lay open for a brighter future. Already the apparatus for the Welfare State was being constructed with the Family Allowance Act (1945), the National Health Service Act (1946) and the National Insurance Act (1946). It could have been expected that the value which the government had placed on social work in wartime would have continued in a peacetime setting. But the inexperienced Labour government was far too preoccupied with problems of reconstruction, the major legislation for the Welfare State, the nationalisation of industry and economic problems to make a thoroughgoing statutory review of social work training and policy, and it was through voluntary support that major reviews of social work training were undertaken during this period—the two Carnegie Reports by Eileen Younghusband[1] and the NCSS Report by Professor Simey.[2] Nevertheless, a miniature review of the field of social work was made by the Curtis Committee, which had issued an interim report on the training of residential workers,[3] and which in its main report included an appendix dealing with the training of boarding-out visitors.[4] It was argued that the training should be of a university standing and that it should be established in universities and colleges already providing training for social workers. It is clear that the committees were impressed by the training for psychiatric social work but were also conscious of the importance of the physical health of the child which should be emphasised in training. Between a third and a half of the one-year courses should be practical work, of which the main part would be 'the actual boarding out and visiting of children under skilled supervision'. The long-term effect was to create a further specialised social work role with its own training and whose control would be vested in a new central training council working in liaison with the universities. However, it was a significant achievement that the request for a university training (despite considerable variation in the opinion of witnesses, some of

196

whom would have been satisfied with training on the job) had been won.

All the arguments in favour of a new department also won through, and the creation of a new local government department was recommended, with central government responsibility being vested in the Home Office.[5] The report, with its recommendations for the appointment of a children's officer supported by one or more boarding-out visitors, was eventually accepted and the Children Act 1948 became law. Although we shall look at the general developments of the period shortly, it is relevant to spend more time examining this turning point in child welfare services from the standpoint of the appropriateness of women for the post of children's officer and boarding-out visitor. All the indications were that at a time when some more men were beginning to percolate into social work a new staff pattern would be established mainly attracting women. The Curtis Committee, in discussing the function and importance of the children's officer, thought that the children's officer should be the 'pivot' of the new organisation. When referring to the children's officer the feminine pronoun was used and this was explained thus: 'We use the feminine pronoun not with the aim of excluding men from these posts but because we think it may be found that the majority of persons suitable for the work are women'.[6] The reasoning behind this was by implication associated with the committee's assertion that she would be 'a specialist in child care' and would 'represent the council in its parental functions'. In the event many men were appointed as children's officers, but a large number of women were appointed, more than had ever before held posts as chief officers in local government. The wide-ranging duties of children's departments under the Children Act 1948 were to form the basis of a social work organisation that was not limited by depending upon the medical profession,[7] and were to give opportunities to women for administration and organisation hitherto only available in the inspectorates and to some extent in wartime.

Also by tradition and implication the boarding-out officers would be mainly women. Almoning, psychiatric social work, probation, and posts in the Charity Organisation Society and settlements were occupations already manned by paid, if not always trained, staff. The position in child welfare had been radically different in that the dominant form of care had been residential and community-linked service such as fostering had been tenuous. Apart from a relatively small proportion of paid visitors, few of whom had had relevant training,[8] the main supervision of boarded-out children was the responsibility of boarding-out committees composed of volunteers. This system of supervision, with variations from area to area, had existed from the late nineteenth century. The Curtis Committee found in one area that the committee members[9]

> were largely women, and usually held some recognised position such as magistrate, doctor, local councillor, or councillor's wife; they were usually aged between 50 and 60. All appointments were for three years in the first instance but as most of the members had been visiting for some years the renewal was probably a formality.

There had been a small number of paid assistant relieving officers who had acted as boarding-out officers, and also public assistance boarding-out committee members who had assisted in this work; the employment of paid visitors was, however, on a very limited scale. Other initiatives had come from the voluntary society sphere where Miss D. M. Dyson had been responsible for organising the boarding-out work of Dr Barnardo's, and herself later became director of training in Dr Barnardo's. Miss Clement Brown's experience of training on the LSE mental health course must also have exercised a strong influence on the committee's review of training. Thus the decision to introduce a full-time paid staff of university calibre to operate the child care service was an imaginative innovation comparable to the establishment of a national probation service, but going further than the probation service in standards of training.

The state of social work—Younghusband and Simey

The Curtis Committee had benefited from the experiences of the war, the interest and enthusiasm of an enormous number of individuals and welfare organisations who had given evidence, and their own zeal in visiting many authorities to see the provisions of existing child welfare services at first hand. But it is now necessary to turn aside from child care to comment on the Younghusband and Simey studies. As already pointed out, the initiative for these studies was voluntary and their purpose was to survey the facilities for training for social workers and to examine salaries and service conditions. The two Younghusband reports were especially valuable as giving a picture of social work training before and after implementation of the welfare state legislation in 1948. The information in the earlier survey related to the end of 1945 and estimated demand over the next five years after assessing the situation. In 1945 there were seventeen universities or colleges running courses in social studies and nine professional social work courses in operation. Expansion was advocated, but in nearly every case when Eileen Younghusband examined the situation in her second report, in which the information related to the period 1949–50, she found that the demand for social workers had been underestimated. The main reasons given for this were that the creation of the National Health Service and the local authority children's departments had caused a sudden expansion in demand for social workers which had not been anticipated in the earlier report. This meant that recruitment for training for almoners, for child care workers and personnel officers exceeded the 1945 estimates, recruitment for probation officers was in line with expectations, but recruitment to psychiatric social work and a number of other services was below expectations.[10] Eileen Younghusband felt it necessary to point out that her data on actual recruitment related to intake through professional courses and not to total recruitment to the profession in question: 'It is significant that the estimated annual demand in 1950 is more than double that of 1945; although for three groups—caseworkers, mental welfare workers, youth leaders and a miscellaneous group—no forecast of demand is possible in 1950.'

We have seen that in some branches of social work, particularly probation, men were already playing a significant part. Yet the dominant influence in setting the tone and standing of the profession was the reliance on women's labour. Younghusband analysed the situation in the following way:[11]

Because the professional social worker has developed her skill within the comparatively small voluntary organisation where little administrative experience could be gained, and because she lays stress on the value of the individual services which she performs she finds herself left with both a range of responsibilities and a salary neither of which significantly increases as the years pass by. She does not look forward to any post in which she will share in framing policy and administering a service, as might happen if she had entered the field of medicine or education.[12] It is perhaps significant that one writes of the social worker as 'she'—that 'she' who was alleged to have no dependants to support and to be happy to work for pin money because a sense of vocation would be killed by a decent salary.

The combination of small organisations, and a heavy use of women's labour were both elements in understanding the development of social work at this stage and it is important not to exaggerate the proportions working in statutory organisations. In the 1951 census the numbers of social-welfare workers in statutory services was given in Table 13.1.[13]

Table 13.1 Occupied males and females 15 and over, 1951

	Males	Females	Total
Social welfare workers in national government service	242	348	590
Social welfare workers in local government service	1,782	1,797	3,579
Social welfare workers in other services	2,973	3,113	6,086
	4,997	5,258	10,255*

* Cf. total social welfare and related workers 1951: 22,151.

Thus under half the social welfare workers were employed by statutory bodies even with the impact of increased employment within the National Health Service and children's departments. This makes the contribution of the Simey Report particularly relevant[14] as it was very much alive to the problem of voluntary social work organisations, many of which paid salaries 'adjusted to the amount the society could afford rather than the skill of the social worker' (Simey, 1947, p. 7). It was argued

that many of these associations have depended for their staff as well as for their funds on the services of middle class people, who have either served voluntarily, or for salaries or wages which could be regarded as a supplement to other sources of income. In the coming years however the number of persons in the community with sufficient leisure for such full time occupations is bound to be reduced drastically.

Also it was thought (Simey, 1947, p. 19) that

the pressure of taxation on family income has forced many women into employment who would otherwise be available for this type of service, and even if it has not done so, the task of the housewife is immeasurably more burdensome as paid help has become more and more difficult to find, and the opportunities to take part in voluntary social service become correspondingly more restricted.

As in the Younghusband reports and the Curtis Report there was support for university-based training for professional social workers and in addition an appeal for the 'right balance' between paid professional workers and their volunteer collaborators. Salaries should be at a level more comparable with other work needing similar qualifications (it was suggested that the rates for almoners, psychiatric social workers and probation officers, although not necessarily ideal in themselves, should serve as a standard for all social workers) and the basic grade social worker should receive £300–£350 rising to a maximum of £450.[15] The Younghusband and Simey reports each emphasised the need for better financial arrangements for students.

This, then, was the diagnosis: social work should have a university-qualified staff; salaries should be at a higher level, particularly to attract more men; men should move into fields hitherto mainly staffed by women (i.e. individual casework as well as community work, group work and personnel management); the finance of training should be strengthened to attract a range of workers from a wider social stratum. To a limited extent these recommended changes were already occurring. Cavenagh found that in the decade 1940–9, particularly from the end of the war, more men were taking social studies courses at Birmingham University and that 71 per cent of the men were aided, the majority fully aided. Although the numbers of men were small (38) compared with 250 women giving this information for the same period, only 32 per cent of the women were aided, the majority of these being partly aided and more likely to be aided from private funds (in contrast to the men who were more likely to be financed by public funds). Another interesting feature brought out by the Cavenagh survey was that in the decade 1940–9, although children of professional people formed the largest group of students, there was an increase in the proportion of children of people directly engaged in industry, artisans and skilled technicians. In the decades 1930–9 and 1940–9 it was noticeable that an

increasing proportion of students had had mothers who were themselves trained or had been in paid employment of some kind
(especially teaching).

Before going on to examine how much progress in dealing with
these problems was made in the following two decades, three other
topics will be dealt with briefly to establish the context of later
discussion: the break-up of the Poor Law; training in the universities;
and professional developments.

Social work and the vanishing Poor Law

We have observed at many points how social work in the nineteenth
century and in the early decade of this century was involved with
material and financial problems, and how it was considered a mark
of progress in almoning and a virtue in psychiatric social work to be
able to leave this 'phase' behind. This was inextricably tied up with
the piecemeal development of social insurance and health services
which relieved the worst poverty. In a wider interpretation we can
safely assert that this was part of a process in which social workers
in a variety of settings wished to establish an existence which was
independent of relief-giving agencies, health services, or housing,
which could be potentially available to the whole community. The
new children's departments epitomised this feeling. Just as in the
1930s ordinary people had revolted against receiving help from the
Poor Law because of unemployment, and during the war services
dealing with homelessness were removed from Poor Law administration, there was now an urgency to break up the Poor Law and
apply a concept of universality to social services. Applied to social
work services this meant that local authorities had a duty to meet
social needs wherever they occurred and not only for assistance
clients. There was a separation of assistance from other services not
invalidated by the existence of limited charges according to income.
The National Assistance Act and the consolidated insurance services
potentially gave the opportunity for social workers to finally divest
themselves of a relief-giving function, reinforcing the earlier developments. But this would only be possible if these services were maintained at an adequate level. Initially, and the Rowntree and Lavers
survey of 1950 fed this belief, it was believed that the cloak of
poverty had been cast off with the dismantling of the Poor Law and
it was only later that the effectiveness of the broader measures was
seriously questioned.

Universities and social work

The second point is concerned with the concept of universities being responsible for the brunt of training for social work in this country. It has been shown that the role of the university in practical training and the relation of theory to practice was debated from the beginning of the century and during the Second World War. A related issue was the poverty of research into social work practice, which did not enhance the standing of social work in universities, and the fact that the tutors were nearly all women and not, because of lack of time or ability, notable for their academic output. The universities were largely staffed by men, and women even in 1961 only formed 13 per cent of all university teachers.[16] Eileen Younghusband was well aware of developments in America and other countries and in her 1947 report devoted much space in her conclusions emphasising the need for research into casework and group work and for the establishment of a 'School of Social Work' as a graduate professional school within the university.[17] Her 1951 report, looking at the 1950 situation, found a substantial increase in social studies training but enormous variations. Thirty-two courses were being offered as against seventeen in 1945 and one of the major shifts had been to recognise social administration as a basic subject on nearly all courses; but only in ten courses was there a compulsory subject 'Social Work Principles and Methods'. Miss Younghusband wrote:[18]

> It is the glory of the British courses that they offer syllabuses in these subjects which are on the whole balanced (i.e. giving a basic grasp of the social sciences). It is their weakness that they fail to teach students to practise the art of which they have learnt the basic theory.

She concluded her review of developments in the universities by the following remarks (1951, pp. 137–8):

> The conclusion of any general survey of the variety of preparations of social work seems to be that the situation has got out of hand. Academic freedom, coupled with the rich luxuriance of professional training bodies, have led to something approaching chaos. . . . In view of the recognised place of social workers in the welfare state, and the value of their preventive and curative function, the importance of using limited manpower and financial resources to the best

advantage, the unsatisfactory multiplicity of training and the conflict of aims in training, there seems to be a strong case for an authoritative committee to review the situation as a whole. . . . The one essential would be that the enquiry should be sufficiently thorough and the persons who composed the committee such that its findings would command general respect and acceptance.

These comments have been recorded at length because if acted upon, they would have radically altered the fact of social work in this country within a decade, and at this early date presented the social work profession with ideals towards which it could work, if only slowly at times. Sadly, the clearly argued case was not taken further by the government which had acute political problems to deal with. As it was, the universities had to be coaxed, cajoled and persuaded by tutors, professional bodies and inspectorates in the attempt to bring some order from chaos. But the social studies course tutors had little power to initiate and create a true social work department, in the existing power structure. It was reported to the Clapham Committee[19] by one Professor of Social Science 'that he had more difficulty in getting support for his studies than his colleagues in, say economics, because they were not yet thought academically respectable'. The idea of a school of social work had had a mixed reception and in her 1951 report Miss Younghusband replied to the objections and set out slightly modified proposals for a differentiated programme of social work training at varying levels, including a research institute in applied social studies which should also train professional social workers. Developments in training during the next two decades were the realisation, however imperfectly, of the fundamental thinking embodied in these reports and it is difficult to find in any of her later reports fundamental advances in the analysis of objectives and methods of training; rather there are peripheral modifications and adaptations according to limited terms of reference and the political context.

In understanding the discussions about social work training in the early post-war period it is important to realise that Eileen Younghusband's visions for the future of social work in this country were not universally accepted by universities or by social workers. As already mentioned, she was strongly influenced by the model of the American schools of social work in which social administration was seen as part of the equipment of the social worker. In England the future of social work as an academic discipline was bound up with the developments in social studies departments where there was a growing focus on the need for strengthened social administration training which would supply staff of high calibre to administer broad social services, as well as social workers. The old social science certificate or diploma which had provided the basic training for social workers for forty years was now seen as too vocationally biased and social studies departments wished to establish a pattern of social studies degrees which would lead to a variety of professional trainings, not only that of social work; already Manchester had established a degree course in social administration in 1937 and Birmingham followed in 1947. Those involved in the development of social administration as an applied social science saw their discipline as a bridge between the basic social sciences and social work.[20]

Nowhere are these tensions better illustrated than in the attempts to gain a grant for the establishment of a school of social work from the Carnegie United Kingdom Trust which had sponsored Eileen Younghusband's surveys.[21] The trustees were not enthusiastic about the recommendation of a school of social work and had constituted a special advisory committee of social workers and other interested parties to examine the idea. From their deliberations it was clear that the matter was highly controversial. The Joint University Council had supported the idea of a central institution but not along the lines suggested by Eileen Younghusband. No decisions were made and in 1951 Professor Titmuss and Eileen Younghusband submitted a new proposal asking for £75,000 over ten years for the creation of an institute for applied social studies with four main aims: to develop basic social science training at a higher level than was currently available; to promote refresher courses for senior social workers; to promote in-service training for civil servants and similar people; and to conduct research into teaching methods in social studies. This proposal was submitted to four trustees—Sir George Dyson and three vice-chancellors, Hetherington, Wolfenden and Morris—who argued that improvements in the universities made the proposal unnecessary and that the JUC should carry out research. Hetherington 'made it clear that there was a great divergence of opinion among the experts about the training of social workers'. However the door was left open for a new proposal not involving a new institute. Professor Titmuss and Eileen Younghusband produced another memorandum emphasising the weakness of over-specialisation in social work and social work training and asked for finance for five years for a completely new post-graduate diploma in social work which would produce good 'general practitioners in social work'. This final scheme was accepted and the trust voted £20,000 for the generic course at LSE, which started in October 1954. Other training developments are dealt with later, but these negotiations demonstrate the flux of opinion at the time and the concern in this country that social work should have a coherent relationship with the wide range of social services rather than pursue an independent development as in the USA.

Developments in probation, almoning and psychiatric social work

Within the different branches of social work a number of developments were occurring, each of which marked a small step towards improved standards. Within the probation service there was a strong emphasis on improving the strength of the association and getting better salaries; there was still a substantial differential in salaries between men and women, the maximum for men in 1950 being £570 and for women £460. NAPO had made representations to the Joint Negotiating Committee for the Probation Service in England and Wales when it was established in 1950, to ask for equal pay, but this was not acceptable to the government at the time. The preoccupation with salaries centred round the impetus given to the probation service by the Criminal Justice Act 1948. Probation was the only public service employing trained social workers where demand was roughly in line with supply, but there were difficulties in recruiting candidates of university calibre, particularly women. By June 1950 there were 1,026 full-time probation officers, of whom 377 were women, and 129 part-time officers (including 73 women). The Criminal Justice Act 1948 had made it compulsory for each probation committee to appoint at least one woman officer to each petty sessional division in the area, thus completing the work embarked on ten years before.

In almoning an emergency course was established following the war, in which four men took part, but there was no general influx of men into this branch of social work, which remained the most popular form of social work during the immediate post-war years. Out of 1,308 members of the institute at the end of 1949, 906 were working in some form of social work. Annual wastage from the profession was about 9 per cent, two-thirds of which was due to marriage. In spite of the steady recruitment to the profession[22] it was estimated in 1951[23] that 3,000 to 3,500 almoners were needed to provide a satisfactory service within the National Health Service structure, i.e. the service was only at a third of its desirable strength. Nevertheless, the institute's training earned high praise from Eileen Younghusband: 'Better planned teaching of casework is now being given in this training than in any other, except psychiatric social work and the in-service training of workers in the Family Discussion Bureau' (1951, p. 115).[24]

Almoners felt that the National Health Service Act had not made any great difference in day-to-day operation of the almoning departments, but in circulars to the hospitals and local authorities they were officially relieved of the duty of assessing payments so that they could concentrate on social work.[25]

Psychiatric social work expanded only slowly because, even with the courses started at Edinburgh University and Manchester University, training places were scarce. Only 224 psychiatric social workers were trained in the period 1945-9. More men were coming into the field, but one of the most significant developments was the influence upon child care training by the fact that up to 1951 all the tutors appointed to be in charge of child care courses had been psychiatric social workers. Unlike the Home Office, which pressed for the support of training in the universities for probation officers and boarding-out visitors, there was no corresponding initiative from the Ministry of Health. It was officially decided not to assume the status of medical auxiliaries within the health services, which in the long run proved a wise decision.[26]

If we consider these three branches of social work and also child care, we have four branches where the balance of the sexes varies from the extreme of almoning (almost entirely women), to child care and psychiatric social work where, despite the predominance of women, men might well extend, and to probation, where the balance was weighted to men. The development of these branches during the next two decades will later provide us with evidence to test some hypotheses about women's position in social work.

The period 1945-51 had been one of immense activity and opportunity in social work. Unlike the period after the First World War, there was full employment and returning servicemen did not displace women from their jobs; there was room for men and women in social work and a need to make the best use of all available manpower. So far there had been no large social work organisation to provide a career structure, and correspondingly few senior appointments, but there was the germ of this in the new children's departments. W. E. Cavenagh in 1950 characterised the stages that social work had passed through by making three divisions (1950, p. 33):

(*a*) In the earliest period paid jobs were more likely to be organisers, but most social workers were voluntary.

(*b*) The next development was that of casework as a paid job, mostly singlehanded.

(*c*) The next stage was the development of specialist fields to an extent that more organisation was necessary and possible (e.g. organising secretary, inspectors, head almoners).

The development of any larger organisation in a fourth stage would test whether women could compete with men on an equal basis for posts at all levels, or whether the dependency upon men which has been observed even in the ostensibly female branches of social work, would reveal itself in the career positions that women were to hold at different levels in social work. So far we have seen that the statement that social work is a woman's profession has a variety of meanings and has given rise to a number of myths, particularly the one that women have had authority and control of the destiny of social work. The activity of women cannot be denied, nor their imagination and ideals. But, as in the family, they were subject to financial decisions of the breadwinning male, having to adopt a suppliant stance however vigorously they argued their case. Therefore the influx of men into psychiatric social work and child care in the next period may be regarded as a naturally occurring experiment, where the impact of more men in the profession can be observed. Up until this period the majority of men had been in posts with a strong emphasis on authority (for example, NSPCC, probation, mental welfare) with administrative bias (such as wardens of community centres, settlement wardens, youth work), overlaid with the strong tendency to work with men or boys. The heart of the question was would men acquire the ethos and attitudes of the women in the casework services or would they transform the individual casework services in the direction of bureaucratic organisations?

Two decades of training 1951–71

New demands and limited resources

The process of adding to the duties of social workers through legislation and thereby stimulating the demand for social work staff continued through the next two decades. Governments, particularly the long-standing Conservative government, revealed an immense capacity for increasing the responsibilities of social workers in a variety of fields without being willing to take the organisational and administrative steps necessary for implementation. The major series of Acts was: the Mental Health Act 1959; the National Assistance Act 1962; the Children and Young Persons Act 1963; the Children and Young Persons Act 1969; the Health Services and Public Health Act 1968; the Chronically Sick and Disabled Persons Act 1970; and the Local Authority Social Services Act 1970.

It was evident that the failure to expand professional social work training sufficiently, already seen 1945–51, would become a characteristic of the period as a whole. This is clearly demonstrated by Kathleen Jones's survey of social studies departments.[1] From 1950–1 to 1962–3 the number of students entering professional social work courses increased from 98 to 302 (an increase of 208·2 per cent), representing in 1950–1 12 per cent and in 1960–2 24·8 per cent of all students entering social studies departments. To accomplish this limited expansion the number of departments offering courses leading to a professional qualification had increased to seventeen (including four seventeen-month courses). The uneven concentration of courses was still very evident (Jones, 1964, p. 36):

> As far as professional social work courses are concerned, the field is still dominated by LSE and Liverpool, which in 1962 took 34·8 per cent and 16·9 per cent of all student entrants respectively, more than half the total. No professional course had less than eight students but the average for other departments was sixteen as against LSE's 105 and Liverpool's 51.

For a stimulating analysis of this situation in the 1950s we can

H

turn to Eileen Younghusband's assessment, from which the following passage is worth quoting (Morris, ed., 1955, pp. 208–9):

> The total output of men and women from the social science departments . . . is about five hundred a year; this is of course quite inadequate to meet the increased demand for social workers and to replace normal wastage. The fault does not lie wholly at the doors of social science departments; these find their numbers restricted by their own teaching facilities and by the lack of suitable vacancies for practical training. The fundamental cause, however, is the lack of good candidates for training; as things are at present it could only be done by accepting the unsuitable and those whose lights are very dim. Moreover the situation is made worse by the lack of grant aid at the first stage of training. . . . Furthermore, older people wanting to enter professional social work after some other career can only do so by their own financial efforts or by else choosing one of those branches, of which probation and child care are the chief, which will give them the necessary help to train. Such people are a grave loss to social work which essentially demands maturity and responsible judgement even at the training stage.

The still limited access to university training, and its still predominantly middle-class character, was closely allied to the predominance of women amongst trained workers, and it is to this feature that we must now turn. The proportion of men completing social studies courses in 1950, 1955 and 1960 was just under one-third, although a much smaller proportion completed social work training. Of all the women entering social studies courses in 1950, 1955 and 1960, 94 per cent were single.[2] If anything the proportion of married women taking training was decreasing (Jones, 1964). Overall the impression is of no enormous increase in the number of men wishing to undertake social work training during the 1950s. Those men taking certificate courses were much more likely to proceed to social work training than those studying for degrees in social studies, but as the old social studies certificate declined, more men took post-graduate diplomas in social work and social administration. Barbara Rodgers found that among the men in her sample of social studies students (1950, 1955, 1960) probation was easily the most popular form of training, with training for psychiatric social work and for the other casework professions attracting only a few of the 1950 and 1955 graduates; however by 1960 the applied social studies courses were beginning to attract more of them.[3]

Women in social studies departments

One possible interpretation of the slow developments is afforded by the high proportion of women as staff of university social work courses and their relatively low status within their departments. Kathleen Jones found that 78 per cent of the sixty university staff primarily concerned with social work teaching were women (compared with 48 per cent of women in the whole social studies group) who tended to be older than other staff members. Only one of the social work teachers had a higher degree (although fifty had a postgraduate vocational qualification, mostly in social work). Half were engaged in research in 1962, but only seven (12 per cent) were senior lecturers, with one woman who was a professor at a women's college. It is reasonable to argue that the high proportion of women in the social studies departments and particularly the sub-departments of social work did not put them in a good position to acquire a greater share of university resources for expansion. In fact the percentage increase in the staff of social studies departments in the period 1950–62 was only half that of the increase in students. Also important was the age of female social work tutors, three-fifths of whom were over forty (in 1962) and eighteen of whom were psychiatric social workers.[4] Their training experience would mainly have been in the 1930s and 1940s and the traditional concern with individual dynamic psychology would have been of prime importance to them in the teaching of human growth and development and casework. A combination of a worsening staff/student ratio in departments and the efforts in developing higher standards of teaching in practical work placements were also responsible for the difficulties in producing any substantial research into social work practice.

The Younghusband Report, 1959

As was the case in so much social work practice, the problems in the structure of social work training were clearly recognised by those in the social work field, but the solutions were less obvious. Eileen Younghusband's suggested school of social work did not materialise, the universities were incapable of expanding professional training fast enough and the government was not yet ready to take a comprehensive view of social work training. The response to the scarcity situation was a succession of reports, sponsored by government departments and private agencies, into the training situation in different fields.[5] All the reports revealed serious shortages in trained staff but the first to make an impact on training programmes was the Younghusband Report in 1959, appointed in 1956 whilst the Royal Commission on Mental Illness was still sitting and when the shortage of social work staff was acute. Although this was a further piecemeal approach to the problems of social work training, the significant departure was the proposal for a non-university-based training, as the middle part of a three-tier system of training geared to different levels of work; the lowest tier was to be a welfare assistant grade and it was suggested that professionally trained university graduates should head the service.[6] Within health and welfare departments there were substantial developments in the employment of welfare assistants. The proposal for a non-graduate training was implemented and the Council for Training in Social Work was established by the Health Visitors and Social Work (Training) Act 1962. The Younghusband Committee had been faced with a difficult task, for in 1956 93 per cent of local authority staffs were untrained. One section of the report clearly implied that a three-year training for the non-graduate middle-level tier might be desirable,[7] but the needs of the service (with the enlarged conception of community care in the Mental Health Act 1959) made it essential to get a quick supply of trained workers to local authority health departments which the universities seemed unable to supply. A further important factor was that psychiatric social work was still predominantly a female profession. The women in the profession showed a strong preference for child guidance or hospital settings rather than local authority mental health work. Although male psychiatric social workers were much more attracted to local authority work, their small proportion of the total profession meant that an exceptionally large increase in the number of university-trained psychiatric social workers would have been necessary to significantly influence the local authority staffing situation. Expansion of the certificate courses was rapid, and by 1967 217 certificates were awarded for candidates completing the two-year course and fifty-seven certificates were awarded for those completing the one-year course. The new workers did not only carry out mental health functions but it is significant that in five years the new certificate courses had attained a supply of trained workers five times as large as the average annual output of psychiatric social workers in the period 1945–59.[8] The colleges of commerce and further education (many of these later to become polytechnics) welcomed the opportunity to establish courses in an expanding field.

A general critique of social work services and training not limited to health and welfare was undertaken by Barbara Rodgers and Julia Dixon and published in 1960. Their research into the social work services in a small northern town also demonstrated the need for more training and for a variety of trainings, the higher level to be trained in the universities and the bulk of the workers outside. For the highest-grade worker the emphasis was on his or her need for skills in organisation and administration in addition to under-standing of personal problems, rather than on Eileen Young-husband's division which tended to concentrate on the greater skill and sophistication in the analysis and treatment of personal problems.[9]

Training in child care and health and welfare

Simultaneously there was a comparable development in child care training. After the Curtis Report training for boarding-out visitors had started at four universities, which increased to six for 1948 and 1949 but fell to four again in 1950 (Birmingham, Liverpool, Notting-ham and LSE; the courses at Leeds and Cardiff closed).[10] By 1951, 216 students (211 women and five men) had qualified, and in 1950 seventy-eight people (seventy-three women and five men) entered training. Expansion was slow in spite of the fact that many children's departments had begun to take an increasingly broad view of their responsibilities towards families where there was a possibility that the children were at risk of being admitted to care. Up to the end of 1960, 681 women and sixty-seven men had successfully completed their courses but there was a disturbingly high wastage rate, one suspects because of marriage.[11] A higher proportion of staff were qualified than in the health and welfare fields, but there was still a grave shortage. As a result of discussions between the LCC and the Home Office the first two-year non-graduate course for child care officers was established at the North West London Polytechnic in 1960, followed by the establishment of courses in Manchester and elsewhere. By 1966, two extramural departments and seven colleges of further education were providing courses of this kind, on top of the provision of graduate courses in twenty-three university departments, and contributed significantly to the expansion in output of trained workers qualifying, from fifty in 1960–1 to 242 in 1966–7.[12] The numbers of men coming into child care increased substantially during the decade and by 31 March 1970, of 3,368 full-time field officers, 1,323 (39 per cent) were men.[13]

The increasing popularity of child care was a feature of the 1950s and 1960s and is clearly shown by Barbara Rodgers' study of social studies students (1964). Both the new certificate in social work courses and the two-year child care courses arose out of the total demand/supply position for social workers in the 1950s, with courses supported financially by the Ministry of Health and the Home Office, although the latter was more generous in a number of ways, and child care students received Home Office grants, while the certificate in social work students had to apply for LEA grants.[14] Expanding colleges of commerce and further education were eager to move into the field of social work training and to some extent this development in social work is part of the development of a binary system of higher education. There were differences between the child care and certificate in social work courses. Admission requirements to the certificate in social work courses were generally equivalent to teacher training minimum entry requirements and students were admitted from the age of nineteen years. The two-year child care courses were for students over twenty-five years of age (twenty-three from 1967) who had no formal academic admission requirements, although courses used a variety of assessment techniques to ensure that candidates of suitable ability were attracted to the course. A further factor important for the development of social work was the increasing number of men attracted to these two types of courses.[15] Expansion in children's departments, and to a lesser extent in health and welfare departments provided career prospects that were comparatively rare in hospital social work departments, child guidance clinics, and probation, although the strengthened regional development in probation was improving the situation; moreover local authority pay scales for social workers began to improve considerably in the 1960s.

The establishment of the two kinds of non-graduate social work training was the culmination of a long line of development in which social work training had been mainly based upon a functional organisation of social services, and the gradual though limited acceptance of responsibility for supplying sufficient numbers of social workers to carry out the duties imposed by legislation. The training for child care and health and welfare workers was paralleled by the establishment of the National College for Youth Leadership Training, after the Albermarle Report, which also coexisted with university post-graduate youth work courses (the college's functions were later to be transferred to colleges of education). An additional important contribution to training was the development of one-year courses for serving officers in children's departments and health and welfare departments. Most of the officers attending were men. The prototype for this type of training was pioneered by the National Institute for Social Work Training. In the child care service yet another type of course established in the 1960s and mainly attracting men was that of the emergency training scheme at the North West Polytechnic in London, later extended to the polytechnic at Leeds and the Llandaff College of Further Education in Cardiff.

Generic training

Alongside these developments in providing different forms of training in a variety of fields sprang up the debate about generic training. Already many social workers were concerned in the late 1940s and early 1950s with the fragmentation of agencies and training. Mrs McDougall at the LSE was a prominent leader of this movement and the matter was discussed much at LSE and within the Association of Psychiatric Social Workers.[16] In October 1954 a one-year course in generic social work was started at the LSE, open only to students with a social science qualification; for the first four years the course was financed by a Carnegie grant. In 1957 the Association of Psychiatric Social Workers working party on generic courses reported to the executive and a proposal for acceptance of generic social work courses as a qualifying course was accepted at the annual general meeting, with the provision that for membership of APSW a further complementary psychiatric placement of four months would be necessary. The first applied social studies course to include psychiatric social workers started at Southampton in 1958 and the pattern then developed steadily at LSE, Bristol and other universities. Thus within the universities one had the pattern of students intending to practise in a variety of fields following a basic core of lectures, with some variation according to the future work setting of the student. Similarly, although the functions of the practical work placements would be essentially the same at each stage of the course, there would be a bias towards at least one practical placement in the student's work setting. A long period of disintegrated development had produced a countering impetus towards unification.

Other interesting changes which strengthened the position of social work were taking place in the universities during the 1960s. Mrs Elizabeth Irvine at York University and Mrs Kay McDougall at LSE became Readers. Departments of social work and social administration were formed at York University and also at Bristol University. Schools of social work were established at Bradford and Leicester universities and at University College, Cardiff. At York and Bristol the departments are headed by Professors of Social Administration (Kathleen Jones and Roy Parker); similarly, the Professor of Social Administration at Cardiff directs the School of Social Work. There are now four Professors of Social Work: Noel Timms at Bradford, Derek Jehu at Leicester, Phyllida Parsloe at Aberdeen and Dorothy Stock Whitaker at York. Although social work training in universities is still generally within departments of social administration, these developments indicate a search to establish social work as a theoretical discipline in its own right and for it to be free to achieve a better integration of social science, social administration and social work teaching. The potential for developing higher degree work and research into social work is being established, but it remains to be seen whether the research into social work practice so badly needed will result on a sufficient scale. A further innovation in the 1960s was that of the four-year degree courses at Keele and Bradford.

Fieldwork teaching

Throughout this period there has been continual discussion in professional associations and amongst teaching staff and practitioners about the use of field work experience during training. It was true that the old apprenticeship concept of training had been largely superseded, but the 1950s and 1960s saw an increasing emphasis on the teaching role of the student supervisor. Also there were increasing attempts to draw fieldwork supervisors closer to the educational institutes to achieve a closer link between the theory and practice of a student. Dr Jean S. Heywood, after spending a year at the Chicago School of Social Work in 1961–2, wrote the first British book on student supervision in 1964, although parts of it had appeared earlier in *Case Conference*.[17] The book is particularly interesting because it embodies an introductory text to casework as well as being an introduction to supervisory skills. Its emphasis on detailed recordings of social work practice and the teaching method arising from discussing them were particularly appropriate when most supervisors of students were still not conversant with ego-oriented casework. Its aim therefore was to teach supervisors casework as well as skills in supervision. Psychoanalytic theories were the basis of the psychological part of the social diagnosis and Anna Freud's *The Ego and Mechanisms of Defence* was essential to understanding client or student reactions to people and situations. Other key concepts were transference and identification, equally applicable to the student or client situation. Most supervisors (apart from psychiatric social workers after the last war) had not been taught this psychological base to social casework and it was necessary to bring them up to date with current theory and teaching. The problem of ensuring that students in agencies were supervised by social workers in tune with casework theory should not be minimised. Before Noel Timms' *Social Casework* appeared in 1964 there was no British text on casework apart from *Social Casework in Great Britain*, edited by Cherry Morris in 1954. No textbook of the weight of Helen Perlman's *Casework—A Problem Solving Process*, or Gordon Hamilton's book *Social Casework* had been written.

In order to communicate with supervisors, it became a regular pattern with most social work courses to have short courses on supervision for beginning supervisors, advanced seminars for experienced supervisors, and two or three meetings of supervisors during student's placements. In agencies also there was a growing awareness of the importance of student training as a part of their total function, as well as a means of recruiting future staff. Many larger departments began to appoint full-time training officers to co-ordinate training activities within the department and to appoint student supervisors with student supervision as a part or whole of their workload.[18] The establishment of specialised posts for training and supervision within the agencies in the 1960s provided a springboard for the growth of in-service training. The expansion of full-time training made apparent the needs of untrained staff who were either too old or for some other reason unable to undertake full-time training and the needs of new entrants to social work departments before they undertook training. Training officers and super-

H*

visors became involved in formulating a great variety of in-service schemes according to the needs of the department and the teaching resources they had available. A great many posts of training officer or student supervisor were taken by women who found this a more satisfactory promotion avenue than administrative seniority. Of special importance was the liaison between the training staff in agencies and social work teachers. Training officers controlled courses' access to training resources and were under continued pressure to accept more students; they were also able to judge a caseworker's ability to undertake supervision and assess their chances of promotion. Training officers talked the same language as the social work teachers and had the tricky task of interpreting course needs to other senior staff and committees and balancing agency and training priorities. The whole range of these functions was often described as 'staff development' and this became a familiar theme in many articles in the mid-1960s and was emphasised in the reports of the Williams Committee and the Seebohm Committee as a desirable growth point in agencies.

Central government reorganisation and the National Institute for Social Work Training

After a long and difficult process of gestation, during the 1960s social work training at last seemed to be growing rapidly enough to increase substantially the proportion of trained workers in social work departments.[19] But the multiplication of new courses in large cities conflicted with the concept of generic training and was also a measure of the irresponsibility of the three central training councils in not attempting to create a unified strategy for training. Therefore when the Seebohm Report examined social work training it took the same view as it took of the local authority personal social services. There should be a unified structure for social work training. This should be achieved by a new central council for all social work training. After many discussions with interested bodies the Local Authority Social Services Act 1970 made provision for the establishment of a new Central Council for Education and Training in Social Work to replace the existing training councils in 1971. The council is responsible for drawing up a social work training programme for the whole country.[20] It is to be expected that it will incorporate all the elements that have been described so that a wide variety of training needs can be met. Geographically there will be a tendency for courses to plan jointly wherever possible and for informal links to be strengthened even where administrative integration is not possible. The pattern for the 1970s seems certain to be a blend of generic training with opportunities to specialise by social work method or administrative setting according to the size of the course and the specialised teaching resources available. One effect of this should be the increase of opportunities for advanced study and research. A key institution which supported many of the changes during the 1960s and became a catalyst after much thinking about the future of social work was the National Institute for Social Work Training. The National Institute was a further embodiment of Eileen Younghusband's proposals in 1951 and 1959 and became a centre, under the direction of Huw Jones, formerly of Swansea University, for the training of tutors for advanced studies, and for research. Its series of publications has done a great deal to remedy the lack of literature and to bring articles not easily available into circulation. Its advanced courses cover a variety of areas—research, group and community work, management and administration—and it also engages in social work research.

Training as a special field for women

If we try to draw together the strands in the training developments, we first find that as from the nineteenth century onwards women were heavily involved in training. They recognised early on that education and training were a vital part of establishing a profession and determining its values, but were denied the resources to develop a body of practical research that would give status and power in universities. Women's involvement was great in lecturing, in writing about training, and in field work teaching. Kathleen Jones's study revealed that the women tended to be at lower grades than the men in social studies departments; in 1968 there were eight male professors and four male readers, one woman professor and ten women senior lecturers (compared with six male senior lecturers).[21] Social work lecturers, who were mainly women, were less likely than other social studies teachers to be engaged in research. The universities had never taken account of the administrative duties involved in arranging social work practice for students and, unlike medical lecturers, they had no teaching hospital within the university. Thus, in the university as in the town hall, women met with the suspicion and sometimes hostility that the early women social workers met with in their first incursions to the inspectorates. Not given the resources and freedom to conduct research and write on a sufficient scale, their failure to produce results was used as a reason for maintaining their low status. Women's interest in training may also be partly viewed as a displacement in that within social work it presented the possibility of a senior post without management responsibilities. Alternatively or complementarily, it may represent a displacement because of the unwillingness of employing bodies to appoint them to other kinds of senior post. It would also be wrong not to emphasise the caring nature of the teacher of social work, and that one of the hallmarks of women teachers of social work has been the disciplined personal involvement with their students which has blended something of the parent, nurse, and social worker in the teaching task.

Above all, one woman, Eileen Younghusband, played a dominant part in conceptualising the required development of social work training in the post-war period. From her Carnegie reports onwards she pursued the objectives of a rational, but differentiated system of social work training, by her chairmanship or membership of committees of enquiry (including the Morison Committee on the Probation Service), her writing and by her influence in course curriculum planning.

15 Women in social work agencies and the social work profession: the male threat

The wider pattern of recruitment and employment

In staffing social work agencies the gradual influx of men into child care and psychiatric social work provided a naturally occurring situation in which it could be tested whether all the factors of male prejudice, early marriage and difficulties of married women working would lead to an unequal representation of women in senior positions. An even broader view may be taken, and it is possible to provide mutually supportive evidence from census data, analysis of particular fields of social work and from studies of particular local authorities. During the nineteenth century and until the First World War, social work formed one of the many professions in which women had a special contribution to make although, as we have found, men were far more involved than is usually acknowledged. During the inter-war period and particularly in the 1960s more men entered social work positions that had been thought to be particularly appropriate to women. This was welcomed by women and to some extent the encouragement the men received was the result of earlier marriage and the short length of service which women could give. Cavenagh had shown in 1950 that amongst women students from the Birmingham course who had married, few continued working after the birth of their first child.

Barbara Rodgers carried out a similar study of all students at Manchester University Social Administration Department during the period 1940–60, the majority of whom had studied for the BA(Admin) pass degree.[1] 435 students passed through the department, of whom 368 took degrees; 401 students were women. A 90 per cent response rate was achieved. The most popular forms of training for students completing their course at different periods were as shown in Table 15.1.[2]

An increasing trend towards early marriage was found in the groups of women students completing their courses 1950–60, a fall in the proportion giving up work in marriage for those women completing courses 1940–55, and a reduction in the average number

221

Table 15.1　The most popular forms of social work training, 1940–60

		Year of completion of course					
A 1940–45		B 1946–50		C 1951–5		D 1956–60	
1 Almoning	14	*1* Almoning	20	*1* Almoning	12	*1* Almoning	18
2 Personnel		*2* Personnel		*2* Personnel		*2* Child Care	7
management	9	management	17	management	7		
3 Housing		*3* Psychiatric		*3* Psychiatric		*3* Psychiatric	
management	5	social work	11	social work	7	social work	5
				Probation	4	Probation	5
						Family	
						casework	5

of years worked after marriage and between graduation and the first 'career break'. The career break was much more likely to be the result of the birth of the first child than because of marriage. These findings were confirmed by Barbara Rodgers's national follow-up study (1964) of all those completing social science courses at British universities in 1950, 1955 and 1960. Fifty-nine per cent of the women completing courses in 1955 were married within six years compared with 49 per cent of the 1950 group.

The broad picture for England and Wales is given in Table 15.2 which shows the numbers of men and women social welfare workers entered as managers and operatives.[3] This clearly demonstrates that men took double the proportion of managerial appointments in relation to the sex distribution in the profession. The effect of early marriage is demonstrated by the age distribution. At every age in

Table 15.2　Employment status of social welfare workers, 1951–61

1951	Employers	Managers	Operatives	Workers on own account	Out of work	Total
Male	—	259	8,989	29	141	9,418
Female	—	182	12,196	33	322	12,733

1961	Employers and managers		Foremen and supervisors		Out of work	Total
Male	5,730		14,050		210	19,990
Female	1,650		16,210		240	18,100

1951 there were more women than men social welfare workers, and in 1951 and 1961 there were double the proportion of women to men in the age group 20 to 29. However, in 1961, for all age groups above 20 to 29, there were more men than women. Also the proportion of women in the age groups 35 to 44 and 45 to 54 had reversed between 1951 and 1961 (see Table 15.3).

Table 15.3   Women social welfare workers aged 35–44 and 45–54, 1951 and 1961

	Age groups	35–44	45–54
Percentage of total women	1951	30	27
Percentage of total women	1961	24	32

Psychiatric social work

In psychiatric social work the small group of men who had entered the profession before the Second World War increased, but the majority were still women. In the total profession, even in 1961, there were not many more than 600 psychiatric social workers working and of these a quarter were working in fields other than mental health.[4] Noel Timms examined the cohorts of workers who had qualified in 1947–8 and 1952–3; men formed 12·5 per cent of the former group and 15 per cent of the latter group. Overall men in 1962 formed 12 per cent of the profession. Looking at the service of the two cohorts Timms found a slight increase in the number of women marrying after qualifying and a corresponding decrease in the number of women married when qualifying. There was hardly any change in the proportion of single women. An interesting feature to arise from this analysis was the high proportion of childless marriages up to 1960. Approximately one-third of the 1947–8 group marriages were childless and one-half of the 1952–3 group marriages. A general change was the increasing job mobility of the second group apart from the group of women already married when qualified.

In spite of the small proportion of male psychiatric social workers, Timms thought that 'they have in fact an influence on the profession out of all proportion to their numbers'. The men tended to be academically less well qualified than the women and were more likely to have a non-social work background, and to have come from an industrial or clerical background. Their influence was detected in salaries questions, interest in community care and the development of psychiatric social work in the local authority health departments. Moreover, although they were only 12 per cent of the profession, of those holding senior psychiatric social work posts over 30 per cent were men. It is possible to interpret these facts by the unwillingness of men to play the subordinate position in the hospital or child-guidance settings and by the promotion appointments in local authorities, where mental welfare work was predominantly the concern of male duly authorised officers. Conversely, women psychiatric social workers might well have been avoiding the authority role of the local authority mental health worker; the fact of poorer clinical support in many local authorities may well have been involved also.

Medical social work

Problems which had beset almoning in its earliest days continued throughout the post-war period. As with psychiatric social work there remained a heavy concentration of workers in London and the south, particularly in the teaching hospitals.[5] There was also evidence that the difficulties which almoners had experienced in defining their function and role in hospitals did not disappear when the institute changed its title to the Institute of Medical Social Workers at the beginning of the 1960s. Z. Butrym's (1968) study of medical social work at the Hammersmith Hospital in 1964–5 gives many valuable insights into the problems of medical social work. Medical social workers at Hammersmith Hospital felt that they had too much routine welfare work to do with insufficient administrative and clerical support; the research showed that about half the departmental caseload did not require the services of a trained medical social worker and that this related to the excessive caseloads of the social workers. Communication between consultants and other medical staff was felt to be poor in spite of the fact that medical staff—like the patients—were generally very satisfied with the service they received. The social work staff felt unable to practice sufficiently the casework techniques they had been taught, and that the nature of their casework skills was inadequately understood.[6] In view of the similarity between these difficulties and those experienced by the early almoners, and the fact that medical social work has remained an almost completely female branch of social work, it is particularly notable that Butrym, in discussing her findings, focused on the difference in authority between medical staff and the medical social work staff. She found that statements by some doctors and ward sisters confirmed an American study in 1957 which (Butrym, 1968, p. 107)

> showed that a number of doctors recognised the value to patients of a helping relationship which was different from the relationship with the doctor and lacked the authoritative aspects of the latter, thus enabling the sick person to feel more secure and self-confident, and freer to determine what he wants to do about his situation.

The majority of medical social workers continued to be employed in the hospital setting and, although in the late 1960s there was a slight shift towards local-authority work, even in 1969 only about one-tenth of practising medical social workers were in local authorities.[7] Medical social work was less popular in the 1960s and the number of practising medical social workers was almost the same in 1969 as in 1951. The expansion of university training courses providing an option in medical social work (in 1961 Edinburgh University ran a full medical social work course and six other universities included training for medical social work in their applied social studies courses) put the institute's own course in an anomalous position and 1969–70 was the last academic year in which the institute ran its course.

Another important development was the resignation of Professor Moncrieff as chairman of the institute in 1961. He became president of the institute and for the first time the institute elected one of its own members as chairman—Miss Enid Warren. That this development had come so late is perhaps a further mark of the diffidence of the institute. It would be foolish to read too much into this change, but the annual report of the Institute of Almoners 1960–1 quoted Miss Kelly's comments in the *Almoner*, May 1961:

> Changes in leadership are always important and these particular ones have a special significance. Tradition has been maintained by the election of an eminent medical man as our President, while the increasingly important trend towards identifying ourselves as part of an independent social work profession was underlined when the Council entrusted its leadership to a practising almoner.

Marriage was a further factor affecting an almost completely female profession. In *The First Two Years*, of seventy-four students completing training 1960–1, marriage was the factor most frequently affecting choice of first posts (twenty-three). All these women were already married or engaged to be married, which decided where they must live. At the time of the second (follow-up) interview more than half of the group were marrièd and marriage was the chief cause of resignation. Six medical social workers had already left work for this reason, and a further seven were working their notice. Of eight workers who had moved to other hospitals, five were married women who had changed their posts on account of their husbands' change of work. These changes led to a necessity for part-time employment on a larger scale, and in 1968–9 the institute estimated that over 300 medical social workers—over a quarter of those employed—were employed part-time.[8]

The Institute of Medical Social Workers strongly supported the movement for a British Association of Social Workers and also the creation of local authority social service departments. Nevertheless, the latter development placed them in a dilemma—whether to remain in the employment of hospitals or to become a part of social service departments. Whether being employed by the social service departments would solve their continuing problems of relationships with medical staff is an open question. A more interesting surmise is whether such a change would attract more men to the work.

Child care

In turning to child care, we have seen that it was mainly in the 1960s that more men entered the field, partly as a result of improving prospects and training opportunities for older men through the two-year non-graduate courses (and later through the emergency training courses). Another factor was the changing conception of child care work. From time to time the Association of Child Care Officers had discussed whether to change the name of the association because the nature of the work became so much broader than that of dealing with children. The title 'boarding-out visitor' was dropped in 1954, symbolising the broadening of role. Also boys had always been more numerous than girls in care, and the increasing numbers of committals to care, including older boys, led to frequent expression of the need for boys to have a father figure. Of course children's officers were keen to attract men to provide stability of service.

Because of the heavy dependence on women's labour and the drive for expansion in children's departments there was a need for good-quality statistics on staffing and wastages. The fast influx of men to child care make it an especially important case study in looking at the careers of men and women in social work.[9] The increasing numbers of men was illustrated by the fact that in 1966 of the 396 students entering training 155 were men and 241 were women; in 1968 of 705 students entering courses 303 were men and 402 women (Boss, 1971). As would be expected, the wastage rate for women was much higher than that for men; for field officers wastage in 1969–70 (excluding promotion in the field and transfers in the field) was as shown in Table 15.4.[10]

Table 15.4   Wastage in the child care service, 1969–70

	Total %	Men %	Women %
All staff	15·8	9·4	20·0
Holders of letter of recognition	13·7	8·2	16·8

Of 716 vacancies occurring at fieldwork level 1969–70, the largest single group was 154 women who left for domestic reasons or pregnancy. Of the other reasons for leaving, women were more likely than men to have transferred within the service, to be undertaking other social work or unrelated work, to be undertaking other child care work (including tutorial appointments) or to be undertaking child care training not on secondment. The men were more likely to have been promoted in their department or on transfer. During the same year, of all field officer appointments made 325 were men and 677 women. Although men formed two-fifths of fieldwork staff at 31 March 1970, when we examine the 696 senior staff in grades paid on APT4 or above we find that 369 were held by men and 327 by women. By combining the fieldwork appointments the situation shown in Table 15.5 emerges. In addition to these full-time appointments there were 309 part-time appointments, 298 of which were women.

A possible indication of ambition acting as a stronger motivating force for men than women is given by the fact that of fifty-eight

Table 15.5   Senior appointments in children's departments, 1970

		Men	Women
(a)	Field officers	1,323	2,045
(b)	Other staff in grades paid on APT4 or above	369	327
(c)	Total	1,692	2,372
	(b) as % of (c)	22	14

people in children's departments on 31 March 1970 who were paid on APT4 or above and who held other professional social work qualifications (such as for psychiatric or medical social work and probation) forty were men and eighteen were women.

Probation

In the probation service, because the caseloads tended to be differentiated by sex one might have expected that proportionately within the ambit of their work there would be a comparable number of senior posts. In 1945, however, there was only one woman principal probation officer. NAPO had taken its quest for equal pay to its conclusion and was the first body outside the Civil Service to apply for the introduction of equal pay in 1955, after the Chancellor of the Exchequer's announcement that he was introducing it as a general principle in the Civil Service.[11] Also in 1955 the association had elected for the first time a woman probation officer, Miss Phyllis Corner, to be chairman of the association. Women had to some extent always had a privileged position in the probation service in that their caseloads had been maintained at a lower number than men, ideally ranging between thirty-five and forty-five compared with the accepted norm of fifty to sixty for a man.[12] Women's caseloads had remained relatively stable since the war, but men's had risen steadily. The Morison Committee, 1961, discussed the differential caseloads and decided that there was no good reason for continuing it (Morison Report, p. 108):

> This lower figure than for men rests, we understand, on the assumption that women officer's caseloads will include a high proportion of adolescent girls who are among the probation service's most difficult cases. There is no reason for regarding

a woman officer's working capacity as less than that of a man, and, indeed, the contrary has been asserted by the introduction of equal pay for men and women. It follows therefore that the work which a woman officer is expected to undertake should depend upon the nature of her cases. If, for example much of the officer's work is with small boys and their families there is no good reason why she should have fewer cases than a man colleague.

Having achieved equal pay in departments, how did women fare in getting promotion? This subject was discussed in detail by NAPO within the context of a broader investigation into seniority in the probation service.[13] The NAPO working party found that in 1965 the number in supervisory grades were as shown in Table 15.6.

Table 15.6   Senior appointments in the probation service, 1965

	Men	Women
Senior probation officers	219	38
Deputy and assistant principal probation officers	21	4
Principal probation officers	68	
Ordinary officers (excluding part-time officers)	1,410	597
Ratio	4·56	14·21

Concern was expressed over this situation in the following passage (p. 10):

We feel that attention should be drawn to the very great imbalance between the number of men and the number of women who achieve senior officer posts. Amongst the women who replied to our questionnaire, there were a number who suggested that there was some prejudice against employing women officers as seniors. It is difficult to say how real this prejudice is and such evidence as we have suggests that women are less interested in applying for senior jobs than men. We would like to stress that in our view women have as great a contribution to make to the service as men and the opportunities for promotion should be equal for both groups. Appointments should be made solely on ability and, except where special circumstances apply, without reference to the sex of the applicant. . . . The Working Party considers that more women would be encouraged to apply if advertisements normally stated that the post would be open to men and women applicants.

In the Morison Report there was an implicit assumption that women would work for less money than men, and that men (where the main shortage was) might be attracted. At the time of the Morison Report, probation salaries for the basic grade maximum were slightly better than for the other social casework branches. Nevertheless the report recommended 'a bold increase in salaries which will put the service on a different plane of attraction, and encourage, as can no other measure, interest in the opportunities which the modern service offers for a professional career' (p. 241).

Two factors seem to be operating in the probation service which have general relevance and seemed to be operating in the child care service. First, to attract good-calibre men it was necessary to devise a career structure above basic salaries which would be competitive with other fields; the element of vocation allowed for in men was much smaller than that allowed for in women. Since the major staffing requirements of the service, based on the sex of the clientele, were for men this had a dominant influence. Second, the NAPO study of seniority suggests that in a competitive situation women social workers as a group are less interested in administrative responsibilities and high salaries than men.

During the 1960s the probation service expanded rapidly and the career structure improved as Table 15.7 shows.[14]

Table 15.7   Staff structure of the probation service, 1961 and 1969

	1961	1969
Principal probation officers	61	67
Deputy and assistant principal probation officers	27	56
Senior probation officers	158	430
Ordinary officers (excluding part-time officers)	1,522	2,419

The proportion of basic-grade women probation officers had fallen from 40 per cent in 1951 to 33 per cent in 1961 and 30 per cent in 1969, even though probation was being used for an increasing number of female offenders. Average caseloads of women had hardly changed in the decades (1952, 42·6 per cent; 1969, 42·7 per cent) but a significant improvement in men's caseloads was achieved, the average caseload falling from 60·6 in 1961 to 52·2 in 1969. Women dealt with a higher proportion of juvenile supervision cases and were much more likely to deal with matrimonial work. The Children and Young Persons Act 1969, and the increasing involvement of local authorities with delinquent children and matrimonial work may well have affected women's motivation for probation work.

Beatrice Pollard's research into marital casework in the probation service in 1954 commented on the organisation of work in the probation service, and showed that factors long in operation were still evident (Pollard, 1962). She observed that she had found no evidence that men did casework any faster than women to justify the differential caseload (p. 116): 'Perhaps it [the difference in caseloads] would be found to be based on nothing more recondite than the unexamined assumption that male officers can always deal better with male probationers. . . .' Pollard did not find the difference in the weight of matrimonial work falling on men and women that is so evident later. In her investigations of marital casework she found that many probation officers considered that there were more unreasonable husbands than unreasonable wives, which was bias rather than fact. This bias was attributed partly to the fact that 12 per cent more wives than husbands were interviewed, the bias to women in the legal process and that male probation officers were likely to have a distorting interaction with masochistic wives. Women probation officers were more likely to be diffident in their work and more likely to request a second worker of the same sex as the client, but Pollard summed up as follows:[15]

> The present study offered no evidence of difference between the sexes in the effective practice of marital casework even though some women officers continue to express diffidence. There was indeed evidence to suggest that women officers tended to be better qualified in the formal sense than men. . . .

Local studies

It is possible to look now at how these factors—the national proportions of men in social welfare and the proportions of men in fields of social work—were realised in particular areas. There have been four major studies during the post-war period, two by Barbara Rodgers in a northern county borough, looking at the situation in 1957 and 1969;[16] one by Margot Jeffreys of services in Buckinghamshire in 1961,[17] and a study of a Midlands county borough (300,000+

population) in 1965 by Julia Parker and R. Allen.[18] The studies in the northern county borough gave the distribution of men and women in the two periods shown in Table 15.8.

Table 15.8 Staffing of social work departments in a northern county borough, 1957 and 1969

(a) Summer 1957[19]				Senior appointments	
Agency	Men	Women	Total	Men	Women
Welfare department	4	4	8	1	
Children's department	1	2	3	1	
Mental health department	2	1	3		
Hospital social work		5	5		1
Probation	3	2	5	1	
Voluntary agencies	3	2	5		
Total	13	16	29	3	1

(b) September 1969[20]				Senior appointments	
Agency	Men	Women	Total	Men	Women
Welfare department	2	12	14	2	
Children's department	4	4	8	1	
Mental health department	5		5	1	
Hospital social work		8	8		1
Probation	7	2	9	1	
Voluntary agencies	1	3	4		
Total	19	29	48	5	1

Barbara Rodgers also showed that in the earlier study of appointments since 1948, a higher proportion of the women were untrained and locally recruited and had tended to stay in their jobs longer. Services with a high turnover of staff had been the children's, welfare services and probation departments.

It might be thought that the low level of training and large proportion of locally recruited people (the locally recruited staff tended to be older and unqualified) would be a special problem in a smaller county borough, so that the situation in a wealthy county serves as a useful contrast. Of the 287 men and 102 women in social welfare positions in Buckinghamshire in 1961, a higher proportion of women (20 per cent) were likely to have had fathers in higher professional work than was true for the men (6 per cent).[21] Roughly a quarter of all social workers had fathers in this social class but nearly a half of almoners or psychiatric social workers came into this category. More men had left school early and tended to enter social work later and more often from clerical work administration. However, the proportion of men taking a full-time university course at some stage was the same as for women. Women who were later entrants to the social welfare field were more likely to have come from occupations providing personal services such as nursing, teaching or other forms of social welfare. Men were typically married with children, whilst the majority of women were single (approximately three-quarters), or those that were married were childless. Unfortunately Margot Jeffreys does not analyse the pattern of seniority in departments, but she does make the following comment about the balance of men and women in social welfare:[22]

> While some social welfare services, particularly those
> associated with the treatment of offenders and the mentally
> ill, have employed men, social work from its inception has
> been predominantly undertaken by women. Able men attracted
> to work which involves giving personal services in need have
> chosen professions such as medicine, the law, teaching and the
> Church, rather than the social work professions. There is no
> intrinsic reason, however, why men should not make a
> substantial contribution to the social work field. . . . The only
> substantial reasons why they have not taken up the work is
> that it has not had sufficiently attractive financial rewards or
> ultimate opportunities for planning and administration.

This assessment was to some extent supported by Margot Jeffreys's examination of staff spontaneously commenting on rewarding and dissatisfying aspects of their work. Men seemed to need to feel helpful more than women and were more upset by clients' ingratitude or hostility. On the financial side men mentioned more often the low financial rewards as a point of dissatisfaction; men also seemed to be slightly more status-conscious than women. Julia Parker's and R. Allen's study tends to reinforce the picture given by Barbara Rodgers, with problems of low training, inadequate communication between social workers and a concentration of men in senior positions.[23] Parker and Allen found that in spite of the fact that women predominated in the social work departments, senior posts tended to be occupied by men. Women were better qualified than men, though they had had less experience, and both characteristics were associated to their being younger. This is shown in Tables 15.9 and 15.10. The study also gives evidence of the increasing mobility of staff, particularly qualified workers.

Table 15.9 Social workers in different departments by sex and position

Department	Seniors		Field workers		Total	
	Male	Female	Male	Female	Male	Female
Children's	3	4	2	11	5	15
Education welfare	5	1	5	7	10	8
Welfare	3	2	4	10	7	12
Mental health	1	1	4	7	5	8
Total	12	8	15	35	27	43

Table 15.10 Seniority and qualifications

	Men			Women		
	Seniors	Field workers	Total	Seniors	Field workers	Total
Degree and further training	1	1	2	3	3	6
Professional qualifications	3	1	4	3	5	8
Social science qualifications	1	3	4		10	10
Others	7	10	17	2	17	19
Total	12	15	27	8	35	43

What these studies illustrate, as well as to some extent reinforcing the national situation, is the possible variations between counties, county boroughs and the effects of size and location. The Buckinghamshire children's department was almost entirely staffed by women, and overall there was a higher proportion of women social welfare workers than in the northern county borough. The attractions of a pleasant county, being near to London (the professional social work centre in the country), the facilities available for entertainment, are all features that might well appeal particularly to the highly qualified daughter of professional parents. Another feature of Margot Jeffreys's comments is that they are a complete reversal of arguments used in the nineteenth century. Then women had to fight to have a say in the welfare of groups which men had been dealing with. This, in addition to attitudes towards social relations between the sexes, resulted in women being concentrated in certain welfare areas, which, because women's work was generally less well paid than men's, was self-reinforcing. A century later arguments were put forward for attracting men into the field as though they had been denied the possibility of service. Salaries were not raised to attract more women into the field or to give them a proper reward but to attract men. As we have seen, already men were occupying a disproportionate number of senior positions in the 1950s and 1960s and it seems the fate of social work that it will fall under the dominance of men. Once the special arguments for regarding certain areas of work as women's work disappeared it seemed inevitable that eventually men would step into the major controlling positions.

Directors of social services

For these reasons the appointment of directors of social services in 1970–1, following the Local Authority Social Services Act of June 1970, provided a valuable case study situation. At the end of 1970 the heads of welfare departments and mental welfare departments were nearly all men.[24] In children's departments, of 171 appointments in England and Wales eighty were women. This compared with the situation in 1950, when the number of children's officers in post was 133, of whom ninety-six were women; of fifty-five county appointments forty-six were women, of whom forty-two were single; and of eighty county borough appointments forty-seven were women, of whom forty-one were single.[25] It was perhaps notable that more men were appointed in county boroughs and that the largest of them (for example Bristol, Birmingham, Manchester and Liverpool) tended to have male children's officers. The tendency of men to be more likely to land large authorities has been important. The great variations in the size of local authorities certainly gave women a better chance of appointment in smaller departments. But as the children's departments expanded in the 1950s and 1960s the size of the departments entailed that the job of the children's officer became more administrative and organisational.[26] This may have led local authorities to prefer men, and to women being slightly less attracted to a purely administrative post; hence the reduction in the number of women children's officers in the two decades.

Nevertheless, during the period following the 1948 Children Act women children's officers had compared favourably with men in leadership and management skills in operating an expanding service. However, the special arguments in the Curtis Report for the appropriateness of women's appointments were now gone; administrative rather than social work skills were needed. The new social services departments were to have responsibility for a wide range of clients covering all ages, both sexes and many different kinds of problem. In this situation, assuming that women formed approximately one-fifth of all local authority chief officer appointments in children's and welfare departments, one might have supposed that thirty to forty women might be appointed. By April 1971 there had been 160 appointments, of which fourteen were women. Of course there had been an omen of the future because in Scotland, following the Social Work (Scotland) Act 1968, of fifty appointments as directors of social work four were women.[27]

The low number of women appointed as directors of social services caused concern to many women and, despite her antipathy to many aspects of social work—particularly the psychodynamic variants—Baroness Wootton of Abinger raised the issue in the House of Lords on the 3 March 1971.[28] After Lord Aberdare, Minister of State for the Department of Health and Social Security, had told her that fourteen of the appointments were for women, she commented:

> My Lords, while I thank the Minister for his not very reassuring answer, may I ask whether he is not aware that for many years the great majority of social workers have been women, mostly earning very modest salaries? Does he not think it is a matter for concern that when at last there is a reasonable career structure in this profession, the skill and experience of these women has been so poorly utilised in the highly paid appointments at the top of the hierarchy?

Lord Aberdare replied:

> My Lords, I certainly recognise the most important part played by women in the field of social work. However, I must point out that these appointments were made by local

authorities. In every case so far they have been filled by open advertisement, and it has been up to the local authority concerned to choose the person who, in their opinion, was best fitted for the post.

Baronesses Bacon and Summerskill joined in the debate, the latter observing: 'My Lords, the noble Lord said that this tiny proportion of women were chosen by the local authorities. Is it not a fact that ninety-nine per cent of the local authorities are men?' Lord Aberdare replied: 'My Lords, that is up to those who elected them.'

Lord Aberdare, in spite of a further attempt by Baroness Wootton to persuade him to advise local authorities by circular to give more consideration to women, insisted that he could only screen out unsuitable candidates and that any direction to local authorities on this point would itself involve sexual discrimination. He also defended himself by pointing out that his chief adviser on social work was a woman, as was her deputy. At one point Baroness Wootton was shouted down twice by several noble Lords before being allowed to pursue her questioning of Lord Aberdare. In frustration, Baroness Summerskill asked: 'My Lords, may I ask the noble Lord whether he would send a circular if the great majority [of directors of social services] were women?' No reply was forthcoming and Lord Aberdare was clearly relieved when several Lords suggested that no pressure be put on local authorities in making these appointments and he was able to close the debate on Baroness Wootton's question on this note. In total the debate reveals that Baroness Wootton and her supporters of the women's view in the Lords were not fully aware of the details of developments in the staffing of social work services since the war and tended to attribute more to discrimination against women than was warranted. Demographic factors were not sufficiently allowed for. Nevertheless, there was at least the possibility of a grain of truth in the accusation of sexual discrimination which Lord Aberdare could not allow himself to discuss and he washed his hands of any responsibility for the actions of local authorities, other than that of removing completely unsuitable candidates from the lists of applicants.

If one examines this development in the light of the previous analysis, several mutually supportive tendencies in this direction were emerging. First, local government's male domination at senior levels, and lay committee's identification of managerial skills with men, might give a bias towards the male candidates to restore the male club into which women children's officers had been an uncomfortable intrusion at times. The special place which women had had on children's committees would tend to disappear and the chairmanship of the social services committee would become a key political appointment. Second, many of the women children's officers had been in post for many years, if not since 1948, and may have been approaching retirement; their husband's employment if married, and family responsibilities if single, may well have prevented them from applying for many posts other than that in their own authority. Third, at the levels below chief officer there was already a disproportionate weighting of men in senior positions. Fourth, these highly paid posts were extremely attractive to men who applied systematically to a large number of local authorities; many men had in recent years taken short courses in management in preparation. The future of social work in this country, as a part of social care services, now seems to be well and truly in the hands of a male élite and one would predict that the majority of women in senior appointments at second- and third-tier level would be in managing fieldwork services, as professional advisers and as training officers.

Social work inspectors

By contrast, the overall balance of inspectoral positions in central government underwent no enormous change. Up to 1 April 1971 there were ninety-one Home Office inspectors in the children's branch of the Home Office, of whom forty were women. There were also in the welfare section of the Department of Health and Social Security at that time twenty-nine officers, of whom four were men. These were amalgamated to form a unified social work service in the DHSS of 120 men and sixty-five women, of whom the chief officer was Miss J. Cooper.[29] The expansion and development of training in the children's service since 1948 was led by the imagination of two psychiatric social workers who had been tutors on the LSE mental health course, Miss Clement Brown and Mrs C. Winnicott, both of whom had held the position of director of training within the inspectorate in the Home Office.[30] The impact of the inspectorate is dealt with thoroughly by J. A. G. Griffith in his book *Central Departments and Local Authorities*,[31] who was impressed by the progressiveness of the Home Office inspectorate and its relationship with local authorities. It was numerically much stronger than the team of welfare officers in the Ministry of Health and played a more constructive role in the development of children's services. At central government level there was no creation of a series of new jobs but it will be interesting to see the outcome of senior appointments in the creation of the new Council for Education and Training in Social Work.[32] Within the probation services inspectorate women were better represented than in senior positions in probation departments. The position in 1950 and 1969 was as shown in Table 15.11.[33]

Table 15.11 Men and women in the probation service inspectorates, 1950 and 1969

1950:	Principal probation inspector	1 (male)
	Grade 1 inspector	4 (3 men, 1 woman)
	Grade 2 inspector	6 (3 men, 3 women)
1969:	Principal probation inspector	1 (male)
	Deputy principal probation inspector	1 (male)
	Superintending inspector	2 (1 man, 1 woman*)
	Senior inspector	2 (1 man, 1 woman)
	Inspector	24 (17 men, 7 women)

* Director of training post.

These figures seem to illustrate a much better balance between men and women in central government staff, and the question arises whether in fact this is the way in which some women can achieve a position of authority and influence, which they may have been less likely to achieve in local authorities. All inspectoral positions may be regarded as senior appointments and this may be an area which women will be strongly motivated towards in the future as well as the past, especially with the concern of a number of appointments with training.

Voluntary social work

Voluntary social work has been an issue of recurrent interest in the post-war period, beginning with the fears of many people that the Welfare State would sap voluntary initiative. One can distinguish two main trends since the Second World War. First, the expansion of the social work responsibilities of local authorities has led to a contraction and professionalisation of some voluntary organisations such as settlements work, the Family Welfare Association, and children's organisations such as Dr Barnardo's, the National

Children's Home and the Church of England Children's Society. The existence of extended statutory services put voluntary organisations in a competitive situation to provide as good a service, and most voluntary organisations have gradually paid local authority scales and employed a full-time professional staff; the independent woman of means able to do a full-time job has now disappeared. Organisations which expanded, like the Family Service Units, had to offer a service to local authorities to justify the financial grants on which they have increasingly depended. Thus, most voluntary organisations in the social work field employ trained social workers and often act as an extension of statutory services. Financial problems abound and an increasing proportion of finance has tended to come from statutory sources. As an example of some of these changes, the moral welfare movement has been greatly affected by statutory services (Hall and Howes, 1965). In its casework services its functions overlapped with children's department services and probation departments. The numbers trained were small and the main body of workers tended to be older women.[34] Also mother and baby homes were gradually closing down. The work which had developed as a nineteenth-century specialism was now outdated and new forms of social enterprise for the church needed to be found.

The second trend has been the renewed interest, particularly since the mid-1960s, in the use of volunteers, associated partly with the upsurge of interest in community work.[35] Reports such as that of the Aves Committee on volunteers[36] and of the Gulbenkian Study Group on community work[37] illustrate the trend. Social work in the post-war period was identified very clearly with casework and this was the main social work method taught during the 1950s and 1960s. The professional organisations of caseworkers were the strongest and the concern to establish social work as a professional activity, although not antagonistic to voluntary effort, did lead to a preoccupation with defining the role and skills of the professional worker and a lack of attention to the integration of voluntary helpers with professional help; it is only in the late 1960s that caseworkers have given more attention to this problem, gradually realising that this is an important resource. This re-focusing on the use of volunteers—in CABS and marriage guidance work there is a well established tradition—is a healthy sign and a recognition that much voluntary help is being given all the time whether of a neighbourly kind or in a more structured way. J. W. MacCulloch carried out a survey in Bradford in 1967 in which he found that 32 per cent of his sample were giving neighbourly help and just under 8 per cent were working through voluntary organisations.[38] In the overall pattern of voluntary work, people in social class 3 were the greater numerically, but in membership of social work committees women predominated, particularly those in social classes 1 and 2; those men on social work committees were also mainly from the same social class. Although a relatively small group, many of those committee members tended to be represented on several organisations' committees. MacCulloch's findings, although based on a poor response rate, seemed to indicate that many more people were interested in voluntary social work than were actually doing it. This may mean that the extension of volunteer bureaux and training schemes, together with public relations work and the co-operation of professional social workers, may make an even bigger impact on social work patterns of staffing and work over the next decade. It may be that the style of work of the Charity Organisation Society and care committees, with full-time workers supporting teams of volunteers, will become a standard pattern of administration within both voluntary and statutory social service agencies.

Professional organisation

So far the description of the development of social work has shown that the strongest professional organisations in social work were in probation and in almoning, with psychiatric social work, and later child care, growing in strength. The British Federation of Social Workers continued as a not very strong unifying body into the post-war period, organising conferences on current issues and providing a forum for the discussion of social work issues. Miss Bernice McFie took over the chairmanship of BFSW in 1948 and became chairman of the Association of Social Workers in 1951 when it took over the work of the BFSW. She was described in 1959[39] as a person who 'had probably been the steadiest campaigner for professional development of social workers in the last thirty years'. The Association of Social Workers had as the basis of membership associations for whom social studies training was the approved method of entry to the specialised field, and this narrowing of definition excluded health visitors and housing managers. The Association of Psychiatric Social Workers and the Institute of Almoners still felt that the new definition was too wide and decided against affiliation, but reaffiliated to it in 1957, after the ASW had

I

shown its active concern for the development of social work as a profession. The ASW had felt keenly that the increasing employment of social workers during and following the war had not led to a corresponding growth of the social work profession, and convened a standing conference which produced a report on registration in 1954.[40] This was also the year in which *Case Conference* first appeared, under the editorial hand of Mrs Kay McDougall. Because of the dearth of British publications on social work (apart from *Social Work Quarterly*), *Case Conference* was for a decade and a half to provide an essential platform for dissemination of ASW news and publication of many articles on social work practice, administration and history, which encouraged research and analysis into social work and provided a consistent focus for emergent ideas.

Even in 1959 the ASW had only a small membership of 320,[41] but its influence was out of all proportion to its membership, and it established working parties and conferences on important issues. Waldron discussed the future in terms of the possibilities of a national joint training council for social work and registration of social workers. However, there was always the dilemma that until the training of social workers was rationalised and expanded sufficiently, no government would be likely to consider registration as a realistic policy. However, a joint training council with membership of affiliated organisations was set up in 1959.

It was from the ASW that the initiative came for the convening of a Standing Conference of Organisations of Social Workers in 1963, with the aim of establishing a unified profession of social workers. Initially David Jones was chairman, but for the major part of the standing conference's life Kay McDougall was chairman. The standing conference set up a group of working parties, to draw up proposals for organisation, finance, membership, training, salaries and working conditions. After a complicated series of negotiations between standing conference and the separate associations, the British Association of Social Workers was registered in 1970. Of the eight member organisations[42] of standing conference only one, NAPO, decided not to join the BASW. Miss Enid Warren of the Institute of Almoners, who had been vice-president of standing conference, became the first chairman of the new association, and its general secretary was Kenneth Brill, trained as a psychiatric social worker and later a children's officer.

Standing conference had been heavily supported by the strong representation of women, and the representatives of associations

represented the balance of men and women in the individual organisations. For instance, in 1963 the representative members were as
shown in Table 15.12.

*Table 15.12   Men and women representatives, Standing Conference
of Organisations of Social Workers, 1963*

	Men	Women
ACCO	2	2
AFCW	2	1
AMWW		4
APSW	1	3
ASW	2	1
Inst.A		3
	7	14

At this time the chairman and secretary of the joint training council
were women, as were the secretary of the international relations
committee, and the parliamentary and public relations committee.
The general purposes committee had a male chairman as did the
international relations committee. The joint training council had
fifteen women members and five male members, whereas the parliamentary and public relations committee had eight women and
six men members; the general purposes committee had six women
and two men members. The working party on criteria for admission
to standing conference was evenly balanced (two men and two
women) and the working party on salaries and conditions of service
was composed of two men and one woman.

The above information gives an idea of the balance of standing
conference, and why it was so heavily balanced in favour of female
membership. Unlike the employment situation, within the evolution
of professional standards women played their full part, continuing
the tradition so strong from the earliest days of social work. Significantly enough, only in the working party on salaries and service
conditions were women outnumbered by men.

Already the part played by men in improving salaries in psychiatric
social work has been mentioned, and the strong emphasis on
salaries in NAPO was present from the start of the association. A
further useful corroboration of the distribution of roles in the
professional organisations comes from a study of committee

I*

membership in ACCO, disclosing a very strong predominance of men on the salaries and service conditions committee and a pre-eminence of women on the training committee.[43] This is in spite of the fact that the presidentship has been fairly evenly distributed in view of the inflow of men into child care in the late 1950s and 1960s (see Table 15.13).

Table 15.13   ACCO presidents, 1950–69

	Women	Men
1950–4	4	1
1955–9	2	3
1960–4	2	3
1965–9	3	2

At one point, a woman president felt the need to comment on this situation of a male salaries and service conditions committee:[44]

> This is a matter of great personal interest to us all. . . . I do not accept that the pressing for proper recognition of the status and conditions of work of the child care officer should automatically be left to the men. We are extremely grateful to those who do it; but we must all be prepared to be actively helpful.

A strong influence on the development of local authority social services also emanated from the Association of Children's Officers and the Association of Directors of Welfare Services. The different emphasis in these bodies, in which current policies and future developments were discussed, can be seen in the different directions taken by these services. In children's services there was a much greater emphasis on the developments of fieldwork services with casework as the main skill of its workers, whereas in welfare services there was a greater emphasis on residential and day care services. Although this was partly due to the nature of the clientele (children and families, as against the elderly, handicapped and homeless) it was also partly due to the closer liaison of the children's department inspectorate with the Association of Children's Officers and their view of the staffing needed for the departments. There was also close liaison between the Association of Child Care Officers and the Association of Children's Officers. The directors of welfare services, predominantly male, tended to have weaker links with their inspectorate and also had a professionally less well qualified staff. They saw their tasks much more in terms of administration. There was imbalance in both views, and the enormous variations in local authority personal social services which were unrelated to needs demonstrated not only variations in wealth and politics but the general lack of administrative expertise and skills in estimating need and planning provision. The Association of Children's Officers and the Association of Child Care Officers played an important part in the campaign towards a unified local authority personal social service and were more active politically than other associations during the 1960s. It is interesting that the professional associations of almoners and psychiatric social workers and directors of welfare services were much more suspicious of playing pressure group politics in the middle and late 1960s than the professional associations in child care. Caution, therefore, needs to be exercised in interpreting the roles in professional associations purely along sex lines. None the less, the distribution of roles within the professional organisations contributes to our understanding of the effects of the increasing number of men in particular branches of social work and accentuates the concern of women with training and professional development.

16   Problems of women's employment in social work

Defining the issues

During the post-war period the expansion of social services and the increasing demand for social workers created a shortage of workers which was met first by the gradual attraction of more men into social work and, second, by maximising the use of women's labour. The first process was an international one, as indicated in the second International Survey on Training for Social Work: 'It is likewise significant that where remuneration has increased as well as opportunity for more responsible positions, larger numbers of men are seeking social work positions.'[1] Also the wide variations among countries were recognised, comparing social work salaries and other salaries, although only rarely were salaries equivalent to those of the old established professions. In looking at the UK it was felt that[2] the

> salaries of social workers compare favourably with those of
> workers in related professions such as nursing, teaching and
> dietetics, but are still too low to attract men to the social work
> profession in large numbers, as the salaries are not sufficient
> to maintain a family in any degree of comfort.

In Middlesex children's department in 1957 it was complained: 'In general, there is no difficulty in recruiting women to the staff, but it is difficult to get men.'[3] With the men it was unlikely that those highly qualified would enter social work, or be guided towards it by parents, teachers and friends until the gap between its salaries and those in alternative professions was closed.

For the women the problem was different. Even given a parity with basic-grade teaching or nursing, the increasing marriage rate and lower age of marriage introduced problems for social work that had not been experienced on any great scale before. This was part of a general problem facing all professions heavily dependent on women's labour, but interwoven with a revitalised examination of the rights of women to participate in careers on an equal basis with

246

men. A key book focusing on these problems was *Women's Two Roles*[4] (Myrdal and Klein, 1956), which outlined the thesis that women should have the right to work as well as bring up a family. Two phases in the development of the social position of women were distinguished in the present century (p.1):

> The first is characterised by the admission of women to an increasing variety of hitherto masculine jobs, provided on the whole, that the women were unencumbered by family ties. The outstanding feature of the second phase is the growing number of women to combine family and employment. Altogether this amounts to a gradual recapture of positions which were lost when women were squeezed out of the economic process by the Industrial Revolution.

Viola Klein, who had contributed an important study *The Feminine Character* in 1946, later continued her work with valuable surveys and articles. Her general position can be stated in the following terms.

If one accepts that women have the right to work as well as have a family there are a number of practical implications that would be pursued for the realisation of this ideal:

    a Training appointments to take account of their special needs.

    b Part-time work whilst their family is growing (and also special service conditions, e.g. superannuation).

    c Adequate nursery or crèche facilities.

Married women and part-time work

Consciousness of the problems of married women in social work was most clearly focused at the University of Manchester, where from the late 1950s Barbara Rodgers, through her fieldwork for *Portrait of Social Work* set on foot a series of studies concerned with manpower for personal social services. These paid particular attention to the use of womanpower in social work. Viola Klein was a Simon Research Fellow at Manchester before going to Reading University, and Barbara Rodgers stimulated the concern and studies into part-time workers, collaborating closely with the authors of the studies whose results are outlined below. This concern about the problems of married women workers received organised expression in the formation, in December 1959, of the Association of Part-time Social

Workers whose purposes were to press for greater part-time training and part-time employment for training social workers. In 1960 the association completed a survey based on the results of a postal questionnaire completed by over 200 of its members, which suggested that a limited but continuing number of married women could be available for social work if hours and conditions of employment were adjusted to their needs. Particular difficulties were getting suitable workers to the employers and the problem of women in their middle years wishing to enter social work.[5] Employment of part-time workers was on a very small scale and in 1961–2 only 6 per cent of 1,105 social workers employed by statutory and voluntary social work agencies in London were part-time.[6] Although the agencies with the highest proportion of part-time workers were the Citizens' Advice Bureaux and the Family Welfare Associations, and in these areas of social work and in clinics and hospitals, part-time social workers had been using part-time help for a long time. By comparison, the proportion of part-time workers was low in the children's department (2 per cent), welfare department (2 per cent), and mental welfare department (4 per cent) and non-existent in the London Probation Service.[7]

There was a growing awareness by women of social work in the 1950s and 1960s. An analysis of information given by applicants to the University Women's Part-time Employment Agency in the period 1956–8 showed a predominant interest in social work, and in the 1960s the Women's Employment Federation reported that nearly three-quarters of the enquiries they received were from 'mature' women seeking information about social work.[8] To some extent this was related to the increasing concern with social problems shown by women's magazines during and following the Second World War. Cynthia White commented on this phenomenon (1970, p. 131–2):

Starting with the 'quality' section of the market, a new spirit and a new approach, evoked in response to the demands of war and carried over into the peace-time emergency, began to permeate the women's press. During the war women grew in responsibility, resilience and vigour. They discovered at first hand the social condition of Britain and encountered many of her social problems, something they had not the opportunity to do when their world was contained within the four walls of home. As in the nineteenth century when gentlewomen, bent

on dispensing charity to the poor, came face to face with the
festering slums which they had scarcely known existed, so
women of the middle and upper middle classes a century later
had their eyes opened to prevailing social needs, and responded
similarly.

Apart from the women's magazines, during the 1950s and 1960s
the growing awareness of the cracks and imperfections in the Welfare
State was permeating radio and television, and in the 1960s new
voluntary organisations like the Child Poverty Action Group and
Shelter, and established societies like the National Association for
Mental Health, realised the potential of television in conveying the
reality of social problems, touching the springs of concern in women.
In the national press, the women's page in the *Guardian* epitomises
the awareness of social problems as something which would particularly appeal to women.

Tackling the problem of maximising the contribution of married
women in social work in a situation of overall shortage was con-
ditional upon propaganda to create awareness in social work agencies
and study of the position of married women in social work. Barbara
Rodgers's follow-up study of students from Manchester University
(1963) confirmed that opportunities for trained married women to
take up part-time social work after a career break were very limited.
The hours of work in agencies other than child guidance or hospitals
and voluntary agencies were often long and the work was not con-
ducive to regular hours.[9] Barbara Rodgers's 1963 study also found
that some married social workers had taken up part-time work in
other fields, particularly teaching, where part-time work was
established on a firmer basis.[10] Kathleen Gray, writing in 1964
after reviewing the depressing gap between the demand and supply
of social workers in all fields of social work, discerned a ray of hope
for the future:[11]

Gloomy as this picture is we can take some comfort from the
fact that there is a distinct tendency for women to look at
their professional career as continuing intermittently rather than
finishing once for all with the birth of their first child.

Yet there was, in fact, only slow progress in the use of part-time
workers. A national survey of part-time social work in 1963–4
showed that of an estimated 7,500 trained social workers in this
country only 5 per cent were employed part-time. Part-time medical

social workers constituted 6 per cent of their professional association membership compared with 11 per cent of psychiatric social workers. The percentages for child care officers, moral welfare workers and women probation officers were 4, 18, and 5 respectively.[12] The great majority of part-timers were employed because of the difficulty of obtaining full-time workers and most of them did not bring their agencies up to full establishment. Detailed proposals were made to make the employment of part-time workers easier, such as the clarification of work roles, improvement of the status and salaries of part-time workers, advertisement of part-time posts, work-study research to reveal appropriate use of part-time staff, and the development of part-time training opportunities, particularly for older entrants. The authors of the study were firmly of the opinion that,[13]

> A planned policy based on these needs could not fail to have an impact on the recruitment of the older married woman to part-time social work, and meet the needs of women students who increasingly tend to choose a career that they can continue after marriage and combine with family commitments.

In terms of provisions of courses specially adapted to the need of married women, the result was small in the 1960s—one full-time course, a certificate in social work course, and one part-time course in child care in the Extra-mural Department of London University. The Seebohm Committee was aware of this problem and recognised that[14]

> demographic changes will continue to affect recruitment and in particular . . . reduce the number of younger women and unmarried women available for reliable lengthy service. Efforts to attract men and mature women to social work should continue and in this context we wish to acknowledge the valuable work being undertaken by the Social Work Advisory Service. More courses should be provided for married women, whether qualified social workers or with a basic training in social studies to prepare them to return to full or part-time work after their children have reached school age.

The Association of Part-time Social Workers had in the early 1960s succeeded in bringing the problems of married women into the consciousness of the social work profession, and the enthusiasm of a small group of women in close touch with each other and the concern of the National Council of Social Service produced valuable studies of part-time employment. However, the APTW felt that its functions could be best fulfilled within the affairs of the Association of Social Workers, with which it merged in January 1967, and the Social Work Advisory Service, established in 1966. Thus, Helen Curtis was able to write to Barbara Rodgers on 9 December 1966:

> Dear Barbara,
> The accompanying press statement which I am sending for your interest sets out the reasons why the Association of Part-time Social Workers is about to disband. It is encouraging to feel that in the future enquiries concerning the Older Entrant can be dealt with by the Social Work Advisory Service, and anyone wishing to join a non-specialised professional body concerned with the part-timer can now join the Association of Social Workers. I am still in touch with the interests linked with our association as I am now on the Council of the Advisory Service and Executive of the Association of Social Workers. What is specially pleasing is the setting up in the Association of Social Workers of a Committee concerned broadly with the issues we worked for— with four ex-Association of Part-time Workers members, and four Association of Social Workers members. This could prove to be a very useful channel.

Hesitant responses to women's position

In view of the strength of the case presented, one must ask why progress was so slow. One reason was the predominance of men in probation, local authority welfare and mental health work, and the increasing proportion of men in children's departments. In probation and the old local authority mental health and welfare departments it was natural that provision for married women working should only be seen as contributing marginally to the total labour force. The position of children's departments illustrated the strategy that as the supply of single women diminished one looked for men as a source of recruitment, rather than expending energy in maximising the use of married women's labour. Because in teaching and nursing (and within social work in almoning and psychiatric social work) there was a major dependence upon women's labour, the needs of married women with children were considered earlier. The nature of hospital work, with the need for twenty-four-hour manning, facilitated the development of part-time work in

I**

nursing, and medical settings with possibility of sessional work provided the right conditions for part-time medical social work and psychiatric social work. In teaching the school hours and holidays similarly suited the circumstances of married women with children. Moreover, in the teaching profession there was control over an important resource, nursery education, with priority given to women teachers' children in times of scarcity.

The Association of Part-time Social Workers had provided a focus on the issues of special training opportunities for married women and of their employment on a part-time basis. These issues were important in tapping a source of recruitment and in increasing the length of service of younger trained women who married. Both issues were within the control of bodies sponsoring social work training and social work agencies. The issue of providing adequate nursery facilities was much less under the influence of social work, although a central determinant on the ability of women to embark on a career with minimum interruption through having a family. In this country day nursery care and nursery education has never, except in wartime, been extended with the aim of freeing women for work, that is, planned as a universal service (although, as mentioned, education authorities used this scarce resource to help their own labour position). It was a key part of Viola Klein's programme that women would never be able to fulfil their two roles satisfactorily unless such provision was far more widely available.[15]

Day nursery provision has often tended to be associated with a remedial aim and as a provision for families with problems. Similarly, the extension of nursery classes and day nursery care, particularly in association with the recent Educational Priority Area Urban Aid programme, is often seen as focused on children in problem areas, rather than as a way of releasing women for work.[16] In effect pre-school care is often seen as 'residual', to be used by inadequate families, rather than as a normal and legitimate aid to the women wishing to work. The alternative approach, whereby social work agencies provide crèche facilities for their married women staff, does not seem to have been considered. Instead of making special provision for women, social work agencies have preferred to make special provision for attracting men. For instance, in the child care field much more effort has gone into an emergency training, largely for men, based in London and Leeds and Cardiff—from which married women with children are generally excluded because of their inability to live away from home for a year—rather than into establishing part-time courses adapted to married women's needs. There seems to be a deep-seated ambivalence towards married women with children working, which is particularly relevant in the social work profession where for two decades after the war Bowlby's theories on maternal deprivation held sway in their cruder forms. Also, despite the lack of clear evidence, the fears that working mothers were a cause of delinquency and truancy and general family problems may have inhibited the faster development of facilities enabling women with a family to pursue a social work career. It would be easy to emphasise the importance of facilities for the two to five age-group at the expense of ignoring the significance of appropriate hours, easy travelling distance, pleasant working conditions and availability of domestic help. Cynthia Arregger in her study of graduate women stressed the importance of the domestic problem and easy access to work with suitable hours.[17] Audrey Hunt's national study of women's employment found that women with better education gave as their most important reason for working 'opportunities to use qualifications'. 'High wages or salary' were relatively unimportant, coming well behind 'easy travelling' and 'pleasant working conditions'.[18] Both these studies found that more highly educated women were likely to be economically active, and Hunt's study indicated an increasing willingness of married women to return to work in the future and thought that it would be possible to encourage more women to return to work.

In trying to understand the post-war decades of social work in this country and recruitment policies, one key factor seems to have been the acceptance and perpetuation of the myth that social work is a woman's profession, without sufficient recognition of the areas of social work in which men predominated, as in probation and the health and welfare fields. The only major study—unfortunately little referred to in this country—to recognise the presence of men on a large scale was the World Health Organisation study *Health and Social Workers in England and France*.[19] This study referred to the wide range of types of training which gives people of very diverse backgrounds access to the different types of social work:

It is here that the problem arises of the respective places to be occupied among social workers by men and women. There are at present a large number of men employed in various types of social work in England. Perhaps their duties could

be performed just as well by women, but there is no doubt
that many men have a taste for this kind of work and carry it
out with complete competence. It would certainly be a mistake
to eliminate men from all forms of social work.

It must be remembered that in France social work was virtually
wholly a woman's profession, with a unified system of training, and
the authors attributed the presence of many men in social work in
this country to the diversity of training, and thought that 'a simple,
unified type of training . . . would run the risk of becoming specially
adapted to women candidates'.

Although Laroque and Daley pointed out the significant presence
of men in social work in England, their attitude was that account
should be taken in training programmes of the costs to the worker
and to the community, this being related to the average number of
years' service to the community after training. Thus they stated:

> While men remain in service throughout the active period of
> their lives—that is for thirty or thirty-five years at least, women
> often give up social work sooner, particularly when they marry.
> Sometimes many of them—though no precise figure can be
> given—return to social work, full-time or part-time, some years
> later, especially when their children go to school.

There was an acceptance of the economic argument that because
of women's shorter career service as a result of raising a family,
men were a better investment for the community. This argument
cannot be denied on a purely economic basis. But the community
incurs many costs in order that its population may be productive
and has to choose whether it will bear the social costs involved in
enabling women to follow a career with minimum interruption
should they wish to.

Thus, although there was a growing appreciation of the problem
of married women in social work, there were attitudes in existence
unfavourable for any systematic response on a large scale. If men
were already dominant this led to inadequate attention being given
to the problems of recruiting more women of all ages into social
work and accommodating training programmes and working
conditions in agencies to their needs. In child care there was a policy
of attracting men rather than creating special conditions for married
women. It was in psychiatric social work and medical social work,
where the image remained more firmly female and where the work

lent itself to sessional organisation, that most consideration was given to the special needs of women, particularly in making part-time work available.

Women's liberation and social work

Since the late 1960s the new movement for women's rights has gathered steady momentum. Although heterogeneous in composition, its foundation is the realisation that the first movement spearheaded by the attainment of women's suffrage and the right of entry to various professions left many attitudes in society unchanged and only partially achieved changes in women's social position. Ironically, it is these partial improvements and much broader cultural factors such as the redefining of sexual morals and a serious questioning of the moral and economic bases of our industrial culture which sharpened our perceptions of the many remaining inequalities and injustices to which women are subject. Advances in contraception and abortion have also been an important factor. Not only has there been the polemic and analytic writing of Germaine Greer, Juliet Mitchell and Eva Figes, but also the empirical researches by Michael Fogerty, Rhona Rapoport and Robert Rapoport for PEP and sponsored by the Leverhulme Trust.[20] The combined forces of the varied participants in the movement have succeeded in gaining equal pay legislation, in influencing much other legislation affecting women and in forcing the government to accept a commitment to a general Act of Parliament dealing with discrimination, after two unsuccessful Private Member's Bills.

How much have women social workers allied themselves to this movement? Discussion in social work has been almost non-existent and, although a minority of women social workers may be active in or sympathetic to the women's liberation movement, there is no evidence of any general concern. Elizabeth Wilson, writing in *New Society*, observed:[21] 'There may be radical women social workers, but the ideas of women's liberation have had no impact whatsoever on social work.' In 1972 *Social Work Today* organised an essay competition about the role of women in social work and the winning essay by Mrs Sylvia Brooks was published, but it contained no reference to women's liberation although dealing at length with women's caring role and their unequal position in management posts.[22] Mrs Brooks's thoughtful discussion was negated by a facetious accompanying article by male and female contributors. This lack of involvement in the present women's rights movement is in contrast to the position in the late nineteenth and early twentieth century, where at least many women social workers were conscious of the need to think through their position on questions of women's suffrage. Social workers who might not strongly have supported the suffrage movement or any dramatic changes in women's role, were often extremely active in pressing for improved wages and conditions of working-class women; there is little such activity today. To point out these contrasts is not to assume the absolute justification of all the policies emanating from the women's liberation movement but to encourage women (and men) social workers to explore the issues and any relevance for them. In the nineteenth century women concerned themselves with the social problems of women and girls partly because the majority of men ignored them. Although this should not be an exclusive concern of women there is still a sound argument for a similar position today. Elizabeth Wilson affirms in her article 'that women social workers are still seeing themselves as a group distinct from their clients; and yet women social workers are probably the only group who share a similar oppression with many of their clients; and could organise themselves alongside'.

17   Conclusion

In outlining the development of social work with particular attention to the contribution of women, I have tried to avoid overemphasis on the general history of social work and also too great an involvement with the history of women's emancipation. Even within the study of women in social work, it has not been possible to study in detail all branches of social work and I have tended to concentrate on an examination of social work in the casework agencies, the Poor Law and local authorities. However, since even this limited examination provided examples with very varied ratios of men and women, it is possible to derive conclusions and trends which may then be applied to other branches of social work not considered here. Thus in this chapter I will state some of the conclusions and implications derived from earlier material.

Motivation for social work

The earlier period examined showed how social work, like teaching and nursing, was related to female roles within the family. Nursing in sickness, tender love and comforting, education in its broadest sense and child care and nurture all demanded the ideal of personal service. It was, therefore, appropriate that women became involved in forms of social help which corresponded to these roles, as in almoning, psychiatric social work and child welfare. The low value placed upon these domestic activities indicated by the poor status of women in the nineteenth century, can to some extent be held responsible for the slow acceptance of social work as a professional activity. The expression of family roles in social work was most vividly marked by the open reference of social work as providing substitute experience for single women unable to marry, or married women without children. Because of the demographic structure before the First World War and because of attitudes to middle- and upper-class wives working, most of this desire to help was harnessed to voluntary work, and this inhibited the development of social work as a paid professional activity so that it was only an embryonic career before the First World War.

It is relevant to remark that the forms of social work where men predominated—probation, NSPCC, School Board Officers, duly authorised officer, relieving officers—all carried strong elements of authority and control. Thus, whilst it was possible for men to be motivated to social work they tended to hold positions which mirrored family roles of authority, discipline and management.

Differentiation of male and female social work roles

Besides the degree of authority which influenced the proportion of men in a branch of social work there were sexual taboos which dictated that to some extent men dealt with men and boys and women dealt with women, girls and younger boys. This has been particularly evident in probation, child care and above all in residential institutions of all kinds—prisons, approved schools, Borstals, mental hospitals, and homes for the aged. Although in children's homes, homes for the aged and mental hospitals much progress has been made in breaking down this isolation of the sexes, attitudes associated with it die very hard. In my study of the residential care of deprived children it was shown how mixed children's homes were established and how gradually attempts were made to have mixed staffs.[1] Another factor influencing the distribution of men and women in social work was the administrative setting. Men have avoided the hospital setting and preferred local authority social work. This is related to the traditional pattern of female auxiliary staff in hospitals and to the greater career opportunities in local authority work.

Leadership and administrative abilities of women in social work

From the earliest beginnings of social work the power of men in terms of patronage and influence was very strong. Their control of financial resources and dominance of committees are examples of this. Yet there were a set of women who were charismatic leaders and accepted by their male counterparts as equals. Throughout this study there are examples of women with outstanding administrative and leadership qualities, whether one thinks of individuals such as Octavia Hill and Josephine Butler or the whole group of pioneering almoners, or the women children's officers after 1948. The under-representation of women in senior appointments reflects, then, not inferior ability, but institutionalised resistances.[2] It has been amply demonstrated how women had to fight for an opportunity to exercise their helping abilities and how men were resistant to women occupying committee and staff positions of seniority. There was an attempt to define a woman's role narrowly, to confine her to work which would create the minimum of disturbance to the male hierarchy. Management and overall control were male prerogatives and, in spite of some evidence to the contrary, there still seems to be a strong residue of prejudice against women in senior positions. In recent years it is almost as if men were arguing that they could be tender if they wished[3] but women were unable to be managers on any scale. Sufficient evidence has been presented to prove that women have not received a proportionate share in management posts.[4] How much this is due to woman's dual role, how much to her lack of ambition or readiness to take on these responsibilities, and how much to masculine prejudice is much more difficult to say. The evidence dealing with the probation service and directors of social service pointed in the direction of a lack of willingness by women to apply for senior posts. This might be a fear of anticipated prejudice or rejection or a wish to remain in personal work with staff or clients rather than take on purely administrative positions. A factor difficult to evaluate is the effect of selection procedures on courses and of casework teaching on social work courses. It is at least possible that social work tutors may have screened out female students with more ambitious and aggressive traits whilst being willing to accept these in men selected for training. Coupled with an emphasis on client-worker relationships in casework teaching and a non-directive approach to treatment, female workers may have been strongly influenced in the direction of under-valuing administrative skills, seeing administration and policy-making largely as impediments to personal work with clients. The inability of women to obtain a proportionate representation in management has been linked to a powerful contribution in the fields of social work training and the development of professional associations in social work.

In the first half of our period it was natural that a proportion of women pioneers in social work also campaigned for women's suffrage and better education for women as part of a general campaign to create careers for women. It is ironic that after the Second World War when so many of the early battles had achieved improvements in the position of women, with social work a small but important career for them, that changes in the pattern of marriage made it extremely difficult for women to play an equal part with men.

The comments in the preceding sections can be summarised in briefly listing some guidelines for determining the allocation of social work tasks:

Indications for male role	*Indications for female role*
a dealing with men or boys	*a* dealing with women, girls, young boys
b the work involves authority/ control/directive interaction with clients	*b* the work is non-directive, therapeutic
c managerial work/administrative work/financial control	*c* non-managerial work (except in training)
d local authority setting	*d* hospital setting and voluntary organisations
e concern with salaries	*e* face-to-face work with people in need

Future trends

Without fundamental changes in attitudes and policies the following trends are implied by the present study:

a Women will continue to be discriminated against in senior line management posts resulting in a disproportionate number of men in senior social work posts.

b Senior women will be mainly single or married without children.

c If any branch of social work previously dominated by women becomes equally accessible and attractive to men, it will come to be dominated by men. Women will tend to hold lower participant positions.

d Women will tend to be appointed as training officers.

e Women will continue to play a key part in social work education.

Maximising women's contribution

Women's contribution to social work can be enlarged by increasing the number of training courses, equivalent to teacher-training courses, for entry at the age of eighteen or nineteen. Training, taking account of the needs of older married women, should be expanded.[5] Social work agencies should develop a systematic policy for employment of women with families, dealing with hours and appropriate work allocation, part-time work, the development of crèche facilities in large departments, maintainance of seniority during absences due to family commitments, provision of refresher courses for married women, liaison with the Central Council for Education and Training in Social Work in developing training opportunities, and a re-appraisal of attitudes to women as potential assistant directors and directors of social work departments. Such changes may be difficult within the context of the general lack of opportunities for married women to continue a career.

Reinterpreting the history of social work

The present study illuminates some critiques of social work put forward in recent years. First, the growth of the social services and particularly the development of social work in local authorities, has led to a growth in size of social work organisations, with a consequent bureaucratisation of structures. In the training field this has led to an interest in organisation and management reflected in social work literature from the mid-1960s, the provision of middle-management short training courses by the Central Training Council during the same period, and post-graduate management courses. Although the process of bureaucratisation has received attention from theorists[6] and Weber's contribution is acknowledged, it is not emphasised in the analysis how bureaucratic administration developed frequently in the context of patrimonial and feudalistic societies. Also the development of legal authority, superimposed on this pattern of traditional domination, has reinforced the weight given to male domination in our societies by virtue of the power of men in the legal profession as well as politics.[7] In social work there have been notable contributions by women which have particularly emphasised the value of the individual and his or her needs in the face of a perplexing and often harmful social environment. A link can be traced from Octavia Hill, Mary Carpenter and Josephine Butler which was nurtured in a different form by psychiatric social workers and has influenced the whole of social work by the embodiment of ideals and values in the pattern of social work training evolved in this country. Although these values—emphasising the importance of individual and family—were not confined to women and women have been able to demonstrate leadership and administrative abilities, it can be argued that it has been a particular contribution of women in social work to nurture these ideals in action and so maintain a countervailing balance against impersonal bureaucratisation of services. In the immediate future of social work, increasing size and complexity of social work services are giving a large impetus to forward planning and extended formal hierarchies of workers. It is an open question whether social service departments will integrate the blend of qualities which women have brought to social work at all levels in their organisation. Should the pattern of male rationalistic domination be extended rather than diminished, the power of social work as a profession might well increase, but there will be a danger of losing some essential qualities, in offering services to individuals in need. Bureaucracy has many advantages as well as the disadvantages implied above. So far social work, as part of a large network of welfare provisions, has never been developed as a fully integrated aspect of social policy. Serious discontinuities between the reduction of institutional care and the development of community care services have existed, for instance, in penal and mental health services. If social work is to become an effective instrument of help, universally available where needed, it must face the necessity of using the potentialities of larger-scale organisation, rather than simply regarding them as a cross to be borne.

A second aspect of historical interpretation is that given by Paul Halmos in *The Personal Service Society*.[8] He argues that social work is a moral force gradually superseding that of religion. It is part of a group of personal social service professions such as nursing, medicine and teaching, as contrasted with impersonal service professions such as engineering, law and accountancy. The personal service professions have been expanding faster than impersonal service professions. Whilst Halmos uses census data and social work is included under the category 'social welfare and related workers', which is a broad category, he fails to point out that, with the exception of the medical professions, classified as a personal service profession, the impersonal service professions are male-dominated and the personal service professions have a high proportion of women: nursing and teaching have a much higher proportion of women than social welfare and related workers, which is now an evenly mixed profession. Thus, in the broadest sense in this country women have made their greatest contribution in professions with functions arising from family roles. In social work we can best describe this contribution as one in which a sensitive awareness of individual worth is used to relieve and overcome human suffering; allied to this has been great skill in individualising broadly-based social services. Even in positions of seniority it may be that women rather than men are able to retain the attitudes upon which this contribution rests. The resistances to women in the impersonal professions have led to women trying to secure areas of work peculiarly their own, and in social work, because women have consistently had a tradition of a higher level of training than men, there has been an element of élitism. In almoning, psychiatric social work and child care women formed a spearhead for professional development and it is a great irony that in a profession so largely fought for over many lifetimes by women that there should be the prospect of long-term subjection to men, and the fact that principles carefully nursed may be in danger of disintegration from mechanical managerial and planning systems. Social work, because it is such a mixed profession, now has the possibility of a creative blending of the qualities brought by men and women. In the past these qualities have often been channelled into separate streams by social conventions. One of the greatest challenges facing social work is whether consciously some of these conventions can be broken down, leading to a new and vital fusion of male and female qualities in the service of those in need.

Notes

Introduction

1 Just one example is that of Margaret Mead's study, *Sex and Temperament in Three Primitive Societies*, George Routledge & Sons, 1935.
2 H. M. Bartlett, *Analysing Social Work Practice by Fields*, National Association of Social Workers, 1961, p. 11.
3 N. Timms, *Social Casework*, Routledge & Kegan Paul, 1964, p. 2.
4 Bartlett, op. cit., p. 9.
5 C. R. Attlee, *The Social Worker*, Library of Social Service, 1920, p. 15.
6 A. F. Young and E. T. Ashton, *British Social Work in the Nineteenth Century*, Routledge & Kegan Paul, 1956, p. 1.
7 Barbara N. Rodgers and Julia Dixon, *Portrait of Social Work*, Oxford University Press, 1960, p. 11.
8 Attlee, op. cit., p. 10.
9 Attlee, op. cit., pp. 221ff.
10 Related to the concept of role is that of 'adequate social functioning' or 'social competence'. For a full discussion see H. M. Bartlett, *The Common Base of Social Work Practice*, National Association of Social Workers, New York, 1970, pp. 84ff.

Chapter 1 Employment and education for women

1 Alva Myrdal and Viola Klein, *Women's Two Roles*, Routledge & Kegan Paul, 1956, p. 5.
2 Information from general report, 1871 census.
3 Including women employed as follows: civil servant; prison officer; municipal, parish or Union officer; missionary, scripture reader; nuns and Sisters of Charity, church and chapel officers; midwives; subordinate medical services; doctors and physicians.
4 Summary tables, 1891 Census, p. 11.
5 Asher Tropp, *The School Teachers: the growth of the teaching profession in England and Wales from 1800 to the present day*, Heinemann, London, 1959, p. 22. (The number of pupil-teacher certificates awarded rose from 3,850 in 1849 to 15,224 in 1859.)
6 C. L. White (*Women's Magazines 1693–1968*, Michael Joseph, 1970, p. 53) comments on the way in which some women's magazines in the mid-nineteenth century devoted increasing space to the problem of single women finding employment. Ladies' magazines (e.g. *Queen*) also began to carry articles about philanthropic enterprises.

7 B. Abel-Smith, *A History of the Nursing Profession*, Heinemann, 1961, p. 4.

8 Abel-Smith, op. cit., p. 10.

9 K. Woodrooffe, *From Charity to Social Work*, Routledge & Kegan Paul, 1962. See particularly Chapter 1 'In the Midst of Victorian Plenty'.

10 B. R. Parkes, 'Industrial Employment of Women. A Year's Experience in Women's Work', *National Association for the Promotion of Social Science Transactions*, 1860, pp. 811–19.

11 For a full account of the development of higher education for women see Josephine Kamm, *Hope Deferred*, Methuen, 1965.

12 The history of the council and Josephine Butler's part in it has been written by S. Lemoine, 'The North of England Council for Promoting the Higher Education of Women 1867–1875/6', M(Ed) thesis, Manchester, 1968.

13 J. C. Scott, 'Bradford Women in Organisation', MA thesis, University of Bradford, 1970.

14 Ibid., p. 14.

15 G. E. Maurice, *Life of Octavia Hill*, Macmillan, 1914, pp. 209–11.

16 J. Estlin Carpenter, *The Life and Work of Mary Carpenter*, Macmillan, 1881.

17 For example, Miss Mary McNichol Sharpley took the Moral Sciences Tripos at Cambridge, and immediately went to work at the Southwark Charity Organisation Society in 1894. Her outstanding qualities in the Charity Organisation Society led to her appointment in 1897 as lecturer to the Joint Committee on Social Education. In 1907 she became warden of the Women's University Settlement. Details from her obituary in the *Charity Organisation Quarterly*, July 1933, p. 98.

Chapter 2 Women as innovators in social work

1 C. S. Loch, 'The Confusion in Medical Charities', *Nineteenth Century*, August 1892, pp. 298–310.

2 Canon Barnett, 'Universities and the Poor', *Nineteenth Century*, February 1884, pp. 255–61.

3 A. F. Young and E. T. Ashton, *British Social Work in the Nineteenth Century*, Routledge & Kegan Paul, 1956, pp. 172ff.

4 D. Bochel, 'The Development of the Probation Service in England and Wales', MA(Econ) thesis, University of Manchester, 1963, pp. 31–2.

5 J. S. Heywood, *Children in Care*, Routledge & Kegan Paul, 1959. See Chapter 4, 'The Philanthropic Care of Children'.

6 R. Waugh, *The Life of Benjamin Waugh*, T. Fisher Unwin, 1913.

7 E. Moberly Bell, *Octavia Hill*, Constable, 1942. For insight into her ideas see her *Homes of the London Poor*, now reprinted in the Cass Library of Victorian Times, no. 6, 1970.

8 See the biography by J. Estlin Carpenter, *The Life and Work of Mary Carpenter*, Macmillan, 1881. For assessments of her contri-

bution to social work see J. S. Heywood, op. cit., pp. 40–7 and Josephine Kamm, *Rapiers and Battleaxes*, Allen & Unwin, 1966, pp. 31–5. For a more critical view see J. Carlebach, *Caring for Children in Trouble*, Routledge & Kegan Paul, 1970.

9 *Reformatory Schools for the Children of the Perishing and Dangerous Classes*, Bennet, 1851, and *Juvenile Delinquents, their Condition and Treatment*, Bennet, 1853.

10 See A. S. G. Butler, *Josephine Butler*, Faber & Faber, 1954, and E. Moberly Bell, *Josephine Butler*, *Flame of Fire*, Constable, 1952. For a brief assessment of her contribution see E. M. Turner, *Josephine Butler, her place in history*, Association for Moral and Social Hygiene, undated.

11 'Colour, Space, and Music for the People', *Nineteenth Century*, May 1884, pp. 741–52.

12 Mary Carpenter, 'Reformatories for Convicted Girls', *National Association for the Promotion of Social Science Transactions*, 1857, pp. 337ff.

Chapter 3　Women in social work organisations

1 Dated 26 November 1874. Manuscript in the Fawcett Library.

2 Fawcett Library. Manuscript letter.

3 For a description of 'ladies' and their characteristics, see Mary Stocks, *A Hundred Years of District Nursing*, Allen & Unwin, 1960.

4 E. M. Ross documents fully the contribution of women to the humanising of the Poor Law in 'Women and Poor Law Administration, 1857–1909', MA thesis, University of London, 1956.

5 Harriet McIlquahan, *Local Government in England and Wales*, 1896, pp. 1–2.

6 Ross, op. cit., pp. 235–6.

7 Original at the Fawcett Library.

8 *Work and Leisure*, vol. XIII, No. 6, June 1888, leader article.

9 Ross, op. cit., p. ii.

10 Abel-Smith, op. cit., p. 14.

11 Hilda Martindale, *Women Servants of the State, 1870–1938*, Allen & Unwin, 1938, p. 24.

12 *Transactions of the National Association for the Promotion of Social Science*, 1866, pp. 523, 590.

13 Martindale, op. cit., pp. 30–32. Octavia Hill was a friend of Mrs Nassau Senior and influenced Stansfield in making the appointment. See her letter to Mrs Nassau Senior in 1872, G. E. Maurice, *Life of Octavia Hill*, Macmillan, 1914, pp. 274–5, 277–8.

14 The Liberal government fell in 1874 and Disraeli's Tory government came into power. Stansfield had made Mrs Nassau Senior's appointment permanent before he left office, as a precaution against dismissal.

15 Martindale, op. cit., pp. 58–63.

16 See Martindale, op. cit., pp. 51–8.

17 As an indication of feeling shortly before the appointments, see
Work and Leisure, vol. XV, no. 10, October 1890.

We are glad that the need which exists for female inspectors of
factories has been brought to the notice of the Trades Union
Congress at Liverpool by Miss Wyte one of the Metropolitan
Labour delegates. During the last twenty years the employment
of women has extended itself so rapidly in all directions that
hundreds of workrooms entirely devoted to female labour, have
been opened in London alone, and to prevent overcrowding, and
to ensure adequate sanitary arrangements and ventilation, it is
imperatively necessary that the Factory Acts should be rigorously
enforced. We venture to urge upon the government the importance
of this question and as a beginning the Home Secretary would
be doing good service if he appointed experimentally, a Lady
Inspector for the Metropolis.

18 Countess of Aberdeen, ed., *International Congress of Women, 1899*,
vol. I, *Women in Professions*, Fisher & Unwin, 1900, pp. 96ff.
19 Ibid., p. 101.
20 M. P. Hall and I. V. Howes, *The Church in Social Work*, Ch. 1,
'Rescue and Reform', Routledge & Kegan Paul, 1965.
21 J. C. Scott, 'Bradford Women in Organisation', unpublished MA
thesis, University of Bradford, 1970.
22 Ibid., p. 177.
23 Hall and Howes, op. cit., p. 23.
24 Born 1836, daughter of a Cambridge mathematician.
25 *Manifesto of the Communist Party, 1872*, in K. Marx and F. Engels,
Selected Works, Foreign Languages Publishing House, Moscow,
1958, vol. 1, p. 41.
26 Loch in his article of 1892 (C. S. Loch, 'The Confusion in Medical
Charities', *Nineteenth Century*, August 1892, p. 304), had not
confined almonership to women:

For almonership in general charity a trained and experienced
person is wanted, a man or a woman of some insight, prompt
decision and firmness. This is a new field of work, but slowly
people are being trained for it; and the cost, which might be
met from other than hospital funds, would not be greater than
that of an enquiry officer. If such an aide be forthcoming, we
would connect him or her with one or more hospitals as the
need arises.

27 Miss H. Nussey, almoner at Westminster Hospital, had described
one of the reasons for the success of almoning that the 'social status
of those who attend is gradually becoming what it should be—that
of the respectable poor'. See H. G. Nussey, 'The Work of a Hospital
Almoner', *Charity Organisation Review*, no. 74, February 1903,
pp. 79–97.
28 First annual report, Hospital Almoners Council, 1907, p. 2.
29 Report by Miss Brummel, almoner, Royal Free Hospital, 11 May
1901, pp. 2, 3.

30 First annual report, Hospital Almoners Council, November 1907–December 1908.

31 Ibid.

32 Report, Hospital Almoners Council, 1909, p. 2.

33 Ibid., p. 4. Candidates for training had to be between the ages of twenty-five and thirty-two.

34 Annual report, Hospital Almoners Council, 1913–14, p. 3. By this time the Council Executive included; Miss H. Jex Blake, Lady Margaret Hall, Oxford; Miss G. Penrose, Somerville College, Oxford; Miss Tuke, Bedford College; Miss White, Alexandra College, Dublin.

35 Between 1907 and 1912, twenty-one almoners were trained by the Institute, the training lasting twelve to eighteen months. J. Snelling, *The Contribution of the Institute of Medical Social Work to Social Work Education*, Association of Social Work Teachers, 1970.

36 Annual report, Hospital Almoners Council, 1910–11, p. 2.

37 R. Lubove, *The Professional Altruist*, Harvard University Press, 1965, pp. 24–6.

38 Ibid., p. 30. For a detailed account of efforts of early hospital almoners see E. Moberly Bell, *The Story of Hospital Almoners*, Faber & Faber, 1961.

39 For an account of early developments see A. F. Young and C. T. Ashton, *British Social Work in the Nineteenth Century*, Routledge & Kegan Paul, 1956, pp. 172–80, and Cherry Morris, ed., *Social Casework in Great Britain*, Faber & Faber, 1955, pp. 132–4. F. V. Jarvis has recently written a short history of the probation service: *Advise, Assist and Befriend*, National Association of Probation Officers, 1972.

40 Report of the Church of England Temperance Society Council for the Diocese of Liverpool for the year 1884. Quoted H. H. Ayscough, *When Mercy Seasons Justice*, CETS, 1928.

41 From the Minute Book, National Association of Probation Officers.

42 Reported in the *Birmingham Post*, 5 February 1914.

43 Mrs E. Hutchinson, 'Women in the Police Courts', *The English Woman*, vol. 20, October 1913, pp. 25–30.

44 It is relevant to recall the efforts of the Charity Organisation Society, at the time of the Royal Commission on the Poor Laws, to get themselves established as a national service acting as agents for the state.

45 C. R. Attlee, *The Social Worker*, Library of Social Service, 1920, pp. 187ff.

46 Canon Barnett, 'Universities and the Poor', *Nineteenth Century*, February 1884, p. 253.

47 Ibid., p. 256.

48 Ibid., pp. 260–1.

49 Ibid., p. 258.

50 Mrs Barnett had stayed at Newnham, at Miss Clough's (principal) invitation and had talked about the work at Toynbee Hall.

Mrs S. A. Barnett, *Canon Barnett: His Life, Work, and Friends. By his Wife*, John Murray, 1921, p. 423.
51 Altogether it was estimated that there were forty-six settlements in England in the early twentieth century (ibid., p. 442).
52 Ibid., p. 422.
53 Ibid. Jane Addams in 1910 became President of the National Conference of Charities and Corrections and took social work to task for its lack of recognition of the relationship of poverty to modern industrialism. She was a strong participant in the movement for women's suffrage in America. See her two books, *Twenty Years at Hull House*, Macmillan, 1910, and *The Second Twenty Years at Hull House*, Macmillan, 1930.
54 Mrs S. A. Barnett, op. cit., p. 433.
55 Article on Birmingham Women's Settlement in the *Bournville Workers Magazine*, February 1910.
56 The Barnetts had first come to know Beatrice through her sister Kate Potter who had worked as a rent collector in St Jude's Parish 1875–83 (Mrs S. A. Barnett, op. cit., p. 106). The Barnetts 'empirical socialism' had a strong influence on her and confirmed her dislike of Charity Organisation Society methods.
57 Mary Stocks describes the beginning of Manchester University Settlement in 1895 in her *Fifty Years in Every Street*, Manchester University Press, 1945. In it she tells how the period 1902–9 represented a golden age with a great emphasis on cultural and educational work in the settlement.

Chapter 4   Women and social work education

1 J. R. Green, *Stray Studies in Pauperism in the East of London*, 1887; quoted in Helen Bosanquet, *Social Work in London, 1869–1912: a History of the Charity Organisation Society*, John Murray, 1914. The other one-tenth were extremely important. For instance, C. R. Attlee's mother was a church district visitor and responsible for his education until the age of nine (C. R. Attlee, *As it Happened*, Heinemann, 1954, pp. 4, 19).
2 The following account relies heavily on Marjorie Smith, *Professional Education for Social Work in Great Britain*, Allen & Unwin, 1965. It should be borne in mind that directions to visitors had been the concern of earlier workers such as Thomas Chalmers. See A. F. Young and E. T. Ashton, *British Social Work in the Nineteenth Century*, Routledge & Kegan Paul, 1956.
3 *Charity Organisation Society Review*, no. 73, New Series, January 1903, pp. 37–8.
4 Ibid., p. 54. Professor Foxglove commented: 'There was a wholesome prejudice against mixing up theoretical and practical teaching. It was imperative that the teaching of the university should be free from any suspicion of bias in controversial matters'.
5 Urwick was a strong supporter of the women's suffrage movement. See his *A Philosophy of Social Progress*, Methuen, 1920, pp. 154ff.

Mary Stocks tells how the Diploma in Social Studies students were known as 'Urwick's Harem' and were looked down on by the BSc(Econ) students at the London School of Economics (*My Commonplace Book*, Peter Davies, 1970).

6 Attlee, largely through the influence of Sidney Webb, was appointed lecturer and tutor under Professor Urwick in 1912. His work, 'apart from giving lectures on local government and other subjects, was tutoring students, mostly women—who were about to engage in some branch of social work' (C. R. Attlee, *As it Happened*).

7 Elizabeth Macadam, *The Social Servant in the Making*, Allen & Unwin, 1945, p. 23. See also Marjorie Smith, op. cit., p. 33. M. B. Simey gives a fuller account of the development of training in Liverpool and the relationship of the university, the settlement and the Central Relief Society in *Charitable Effort in Liverpool in the Nineteenth Century*, Liverpool University Press, 1951, pp. 134–6.

8 M. C. Matheson, 'Opportunities for Training for Personal Service', *Women Workers*, vol. 22, no. 3, December 1912, pp. 69–74.

9 Report of conference at Birmingham on 24 June 1910, *Birmingham Daily Post*, 26 June 1910.

10 Elizabeth Macadam, *The Equipment of the Social Worker*, Allen & Unwin, 1925, p. 36. Miss Macadam quoted information from a paper by J. St G. Heath, 'University Social Training Courses' given at a conference in 1918 at Oxford organised by the Association for the Education of Women in Oxford.

11 Ibid., p. 17: 'The carrying out of these new schemes was for the most part entrusted to those without special preparation, though here and there exceptional appointments were made of men and women who had shown themselves qualified by personality, ability and experience.'

12 For a full account of a manager of a Board School see M. Frere, 'The Charitable Work of a Local Manager in a Board School', *Charity Organisation Quarterly*, March 1903, pp. 120–34. Helen Bosanquet in Chapter 7 of her *Rich and Poor*, Macmillan, 1896, emphasises the importance of work on the School Board with truant and sick children.

13 See D'Arcy Cresswell, *Margaret McMillan, A Memoir*, Hutchinson, 1948, and A. Mansbridge, *Margaret McMillan, Prophet and Pioneer*, J. M. Dent & Sons, 1932.

14 By 1911 there were 970 Care Committees staffed by upwards of 6,000 helpers (report of a talk by Miss Matheson at the winter Charity Organisation Society Conference in London, 11 January 1911, *Birmingham Daily Post*, 12 January 1911).

15 In discussing his care committee work at Trafalgar Square School, Attlee comments 'In the local association of Care Committees we used to have great fights against the adherents of the Charity Organisation Society who believed in the Poor Law principles of deterrence' (*As it Happened*, p. 31).

16 See C. S. Loch, *Charity and Social Life*, Macmillan, 1910, p. 445,

for a summary of the Majority Report of the Royal Commission
on the Poor Law and advocacy of Public Assistance Committees
and a related system of Voluntary Aid Committees. Loch also had
some far-seeing comments on the training of volunteers.

Chapter 5 Women social workers, women's suffrage, and social reform

1 The influence of Spencer's organic sociology can be traced in many
  social movements of the time with its emphasis on gradual
  rather than revolutionary changes and its distrust of the effectiveness
  of forced change by government intervention.
2 As an indication of Octavia Hill's attitude to women it is helpful
  to consider her relationship with Ruskin and then read his
  discussion of the attributes of men and women in *Sesame and
  Lilies*, 1864 (Nelson & Sons edn, 1937, p. 80):

  . . . the woman's power is for rule, not for battle—and her
  intellect is not for invention or creation, but for sweet ordering,
  arrangement and decision. She sees the qualities of things, their
  claims, and their places. Her great function is Praise. She enters
  into no contest but infallibly adjudges the crown of contest.

3 Manuscript letter, Fawcett Library.
4 *On Liberty* was published in 1859. Basic arguments stated there
  were elaborated in *On the Subjection of Women* in 1869.
5 J. Butler (ed.), *Women's Work and Women's Culture*, Macmillan,
  1869, p. 36.
6 Ibid., p. 9.
7 29 December 1867. Extract from letter published in full in J. Estlin
  Carpenter, *The Life and Work of Mary Carpenter*, Macmillan, 1881,
  Appendix, pp. 493–5.
8 Undated manuscript letter, Fawcett Library.
9 Undated manuscript letter, Fawcett Library.
10 Undated manuscript letter, Fawcett Library.
11 Manuscript letter, 15 October 1868, Fawcett Library.
12 As late as 9 November 1892 she was writing to Sir George Newman
  about the repeal of the Contagious Diseases Acts in India, saying
  in spite of her illness that she hoped to write in a day or two and
  that 'I have much time for thought, and the present position of
  our own making in the world and its responsibilities occupies my
  thought greatly'. Manuscript letter, Fawcett Library.
13 On 19 October 1892 Josephine Butler expressed this wide concern
  when writing to the editor of the *Women's Herald* asking her to
  review her biography of her husband: 'Although I now have no
  home in England, I continue to read with great interest all that
  concerns women, and their progress, in England' (Fawcett
  manuscript).
14 Manuscript letter, Fawcett Library.
15 See M. Lonsdale, 'Platform Women', *Nineteenth Century*, March
  1884, pp. 414–15:

To rub off the bloom [of true womanhood], to blow away the woman, so soon, alas! get rid of that we appear hardly to be aware any longer of its existence, to banish good taste, the appreciation of what is refined and retiring and fitting in a woman's nature, and to do all this in the name of religion or philanthropy, is this to improve the world at large. . . . It will be objected that these are hard words, that they do not adequately describe many of the cultivated women who speak in public, and who are quiet and gentle in their own homes, and temperate even in their mental attitudes towards others. That such women exist I am well aware, but they are found now chiefly among the old fashioned leaders of what used to be called the 'blue-stockings', and they are fast giving way to the more pushing and exaggerated sort of women. These kindly ladies still get up, spectacled and scientific looking, and read papers at Social Science Congresses, or mildly address young women on abstruse and purely intellectual subjects, but they are not to be spoken of in the same breath with their more advanced sisters.

16 Sidney Webb, in a letter to Mrs Cavendish Bentink on 12 June 1912, maintained that he had always been a suffragist and that he had converted his wife. Manuscript at Fawcett Library.

17 See Mary Stocks, *Eleanor Rathbone*, Gollancz, 1949, for a full account of her life.

18 See Beatrice Webb, *My Apprenticeship*, Pelican edn, 1938, pp. 221ff., 'The World of Philanthropy'.

19 Extract from *Women's Employment*, 8 July 1908, cutting in Fawcett Library. For a picture of general progress in social welfare in Birmingham during this period see, R. Scott, *Elizabeth Cadbury*, Harrap, 1956.

20 Biographical details from *Edgbastonian*, July 1915, no. 490, pp. 483–8.

21 *Common Cause*, 16 February 1917. Copy at Fawcett Library.

22 Alice Crompton, Warden of Manchester University Settlement, was one such woman who eventually left the settlement for the suffrage cause. Mary Stocks details the close connections of many women suffrage workers with the settlement in Manchester before the First World War in *Fifty Years in Every Street*, Manchester University Press, 1945, pp. 34–5.

23 *International Congress of Women*, Fisher & Unwin, 1909, vol. I, pp. 32, 62. A further factor in the impetus given to entrance of women to the medical profession was the need for their services in India. It should be remembered that only in 1859 did Dr Elizabeth Blackwell become the first woman on the British Medical Register and in 1865 did Dr Elizabeth Anderson become the first woman to qualify as a doctor in Great Britain.

24 Ibid.

25 Ibid., p. 33.

26 Ibid., p. 45.

Chapter 6 Overview 1860–1914

1 In an article, 'Training for Social Work', in *Women's Employment*, 17 July 1908, Miss Matheson reinforces this:

> In these days when women are striving to attain a position of social and economic dependence, it is becoming more and more general for the growing generation to realise that one of the evils of life most to be dreaded is a middle-age without means . . . a possible need for economic independence and a certain need of human interests is offered by many of the professions now open to educated women, but it is hardly yet realised how increasingly it is offered by the ever widening field of social service.

2 Dr Blackwell had founded the New York Infirmary for Women and Children and in the 1850s had visited patients at home and hired another worker to train mothers in housekeeping and child care. R. Lubove draws attention to her influence in the eventual establishment of medical social work in the USA in *The Professional Altruist*, Harvard University Press, 1965, pp. 24ff.

3 Manuscript at Fawcett Library, dated 18 April (188–?).

4 *Philanthropy and the State or Social Politics*, P. S. King & Sons, 1908, p. 110. He was referring principally to the Poor Law.

5 *Manifesto of the Communist Party, 1872*, in K. Marx and F. Engels, *Selected Works*, Foreign Languages Publishing House, Moscow, 1958, vol. 1, pp. 50–1.

6 F. Engels, *Origins of Family*, *Private Property and the State*, in Marx and Engels, op. cit., vol. 2, pp. 232–3.

7 Ibid.

8 Ibid., p. 311.

9 Mill was less happy, by implication, with their philanthropic efforts: 'They [the Chinese] have succeeded beyond all hope in what the English philanthropists are so anxiously working at—in making a people all alike, all governing their thoughts and conduct by the same maxims and rules' (*On Liberty*, Everyman's Library, Dent & Sons, 1929, p. 129).

10 Random House, edition, 1934 (first published in 1899).

11 Ibid., pp. 334–5.

12 Ibid., p. 339.

13 Ibid.

14 Ibid., p. 341.

15 Ibid.

Chapter 7 The First World War

1 See also Gilbert Stone (ed.), *Women War Workers*, Harrap, 1917.

2 Annual report, Hospital Almoners Council, 1915–16, p. 3.

3 *Birmingham Post*, 27 November 1914.

4 The munitions work was also significant in the general battle for female emancipation in that in 1916 women munitions workers at Woolwich were awarded equal pay with men—i.e. 30*s*. a week

instead of 20*s*. See A. L. Bowley, *Prices and Wages in the United Kingdom, 1914–20*, Clarendon Press, 1921. Bowley analyses the flow of women into occupations formerly followed by men and boys only and the consequent difficulties in fixing rates of wages. The number of occupied women had increased from 5,966,000 in July 1914 to 7,311,000 in July 1918.

5 In 1916 the Birmingham Women's Settlement combined with the university to establish intensive courses of at least four weeks' duration and lecturers were to include Professors Ashley, Tillyard and Kirkaldy, Dr Beatrice Webb and Miss Matheson; Miss Matheson was to arrange the practical work. *Birmingham Post*, 8 September 1916.

6 See E. Macadam, *The Equipment of the Social Worker*, Allen & Unwin, 1925, pp. 36–7, for a full account of this development.

7 See chapter on 'Welfare Work' by Dorothea Proud in Stone, op. cit.

8 Ibid., p. 246.

9 *The Student Movement*, May 1916, pp. 167–9.

10 'Birmingham Women's Settlement', *Charity Organisation Review*, January 1915, pp. 24–30.

11 Annual report, Hospital Almoners Council, 1915–16, p. 4.

12 Ibid.

13 Annual report, Hospital Almoners Council, 1917, p. 2.

14 Address by Miss Brooks, secretary and warden of the London (Royal Free Hospital) School of Medicine for Women, at the Women's Institute on 21 October 1915. Reported in *The Times*, 22 October 1915.

15 Minutes of executive committee, 10 October 1918. In 1918 a survey by NAPO showed that the salaries of many female missionaries were £60–£80, and of male missionaries up to £100.

16 Minutes of annual general meeting.

17 The details are from J. E. Higson, *The Story of a Beginning. An Account of Pioneer Work for Moral Welfare*, SPCK, 1955.

18 Britain had been noticeable by its absence from the Congress of Criminal Anthropology 1899, the same year as Havelock Ellis's book *The Criminal* was published.

19 M. E. Rich, *A Belief in People*, Family Service Association of America, 1956, pp. 37, 41.

20 Quoted K. Woodrooffe, *From Charity to Social Work*, Routledge & Kegan Paul, 1962, p. 112, Chapter 5, pp. 37, 41, 101ff. ('Social Work Takes Stock'), describes in detail the controversy in the USA about the status of social work.

Chapter 8   Women's social position and career prospects 1918–39

1 Manuscript lodged with the Fawcett Library.

2 Evelyn Gates (ed.), *Women's Year Book 1923–4*, Women Publishers Ltd. This was the only edition of the year book to be published.

3 Ibid., p. 43.

4 Ibid.
5 Sibyl Clement Brown, 'Objects and Methods in Social Work', Lecture I, 1933, unpublished manuscript, p. 14.
6 R. Strachey, *Careers and Openings for Women*, Faber & Faber, 1935.
7 Ibid., p. 6.
8 Ibid., pp. 158–9.
9 Ibid., p. 183.
10 Strachey had commented about prospects in social work: 'Their [university women's] prospects are not materially different from other workers, and indeed, it may be said that none of them have any prospects strictly speaking.' Ibid., p. 182.
11 *Charity Organisation Review*, January 1915, pp. 29–30.
12 Barbara Wootton, *In a World I Never Made*, Allen & Unwin, 1967, p. 56.
13 Ibid., pp. 100–1.
14 For an understanding of the interplay of class, leisure and welfare see the Report of the Royal Commission on Justices of the Peace, Cmd 7463, 1948. At that time there were 3,700 women Justices, 68 per cent of whom had no gainful occupation. 'It must of course be recognised that many of those without gainful occupation are heavily occupied, without reward, in activities which are of service to the state' (ibid., p. 7).

Chapter 9 Women in social work organisations 1918–39

1 See J. C. Pringle, *Social Work of the London Churches*, Oxford University Press, 1937, for insight into his views.
2 Sibyl Clement Brown, 'Social Work in Action 1925–34', unpublished manuscript, 1934.
3 Sibyl Clement Brown, Lecture I, 'Objects and Methods in Social Work', unpublished manuscript, 1933, p. 9. Miss Brown adds the comment: 'Our training for this skill [social work] has, as we know in England been considered a problem for practical apprenticeship rather than specific knowledge and directed analysis.'
4 This account is based on annual reports of the Institute of Hospital Almoners; J. Snelling, *The Contribution of the Institute of Medical Social Workers to Education for Social Work*, Association of Social Work Teachers, 1970; I. F. Beck, *The Almoner*, Council of the Institute of Almoners, 1948.
5 Beck, op. cit., p. 62. This is for almoners working in this country. The 1938 AHA Annual Report mentions that there are now 370 almoners working in this country and about 200 students in training. Miss Snelling gave membership of the association as 46 in 1920 and 600 in 1940.
6 In April 1919 the council had been invited to appoint a representative to serve on the Working Council of the Ministry of Health.
7 Annual report, Institute of Hospital Almoners, 1920.
8 Snelling, op. cit.

9 Annual report, Institute of Hospital Almoners, 1923. In 1923 the trustees of a fund placed £280 at the disposal of the institute for training scholarships. The money was allocated to two scholarships (£100 for two years, £40 for two years) and after advertisement these were awarded 'after careful selection from a large number of applicants'.

10 The Rev. Pringle was on the council 1922–37, and vice-chairman 1928–37.

11 This was the year in which the institute tried unsuccessfully to persuade deans of medical schools that almoners should lecture to medical students. Snelling, op. cit.

12 Annual report, Institute of Hospital Almoners, 1929.

13 Ibid., p. 11.

14 E. M. Batten, *The Principles and Methods of Training Social Workers with Special Reference to Hospital Almoners*, Hospital Almoners Association, 1939.

15 Annual report, Institute of Hospital Almoners, 1926.

16 Annual report, Institute of Hospital Almoners, 1932.

17 The almoners did have some confirmed advocates for their cause in the municipal sphere. In 1935 Dr Tate, MOH for Middlesex, spoke at the institute's annual general meeting and looked forward to the possibility of a great national health service in the future in which the mark of the almoner would have its appointed place (annual report, Institute of Hospital Almoners, 1936). The same annual report referred to the fact that appointments in local authority hospitals were 'in many cases still in the experimental stage'.

18 Annual report, Institute of Hospital Almoners, 1930.

19 Annual report, Institute of Hospital Almoners, 1936: 'Not only have new posts to be filled each year but vacancies frequently occur in Almoner's departments which are already established'.

20 Annual report, Institute of Hospital Almoners, 1937.

21 Annual report, Institute of Hospital Almoners, 1933.

22 *Report of the Departmental Committee on the Training, Appointment and Payment of Probation Officers*, Cmd. 1601, HMSO, 1922.

23 Elizabeth Macadam, *The Equipment of the Social Worker*, Allen & Unwin, 1925, pp. 139–40.

24 This was a very slow development. Even at the end of the Second World War there were only thirty-five probation officers in the Metropolitan Juvenile Courts (of whom over half were women) appointed directly by the Home Office (E. Younghusband, *Report on the Employment and Training of Social Workers*, T. A. Constable, 1947, p. 87).

25 *Report of the Departmental Committee on the Social Services in Courts of Summary Jurisdiction*, Cmd. 5122, HMSO, 1936.

26 The conference was reported in the *Journal of the Association of Probation Officers*, 1919, pp. 193–5.

27 *Journal of the National Association of Probation Officers*, No. 24, February 1926, p. 561. Nevertheless, in 1929, 468 of the country's

1,028 petty sessional divisions were without the services of a woman officer (D. Bochel, 'The Development of the Probation Service in England and Wales', MA(Econ) thesis, University of Manchester, 1963, p. 221).

28 Ibid., p. 92.

29 1936, Departmental Committee, op. cit.

30 For a recent account of some of these factors, see I. Menzies, *The Functioning of Social Systems as a Defence against Anxiety,* Tavistock Institute, 1967.

31 Some people might suggest that the involvement of women doctors in women's hospitals goes against the above argument, but this can be seen more in terms of gaining a medical opening for female medical practice which would be acceptable to men.

32 For detailed accounts of the general development of psychiatric social work, see N. Timms, *Psychiatric Social Work in Great Britain 1939–62,* Routledge & Kegan Paul, 1964, and Noel Hunybun's article 'Notes on the Development of Psychiatric Social Work in England' in C. Morris (ed.), *Social Casework in Great Britain,* Faber & Faber, 2nd ed. 1955, pp. 104ff. The Departmental Committee on Maladjusted Children (1955) also summarises general developments for the end of last century.

33 In the USA psychiatric social work owed its inception to doctors and others concerned with social aspects of medicine. The first scheme of apprenticeship under Mary Jarret was started at the Boston Psychopathic Hospital and the title 'psychiatric social worker' was first used at this hospital.

34 Snelling, op. cit., provides a valuable account of the relation of almoning to the establishment of psychiatric social work in this country.

35 In addition to the sources already mentioned I have drawn on additional material from an undated, duplicated account by Noel Hunybun, *Early History of the Child Guidance Movement in England.* M. Ashdown and S. Clement Brown also give an account in *Social Service and Mental Health,* Routledge & Kegan Paul, 1953.

36 Established in 1926 for the treatment of nervous adult patients. Whilst the Commonwealth Fund negotiations were in hand the Jewish Health Organisation of Great Britain had established a clinic in 1927.

37 For an account of the whole activities of the Commonwealth Fund see *The Commonwealth Fund: Historical Sketch 1918–1962,* The Commonwealth Fund, 1963. For an assessment of the importance of the fund's role in aiding the mental health movement see Nina Ridenour, *Mental Health in the United States: A Fifty Years History,* Harvard University Press, 1961.

38 Unless otherwise mentioned this section is based on Lubove, *The Professional Altruist,* Harvard University Press, 1965, pp. 90ff.

39 Lynde was secretary of the Associated Charities in Cleveland, and he expressed his views in a paper 'Community Agencies and the

K

Clinic' to the National Conference of Social Work in 1925
(Proceedings, pp. 418–21). Quoted in Lubove, op. cit., p. 95.

40 Olive Crosse, 'American Experiences', *Charity Organisation
Quarterly*, January 1930. In the October issue of the same journal
she published an article, 'A Study in Casework'.

41 Elizabeth Macadam had commented five years earlier (op. cit.,
pp. 33ff.) that:

> what may be vaguely described as practical subjects do not
> appear conspicuously in the published syllabus of most
> [British] Schools. Such subjects as 'Casework, Family Work
> and Community Organisation' which occupy an important part
> of the timetable of every American School, do not appear at all.

42 Report presented to the Child Guidance Council by the signatories
who visited the USA to enquire into the work of the child guidance
clinics, 1928.

43 'Child Guidance in America', London County Council, 1929.

44 Timms (op. cit.), in comparing the syllabuses of the London
School of Economics courses of 1932–3 and 1959–60, stresses the
absence of teaching on research method and the lack of
appreciation of the place of research in social work.

45 The field of psychiatry has generally been dominated by men
and women psychiatrists have tended to specialise in children's
problems, for example, the classic case of Sigmund Freud and his
daughter Anna Freud. See the discussion of Freud's Victorian
attitude to women by D. Riesman in *Selected Essays from
Individualism Reconsidered*, Doubleday Anchor, 1954, pp. 183–4.
Freud was not anxious to have women competitors and Riesman
comments:

> Freud seems to have coped with the inconsistency, from his
> viewpoint, of his own daughter's entry upon analytic work by
> assigning to women analysts the field of child analysis—very
> much as women in industrial management today are assigned the
> job of handling the morale problems, not of men and women,
> but of women only.

46 Elizabeth Macadam, *The New Philanthropy*, Allen & Unwin, 1934,
p. 176. She estimated that there were about 900 care committees,
with over 5,000 voluntary visitors and over 100 salaried workers.
Other large cities such as Birmingham, Manchester, Liverpool
and Bristol had similar services.

47 Ibid., p. 175. Compare this with the greater weight of male
mental nurses than male general nurses because of the emphasis
on control and possible physical violence with mental illness.

48 Noel Hunybun, 'Notes on the Development of Psychiatric Social
Work in England', op. cit. The concentration on delinquency was
held in check to some extent by the pattern of referrals. School
care committee workers were present at case conferences and
referred children from the general school population.

49 Dame Evelyn Fox was honorary secretary of the Central Association for Mental Welfare.
50 Association of Psychiatric Social Workers, 1932.
51 Ibid., p. 3.
52 Ibid., p. 13. In fairness, who did understand the right solution to our economic problems?
53 Information from the Society of Women Housing Managers and J. Rowles (ed.), *Housing Management*, Pitman, 1959 (Chapter 1, 'Historical Background', by H. H. Alford).
54 Cmnd. 3703, HMSO, 1968, para 413.
55 Eighth annual report, Josephine Butler Memorial House, 1928.
56 For the long-term effects of difficult finances and ageing buildings see the Memorandum of the British Association of Residential Settlements, pp. 121–34 in Lord Beveridge and A. D. Wells (eds), *The Evidence for Voluntary Action*, Allen & Unwin, 1949.
57 For a detailed account of this period see Mary Stocks, *Fifty Years in Every Street*, Manchester University Press, 1945, and *Manchester University Settlement Diamond Jubilee Brochure*, 1955.
58 Lady Margaret Hall Settlement, *Social Services in North Lambeth and Kensington*, Oxford University Press, 1939.
59 Miss Myra Curtis was one of the women who had entered the administrative class by this arrangement, and was in 1939 one of the three women of assistant secretary rank or above (H. K. Kelsall, *Higher Civil Servants in Britain*, Routledge & Kegan Paul, 1955, p. 175).
60 In 1938 twenty-two women were in charge of districts. Hilda Martindale, *Women Servants of the State 1870–1938*, Allen & Unwin, 1938, p. 136.
61 Dame Lilian Barker—see her biography, *The Better Fight*, by E. Gore, Geoffrey Bles, 1965. After a materially poor upbringing Lilian Barker became a teacher. Then she cared for her mother for seven years. When her mother died she undertook pioneer work with evening classes and became responsible in 1916 for the women and girls at Woolwich Arsenal. In 1923 she became governor of the girls' Borstal at Aylesbury.
62 Civil Service List, 1949.

Chapter 10 Overview 1918–39

1 See Timms, *Psychiatric Social Work in Great Britain, 1939–62*, Routledge & Kegan Paul, 1964, pp. 83ff., who explains this concentration by relating it to the concentration of training facilities and better opportunities in the London area. Elizabeth Macadam (*The Equipment of the Social Worker*, Allen & Unwin, 1925, p. 122), noted that of seventy-four almoners in Great Britain, the majority were to be found in London.
2 A. Salomon, *Education for Social Work*, Verlag fur Recht und Gesellschaft A. G., Zurich, 1937, p. 38:

One of the outstanding characteristics of these schools [British social work courses] and one of their objects . . . defined by the joint university council is that they intend to prepare for voluntary work as well as for salaried posts and it is very striking that most of the programmes of British Schools name voluntary work before professional work as an object of the social work training.

3 NCSS June 1939. The committee had been established in December 1937.

4 Ibid., para. 7, p. 6.

5 Miss Clement Brown delivered a lecture (the second of three) at the University of Birmingham Social Study Department in March 1933, titled 'Research into the cause of Individual Maladjustments and its application to Social Casework'. In the paper (unpublished) ideas of multicausality, and the need for a scientific approach were emphasised.

6 'The Difficulties Encountered in Recruiting and Training Voluntary and Professional Workers in a Social Case Agency', *Charity Organisation Quarterly*, January 1929, pp. 21–31.

7 In the mid-1930s most child guidance clinics were voluntary, as was the hospital setting of almoners. Therefore it was understandable that Miss Milnes should take this line of thought.

8 M. Cosens and Sibyl Clement Brown, *Developments in Psychiatric Social Work*, Association of Psychiatric Social Workers, 1936, pt 2, p. 14: 'The tendency has been to present an eclectic point of view in the academic courses, and to introduce varied interpretation more into the clinical teaching.'

9 Sibyl Clement Brown, *Social Casework in Action, 1924–34*, unpublished, 1934.

10 *Third International Conference on Social Work*, Le Play Press, 1936, Paper on 'Material Welfare', pp. 425–33.

11 *Third International Conference on Social Work*, op. cit., pp. 102–11.

12 Ferens Rajnis, 'The Contribution of Social Casework to other Fields of Social Endeavour', reprinted in *Charity Organisation Quarterly*, 1929, pp. 114–21.

13 See F. G. Waldron, 'The Association of Social Workers', *Case Conference*, vol. 5, no. 7, January 1959, pp. 183–6. Miss Sayles was a member of the Women Public Health Officers Association.

14 N. Timms, *Social Casework*, Routledge & Kegan Paul, 1964, pp. 160ff.

15 The committee membership contrasted with the Council of the British Federation of Social Workers in that there were far more men involved. The full membership was: Dr H. A. Moss (chairman), Mr B. G. Astbury, Mr A. Barratt Brown, Miss E. Black, Miss C. U. Butler, Miss H. E. Clinkard, Sir Wyndham Deedes, Miss Grace Drysdale, Mr W. M. G. Eagar, Miss E. U. Eckhard, Mr H. Justin Evans, Miss M. L. Harford, Mr I. M. Horobin, Mr W. M. Noble, Mr H. Norman, Mrs J. L. Stocks, Mr Z. F. Willins: Secretary, Mr W. D. Hogarth.

16 *Third International Conference on Social Work*, op. cit., 'Current Trends in Social Adjustment through Individualised Treatment', pp. 475–96.
17 Sibyl Clement Brown, 'Looking Backwards: Reminiscences, 1922–1946', *British Journal of Psychiatric Social Work*, vol. 10, no. 4, 1970, pp. 161–9.
18 Sibyl Clement Brown, 'Family Casework and Mental Health', *Charity Organisation Society Review*, vol. 13, no. 1, January 1939, p. 40.
19 Although there was an emphasis on the new insights which psychological knowledge could bring to social work, this did not exclude a concern with social reform. For a discussion of the role of the British Federation of Social Workers during the inter-war period and its concern with social policy see R. Lees, 'Social Work, 1925–50: the Case for a Reappraisal', *British Journal of Social Work*, vol. 1, no. 4, 1971, pp. 371–9.
20 Compare the discussions within the Charity Organisation Society, almoning, and probation about the social worker's functions in relation to material and financial problems.

Chapter 11 The Second World War

1 As examples of the onset of war preventing developments, an abortive Criminal Justice Bill was under consideration in 1939 and inter-departmental meetings had taken place to look at the fragmentation of children's services; inevitably in all forms of residential care there were cutbacks in buildings and maintenance.
2 R. M. Titmuss, *History of the Second World War. Problems of Social Policy*, HMSO, 1950.
3 Ibid., pp. 385–6. The Ministry of Health also encouraged the appointment of social workers in local authorities to deal with welfare problems arising from evacuation, and seventy were employed by the end of the war.
4 Annual report, Institute of Hospital Almoners, 1939. A further circular in December 1940 emphasised the importance of social welfare and after-care work that almoners could do and made financial help available for the establishment of new almoning departments.
5 Annual report, Institute of Hospital Almoners, 1940.
6 Annual report, Institute of Hospital Almoners, 1945.
7 Annual report, Institute of Hospital Almoners, 1942: 'In these cases the mass of financial returns statistics and the work of collecting vouchers for payment overwhelms the work of the department, so that the careful social work needed for many patients is impossible.' See H. Rees, *A Survey made from May to December 1941*, Hospital Almoners Association, 1941.
8 Annual report, Institute of Hospital Almoners, 1942.
9 Annual report, Institute of Hospital Almoners, 1943. At this time some almoners were also working in local authority VD clinics.

10 Annual report, Institute of Hospital Almoners, 1945.
11 See J. Snelling, *The Contribution of the Institute of Medical Social Workers to Education for Social Work*, Association of Social Work Teachers, 1970, for further comments on the union.
12 N. Timms, *Psychiatric Social Work in Great Britain*, Routledge & Kegan Paul, 1964, p. 82. In 1940 over 50 per cent of psychiatric social workers were working within a thirty-mile radius of Charing Cross.
13 Ibid., p. 120.
14 Sibyl Clement Brown, 'An Address to the Association of Psychiatric Social Workers', Burlington House, unpublished, 1942, p. 2.
15 Aubrey Lewis, 'An Address to the Association of Psychiatric Social Workers', Burlington House, unpublished, 1942, p. 2.
16 Sibyl Clement Brown, 'Looking Backwards: Reminiscences, 1922–1946', *British Journal of Psychiatric Social Work*, vol. 10, no. 4, Autumn 1970, p. 167.
17 Sibyl Clement Brown, 'An Address to the Association of Psychiatric Social Workers', op. cit., p. 4.
18 Criminal Justice Bill, 1938. Cl. 2(1) (a), quoted D. Bochel, *The Development of the Probation Service in England and Wales*, MA(Econ) thesis, University of Manchester, 1963, p. 328.
19 *Probation*, vol. 2, no. 7, January 1937, p. 99, quoted D. Bochel, op. cit., p. 328.
20 Home Office circular, 31 August 1939, quoted D. Bochel, op. cit., p. 341.
21 *Probation*, vol. 3, no. 15, August 1941, p. 205.
22 Ibid., p. 213.
23 Ibid., p. 211.
24 Ibid., p. 212.
25 There was much concern lest the education service would eventually see delinquency, prevention, and all aspects of youth work as its province.
26 *Journal of The National Association of Probation Officers*, August 1941, p. 208. Home Office Circular 834,907/1, 4/7/1941.
27 'Social Changes Due to the War and their Significance', report of conference, Caxton Hall, Westminster; the British Federation of Social Workers, 1942, p. 1. The conference was to be preceded by discussion groups of BFSW workers. Similar conferences of social workers were held in 1945 at Nuffield College, Oxford, to consider post-war social work.
28 Ibid., p. 34.
29 Ibid., p. 35.
30 Ibid., p. 37.
31 Ibid., p. 39.
32 Ibid., p. 57.
33 Ibid., p. 45.
34 Ibid., p. 46.
35 Ibid., p. 55. This dichotomy, often discussed, always seems

curious in that we have seen that in much voluntary work there
was a large element of administration.

36 Ibid., p. 59.

37 Ibid., p. 58.

38 Ibid., p. 60.

39 This patronage has always fallen short of adequately financing
voluntary organisations to ensure national standards of
extensiveness and quality in provision.

40 Titmuss, *History of the Second World War. Problems of Social
Policy*, op. cit., pp. 106, 333.

41 See chapter 11 in A. F. C. Bourdillon (ed.), *Voluntary Social
Services*, Methuen, 1945, pp. 194–205.

42 Ibid., p. 190.

43 K. Hardwick, 'Regulations 33B and the Moral Welfare Worker',
Quarterly Leaflet of the Church of England Moral Welfare Council,
October 1946, pp. 6–16.

44 Titmuss (*History of the Second World War. Problems of Social
Policy*, op. cit.), recounts how for pregnant mothers, billeting
households received the lowest billeting allowance of all.

45 *Whose Children?*, London, 1945.

46 It was not until 1945 that the *Report on the Boarding Out of Dennis
and Terence O'Neill* was published (Cmnd 6636, HMSO). Thus
the pressure for a thorough review of the care of deprived children
was already firmly established.

47 *Report of the Care of Children Committee*, Cmd 6922, HMSO, 1946.
The committee was appointed on 8 March 1945.

48 *Quarterly Leaflet of the Church of England Moral Welfare Council*,
March 1942, pp. 3–6.

49 Attlee, a quarter of a century earlier, had made this analysis (*The
Social Worker*, Library of Social Service, 1920, pp. 154–5):

> There are a great many cases of sweated social workers today. A
> local authority will think nothing of asking for a highly
> qualified lady, very likely with a university education, at a wage
> that is barely if at all sufficient to support life. . . . I think the
> real reason [for low wages] is that the desire to work for something
> greater and more absorbing than private profit has created a
> big supply of social workers, and that this desire for social
> service is deliberately or unconsciously exploited against the
> interests of the social workers and also of the work. . . . Social
> workers are entitled to as much pleasure as anyone else.

Chapter 12   The demographic background after 1945

1 D. C. Marsh, *The Changing Social Structure of England and Wales,
1871–1961*, Routledge & Kegan Paul, 1965, p. 155. Similar trends
continued 1961–71. More detailed information about demographic
changes, based on the 1966 Sample Census and provisional data
from the 1971 Census is given in *Social Trends No. 3*, HMSO, 1972.

2 *1961 Census Occupational Tables*, Table 1, p. 6.
3 W. E. Cavenagh, *Four Decades of Students in Social Work*, University of Birmingham, 1950, p. 5.
4 G. Routh, *Occupation and Pay in Great Britain, 1906–60*, Cambridge University Press, 1965, p. 17.
5 The classification of occupations used in the 1951 Census includes the following occupations under the heading Social Welfare and Related Workers: almoner (hospital, etc.), appeals organiser (London Police Court Mission), assistant social science secretaries, attendance officer, authorised officer (mental welfare), chief inspector (RSPCA), club leader, community centre warden, education authority school visitor, employment executive officer, home visitor, inspector (Children's Department, Home Office), inspector (NSPCC or RSPCA), inspector of boarded-out children, moral welfare officer, play centre worker, port welfare worker, probation officer, psychiatric social worker, regional officer (RSPCA), rehabilitation officer, road safety organiser, RSPCA officer, school attendance officer, school officer, secretary (Boys' Brigade, social club, YMCA, YWCA), settlement worker (educational residential settlement), social science secretary, superintendent inspector, superintendent of attendance officers, superintendent (RSPCA), temperance lecturer, visiting officer (Poor Law), visitor (Children's Act), visitor under boarded-out order, warden (educational residential community centre), warden (settlement), welfare officer (industry and commerce—not qualified), welfare organiser, youth leader.
6 Department of Education and Science, *Student Numbers in Higher Education in England and Wales*, Education Planning Paper No. 2, HMSO, 1970, Table 1, p. 11.
7 University Grants Committee, HMSO, 1963.
8 University Grants Committee, *The First Employment of University Graduates 1968–9*, HMSO, 1970, Tables 1 and 3.
9 It should be remembered that because there has been a chronic shortage of places on professional social work courses for graduates, increasingly during the post-war period many graduates have had to wait one to three years before obtaining professional training. This led to the growth of graduate trainee schemes in children's departments in the 1960s.
10 In the four year period 1964–5 to 1968–9 the number of social studies graduates more than doubled, from 6,078 to 12,319.

Chapter 13   Social work under the microscope 1945–51

1 Eileen Younghusband, *Report on the Employment and Training of Social Workers*, T. & A. Constable, 1947; Eileen Younghusband, *Social Work in Britain*, T. & A. Constable, 1951.
2 T. S. Simey, *Salaries and Conditions of Work of Social Workers*, National Council of Social Service, 1947.

3 *Interim Report of the Care of Children Committee*, Cmd 6760, HMSO, 1946.

4 Appendix 1, 'Training in Child Care', in *Report of the Care of Children Committee* (Curtis Report), Cmd 6922, HMSO, September 1946.

5 For a full account of the development of the child care service see J. S. Heywood, *Children in Care*, Routledge & Kegan Paul, 1965.

6 Curtis Report, op. cit., p. 146, para. 443. Her desirable qualities were enumerated on p. 148, para. 446:

> The Children's Officer should in our view be highly qualified academically, if possible a graduate who also has a social science diploma. She should not be under thirty at the time of appointment and should have had some experience of work with children. She should have marked administrative capacity and be able to grasp local government procedures and to work easily with local government committees. Her essential qualities should however be on the personal side. She should be genial and friendly in manner and able to set both children and adults at their ease. She should have a strong interest in the welfare of children and enough faith and enthusiasm to be ready to try methods new and old of compensating by care and affection those who have had a bad start in life. She should have very high standards of physical and moral welfare, but should be flexible enough in temperament to avoid a sterile institutional correctness.

7 Much of the discussion in the Curtis Report trying to distinguish the function of the proposed department from that of education or health—even down to the detail of arguing the case that a health visiting certificate was not a sufficient qualification for a boarding-out visitor—appears again in the Seebohm Report in the discussions favouring the establishment of a new department.

8 Curtis Report, op. cit., p. 117: 'They were usually women of some practical ability between 25 and fifty years of age, familiar with local conditions but often lacking the imagination and resourcefulness of the trained worker'.

9 Ibid., p. 116.

10 Eileen Younghusband, *Social Work in Britain*, op. cit., p. 25.

11 Eileen Younghusband, *Report on the Employment and Training of Social Workers*, op. cit., p. 9.

12 Eileen Younghusband's comparison is slightly misleading, as doctors can earn high salaries whilst remaining in practice.

13 *1951 Census England and Wales. Industry Tables*, Table 7. The overall disadvantages of women in local government service were illustrated by the fact that in October 1948 a sample of employer's salaries showed 11·2 per cent of the men and 1·1 per cent of the women were receiving salaries of £635–£1,000, i.e. were in the four highest grades of the APT division (*Survey of Local Government Service 1950*, quoted Eileen Younghusband, *Social Work in Britain*, op. cit., p. 176). She commented (p. 175), 'It is rare to find a

K*

woman in the higher ranks of a local authority and as the vast
majority of social workers are women this imposes a further
handicap upon them.' Whilst we may disagree with the assessment
of the extent of women social workers, the handicap was real.

14 Professor Simey and B. E. Astbury, general secretary of the FWA,
were members of the NCSS/BFSW committee and the Carnegie Trust
committee.

15 W. E. Cavenagh, *Four Decades of Students in Social Work*,
University of Birmingham, 1950, had found that women social
studies students qualifying in the decade 1940–9, with an average
age of 32·5 years, were earning an average salary of £409, which
was roughly comparable to a two-year-trained woman teacher
(pp. 46–7).

16 *1961 Census Occupational Tables*, Table 1, p. 6.

17 Eileen Younghusband, *Report of the Employment and Training of
Social Workers*, op. cit., pp. 63–72. A detailed account of the
basis of relationship between the Chicago School of Social Work
and the University of Chicago was given. For a detailed account
of the development of an American school of social work, see
Elizabeth G. Meier, *A History of the New York School of Social
Work*, Columbia University Press, 1954.

18 Eileen Younghusband, *Social Work in Britain*, op. cit., p. 155.

19 *Report of the Committee on the Provision for Social and Economic
Research*, 1946, p. 8: quoted Eileen Younghusband, *Social Work
in Britain*, op. cit., p. 176.

20 For an analysis of these changes, and the decline of the old social
science diploma or certificate, see chapters 1 and 2 in Kathleen Jones,
The Teaching of Social Studies in British Universities, Occasional
Paper in Social Administration No. 12, Codicote Press, 1964.

21 E. Robertson, *Welfare in Trust. A History of the Carnegie United
Kingdom Trust 1913–63*, Carnegie United Kingdom Trust, 1964,
pp. 200–3.

22 The staff of the institute had increased in 1951 to a director of studies
and three full-time tutors.

23 Report of the Committee on Medical Auxiliaries, 1951.

24 Hospital almoners, psychiatric social workers and family discussion
bureau workers could maintain and improve standards because there
was no pressure on them (as in child care) to turn out enough
workers to do all the work that an Act of Parliament required to
be done (e.g. Children Act 1948).

25 Annual report, Institute of Hospital Almoners, 1948, p. 1.

26 See K. McDougall, 'The External Ambivalence', *Journal of Psychiatric
Social Work*, vol. 10, no. 2, 1969, p. 90.

Chapter 14 Two decades of training 1951–71

1 Kathleen Jones, *The Teaching of Social Studies in British
Universities*, Occasional Paper in Social Administration No. 12,
Codicote Press, 1964.

2 For a detailed marital status breakdown, see Barbara N. Rodgers, *The Careers of Social Studies Students,* Occasional Paper in Social Administration, No. 11, Codicote Press, 1964.

3 Ibid., pp. 24ff.

4 See N. Timms, *Psychiatric Social Work in Great Britain 1939–62,* Routledge & Kegan Paul, 1964, for a discussion of the contribution which psychiatric social workers made to research publications and teachings.

5 In chronological order the major reports were: *Report of the Committees on Medical Auxiliaries* (Cope Committee), HMSO, 1951; *Report of the Committee on Social Workers in the Mental Health Services* (Mackintosh Committee), HMSO, 1951; *Report of the Committee on Maladjusted Children,* HMSO, 1955; *Report of the Working Party on Social Workers in the Local Authority Health and Welfare Fields* (Younghusband Report), HMSO, 1959; *Report of the Committee on Children and Young Persons,* HMSO, 1960; *Report of the Departmental Committee on the Probation Service,* HMSO (Morison Report), 1962; *Report of the Committee on Allied and Personal Social Services* (Seebohm Report), HMSO, 1968; *Caring for People: Staffing Residential Homes* (Williams Report), NCSS, Allen & Unwin, 1967. A review of the whole field of social work training, was made by Barbara N. Rodgers and Julia Dixon in *Portrait of Social Work,* Oxford University Press, 1960, which looked at the situation in 1957. In addition, a further review completed in 1964 was sponsored by the NCSS and published in 1966, *A Survey of Manpower Demand Forecasts for the Social Services,* K. Gales and R. C. Wright, NCSS. The Seebohm Report reviewed the whole pattern of training in 1968.

6 The essential strategy for a differential training programme for social work was already clearly stated by Eileen Younghusband in 1951. She outlined the need for the following types of course (*Social Work in Britain,* T. A. Constable, 1951, p. 174):

(*a*) a Research Institute in Applied Social Studies which should also train professional social workers;

(*b*) one or two other post-graduate courses in applied social studies;

(*c*) lengthened and improved social science certificate or diploma courses, designed to correlate theory and practice and to break down the alarming increase in specialised trainings;

(*d*) shorter full-time courses of a rather lower academic standard in institutions related to universities in the same manner as teacher training colleges;

(*e*) part-time and in-service training courses planned to give effective training on the job.

7 Younghusband Report, op. cit., para. 897, p. 259:

We are convinced that it could not be done effectively in a shorter period than in the two years full time (or its equivalent) which we recommend. Indeed this may be regarded by many as too short when it is remembered that, to refer to comparable fields, the two year teacher training is to be lengthened to three years, and that the training of a health visitor takes four years and of an occupational therapist three years.

8　See Timms, *Psychiatric Social Work in Great Britain*, op. cit., p. 49.

9　Barbara N. Rodgers, 'New Portrait of Social Work', *Social and Economic Administration*, vol. 4, no. 3, July 1970.

10　Home Office, *Sixth Report on the Work of the Children's Department*, HMSO, 1951, p. 34.

11　In 1957, 25 per cent of 1,037 child care officers were professionally trained and a further 41 per cent had a social science qualification (Association of Children's Officers Bulletin No. 65, August 1957, quoted by P. Boss, *Exploration into Child Care*, Routledge & Kegan Paul, 1971, p. 99).

12　Home Office, *Report on the Work of the Children's Department, 1964–6*, HMSO, 1967, p. 18.

13　*Children's Act 1948, Summary of Returns of Child Care Staff at 31 March 1970*, DHSS, 1971, p. 4.

14　This anomaly was removed in October 1973 when the Department of Health and Social Security relinquished financial responsibility for non-graduate students. After the Local Authority Social Services Act 1970 the DHSS had assumed responsibility for courses and students originally financed by the Home Office.

15　For the changing situation in one two-year child care course see R. Walton and E. Barber, 'Mature Students on a Child Care Course', *Case Conference*, vol. 15, no. 4, August 1968.

16　Eileen Younghusband's contribution is discussed in Chapter 13 above.

17　Jean S. Heywood, *An Introduction to Teaching Casework Skills*, Routledge & Kegan Paul, 1964. Since then three other texts on student supervision have appeared, all written by women: Priscilla Young, Dorothy Pettes, Bessie Kent.

18　In a few cases supervisors were employed jointly by an agency and university department, as in Manchester where the Family Welfare Association and the University of Manchester financed an appointment of tutor/caseworker. There was a similar appointment in Sheffield. In recent years there has been a growing use of student units to cope with the expanding number of students: specially appointed field-work teachers supervise a group of students—usually between four and eight.

19　For a full discussion of the problems of providing good quality practical work placements during a period of fast expansion of social work training, see S. Clement Brown and E. R. Gloyne, *The Field Training of Social Workers*, Allen & Unwin, 1966. This study was based on a national survey of student placements 1962–3 and showed that even at this time children's departments were providing a quarter of practical work placements in statutory agencies, the largest single contribution of any statutory agency.

20 In view of the complexity of present training and the urgent need for more staff this will be a large and difficult task.

21 Jones, op. cit., p. 48. Social studies departments had a lower ratio of senior lectureships, readerships and professorial posts to staff than other academic disciplines (p. 47). Barbara Wootton eventually left Bedford College because the male sociologists were so jealous and prejudiced. See her autobiography (*The World I Never Made*, Allen & Unwin, 1967), pp. 102–3.

Chapter 15 Women in social work agencies and the social work profession: the male threat

1 Barbara N. Rodgers, *A Follow-up Study of Social Administration Students at Manchester University 1940–60*, Manchester University Press, 1963.

2 Ibid., p. 8. If all the jobs held by those completing courses are taken into account, the popularity of child care for groups B, C and D is even more marked.

3 The Census classifications changed from 1951 to 1961, but the situation at each Census is clear.

4 N. Timms, *Psychiatric Social Work in Great Britain*, Routledge & Kegan Paul, 1964, p. 74. Up to 1962 1,202 people had qualified at LSE, Manchester, Edinburgh and Liverpool. Of these 136 were men (p. 48).

5 See *The First Two Years*, Institute of Medical Social Workers, and 'The Deployment of Medical Social Workers' by D. C. Carter, in *Social Work Today*, September 1971.

6 This echoed the findings of *The First Two Years*, op. cit., which had followed up medical social work students completing training 1961–2.

7 The 1968–9 annual report of the institute estimated that about one hundred medical social workers out of more than one thousand were in local authority posts, and that a shift was taking place because of better pay prospects (p. 7). D. C. Carter, in his sample drawn at 30 September 1969, found 11·4 per cent of medical social workers in local authorities.

8 Annual report, 1968–9, p. 7.

9 In 1964 it was agreed with the local authority associations that local authorities should be asked to provide annual returns showing the number of field officers in post and the forecast establishment for the succeeding years (*Report on the Work of the Children's Department, 1964–6*, HMSO, 1967, p. 17).

10 DHSS, *Children Act 1948. Summary of Returns of Child Care Staff*, Home Office, 1971, p. 1.

11 Annual report, NAPO, 1955, p. 5.

12 This was on the advice of the Probation Advisory Committee in 1946.

13 *Seniority in the Probation Service*, Probation Papers, no. 4, NAPO, 1966. A study by M. J. Brown and R. Foren, *Promotion Profiles*,

NAPO, 1970, reinforces the picture of under-representation of women in senior probation appointments. The survey was conducted in 1969 and also showed that women in senior appointments were generally better educated and qualified than men in similar positions.

14 Information from Home Office, *Trends and Regional Comparisons in Probation*, HMSO, 1966, p. 23, and *Probation and After-Care Statistics for 1969, England and Wales*, Home Office.

15 The better education of women in social welfare and related work is shown clearly in the Education Tables, 1961 Census, p. 64. Men with a terminal education age of 17 and over were 5,250 out of 19,990; women with the same terminal education age were 7,510 out of 18,100 (figures based on 10 per cent sample).

16 Barbara N. Rodgers and Julia Dixon, *Portrait of Social Work*, Oxford University Press, 1960, and Barbara N. Rodgers and J. Stevenson, *New Portrait of Social Work*, Heinemann, 1973.

17 *An Anatomy of Social Welfare Services*, Michael Joseph, 1965.

18 J. Parker and R. Allen, 'Social Workers in Local Government', *Social and Economic Administration*, vol. 3, no. 1, January 1969, pp. 17–38. Mrs Parker was formerly Miss Dixon, who had collaborated with Mrs Rodgers on *Portrait of Social Work*.

19 Rodgers and Dixon, op. cit., table 8.

20 Information given by Mrs Barbara N. Rodgers.

21 It should be borne in mind that the Buckinghamshire study included health visitors and home nurses, and caution in interpretation is needed.

22 Margot Jeffreys, *An Anatomy of Social Welfare Services*, Michael Joseph, 1965, pp. 302–3.

23 Parker and Allen, op. cit., pp. 17–38. Note that the composition of the groups differs from that of the northern county borough.

24 There were two women chief welfare officers in 1970–1, Miss S. M. Williams in Devon, and Miss D. Beverly in York (*Local Government Manual and Directory*, 1970–1).

25 *Municipal Yearbook*, 1950, pp. 695–700.

26 This factor is likely to increase in importance with the anticipated changes in local government areas in 1973–4. There will be no 'small' authorities left.

27 The above information was given by Miss Jayne, of the DHSS in a personal interview and I am grateful for a valuable discussion with her about the appointments. The final number of women directors of social services was twenty-one. For a discussion of this and other factors in the appointment of directors see K. Jones (ed.), *The Yearbook of Social policy in Britain 1971*, Routledge & Kegan Paul, 1972, to which Jeff Smith contributed a paper, 'Top Jobs in the Social Services', pp. 16–30.

28 *Parliamentary Debates*, Lords, vol. 315, 1971, columns 1335ff.

29 Information from Miss Jayne, DHSS.

30 In the probation service inspectorate another woman, May Irvine, was influential as director of training. The training divisions of the inspectorates were responsible for the promotion of new courses,

liaison with existing courses and developing overall policies for staffing the probation and children's services. In the health and welfare field this responsibility rested with the Council for Social Work Training, established in 1962. A staff composed mainly of women was headed by a man, Reg Wright.

31 Allen & Unwin, 1966.
32 Miss Priscilla Young, formerly senior lecturer in social work at Leicester University, was appointed director of the new council in the autumn of 1971.
33 Information in a letter from M. Higson of the Home Office, 8 June 1971.
34 The Josephine Butler College stopped admitting full-time social work students in 1970-1, because of the expansion of general social work training.
35 For a survey of the many uses of volunteers see M. Morris, *Voluntary Work in the Welfare State*, Routledge & Kegan Paul, 1969.
36 *The Voluntary Worker in the Social Services*, Allen & Unwin, 1969. Report of a committee jointly set up by the NCSS and NISWT under the chairmanship of Geraldine M. Aves.
37 *Community Work and Social Change, a Report on Training*, The Calouste Gulbenkian Foundation, Longmans, 1968.
38 Morris, op. cit., appendix 3, 'Voluntary Work in Bradford'. Morris estimated that at least 2 million people were active in the United Kingdom at any one time (p. 192).
39 F. E. Waldren, 'The Association of Social Workers', *Case Conference*, vol. 5, no. 7, January 1959, pp. 183-6.
40 *Registration and the Social Worker*, ASW, 1954.
41 The organisations affiliated to ASW in 1959 were: the Associations of Moral Welfare Workers, Children's Moral Welfare Workers in London and South-east England Organisation, Care Committee Organisers (LCC), General and Family Caseworkers, Child Care Officers, Psychiatric Social Workers, the National Association of Probation Officers and the Institute of Almoners.
42 Association of Child Care Officers, Association of Psychiatric Social Workers, Association of Family Caseworkers, Association of Social Workers, Institute of Almoners, Association of Moral Welfare Workers, National Association of Probation Officers, Society of Mental Welfare Officers.
43 Membership of ACCO Training and Salaries and Service Conditions Committee in 1964 and 1968 was:

| | Salaries and service conditions | | Training | |
	Men	Women	Men	Women
1964	9	1	2	11
1968	11	1	3	10

Source: Annual reports, Association of Child Care Officers.

44 M. Joynson, presidential address, *Accord*, vol. 5, no. 1, conference edition, 1959.

Chapter 16   Problems of women's employment in social work

1 United Nations, IV, 9, 1955, p. 9.
2 Ibid., p. 90.
3 *Accord*, vol. a, no. 4, spring 1957, p. 17. In contrast to the earlier departments looked at, seven of the ten area officers were women and two principal child care officers were women (p. 16). An additional important factor is that women tend to be much more concerned with the starting salary, whereas men have much greater concern with career prospects.
4 Viola Klein, *Employing Married Women*, Institute of Personal Management, 1961; *Working Wives*, Institute of Personal Management, 1960; *Britain's Married Women Workers*, Routledge & Kegan Paul, 1965; 'The Demand for Professional Womenpower', *British Journal of Sociology*, vol. 17, no. 2, June 1966.
5 See Phyllis Willmot, 'The Part-time Social Worker', *Case Conference*, May 1961.
6 Helen Curtis and Phyllis Willmot, *Part-time Employment, and some aspects of Recruitment and Training in Social Work: An Enquiry in London*, NCSS, 1962, p. 2.
7 The Morison Report had not thought that there was a shortage of women probation officers and were not anxious to develop part-time work. In 1969 there were only fifty part-time women probation officers.
8 Quoted by Curtis and Willmot, op. cit., p. 14.
9 An unpublished report on part-time work in medical social work (Helen Curtis, 1964, duplicated report) had examined the situation in 1963 and found that the 'structure of the almoning service appears to offer several practical possibilities for part-timers with almost the minimum of contra-indications' (p. 17).
10 The Manchester BA(Admin) was not intended as a vocational social work training, and served as an acceptable basis for teaching in the 1940s and 1950s; nowadays a BA(Admin) would be expected to take a teaching diploma course. Viola Klein had also emphasised that teaching was a good profession for married women to return to and that nearly half of post-war trained teachers not working expected to return to the profession in the foreseeable future ('The Demand for Professional Women Power', op. cit., pp. 184–5).
11 'Women's Contribution to Social Work', *Social Work*, vol. 21, no. 1, 1964, p. 9.
12 Helen Curtis and Catherine Howell, *Part-time Social Work. A Study of Opportunities for the Employment of Trained Social Workers*, NCSS, 1965.
13 Ibid., p. 115.
14 Seebohm Report, p. 170, para. 552.

15 Other writers such as Hannah Gavron (*The Captive Wife*, Penguin, 1966), have also presented similar programmes.

16 For a fundamental discussion on these issues based on survey data see F. A. Ruderman, *Child Care and Working Mothers*, Child Welfare League of America, 1968. Margaret Thatcher's White Paper, *Education: A Framework for Expansion* (Cmnd 5174, December 1972), whilst planning substantial development of nursery education, is not intended to help women return to work.

17 Cynthia E. Arregger (ed.), *Graduate Women at Work*, Oriel Press, 1966, p. 39.

18 Audrey Hunt, *A Survey of Women's Employment*, vol. 1, report, Government Social Survey, SS 379, HMSO, p. 187.

19 P. Laroque and Sir Allen Daley, WHO, 1956. The project was initiated in 1950 and survey work was carried out 1952–4 in France and England. It should be borne in mind that the French *assistante sociale* combines a social work/health visiting function, whereas in England this is not the case and social workers have a wide range of other functions.

20 *Sex, Career and Family*, Allen & Unwin, 1971.

21 Elizabeth Wilson, 'Women Together', *New Society*, 14 September 1972.

22 Sylvia Brooks, 'The Role of Women in Social Work', *Social Work Today*, vol. 3, no. 9, 27 July 1972.

Chapter 17 Conclusion

1 R. G. Walton, 'The Residential Care of Deprived Children', unpublished thesis, University of Manchester, 1967. Even more than fieldwork, residential social work has suffered from the inability of outsiders to see anything other than domestic caring roles for the staff.

2 For evidence on what can happen in a society where these resistances are removed, see B. Q. Madison, *Social Welfare in the Soviet Union*, Stanford University Press, 1965.

3 See I. Suttie, *The Origins of Love and Hate* (Kegan Paul, Trench, Trubner, 1935; Penguin, 1960) for a discussion of the taboos on tenderness in men.

4 This cannot wholly be attributed to problems of married women. E. Younghusband in her 1959 report (p. 330) showed that women held 22 per cent of senior posts in local authority mental health departments even though they formed 41 per cent of the staff. It seems likely that many of the women were single.

5 An analysis of enquirers in 1968–9 by the Social Work Advisory Service showed that three-quarters of enquirers were women, the majority of whom tended to be young with 'O' and 'A' level qualifications. Twenty per cent of the women were married, but this group was heavily concentrated in the south of England and tended to have more university qualifications than the whole sample. Thus there seems to be considerable scope for future recruitment.

See *Analysis of Enquirers*, 1968–9, Social Work Advisory Service, February 1971.

6 The most recent example is R. Pinker, *Social Theory and Social Policy*, Heinemann, 1971.

7 Reinhard Bendix, *Max Weber, An Intellectual Portrait*, Methuen, 1959. See particularly Part Three, 'Domination, Organisation and Legitimacy: Max Weber's Political Sociology'. It is as well to remember the extreme patriarchal structure of the family in Germany.

8 Constable, 1970. This extended the arguments developed in *The Faith of the Counsellors*, Constable, 1965.

Bibliography

Printed sources

Abel-Smith, B. (1961), *A History of the Nursing Profession*, Heinemann.
Aberdeen, Countess of (ed.) (1899), *International Congress of Women*, vol. I, *Women in Professions*, Fisher & Unwin.
Addams, J. (1910), *Twenty Years at Hull House*, Macmillan.
Addams, J. (1930), *The Second Twenty Years at Hull House*, Macmillan.
Alford, H. H. (1959), 'Historical Background' in Rowles, J. (ed.), *Housing Management*, Pitman, ch. 1.
Arreger, Cynthia E. (ed.) (1966), *Graduate Women at Work*, Oriel Press.
Ashdown, M. and Clement Brown, Sibyl (1953), *Social Service and Mental Health*, Routledge & Kegan Paul.
Association of Psychiatric Social Workers (1932), *Psychiatric Social Work and the Family*.
Association of Psychiatric Social Workers (1960), *Ventures in Professional Co-operation: Mental Health in Clinic, Hospital and Community*.
Association of Social Workers (1954), *Registration and the Social Worker*.
Attlee, C. R. (1920), *The Social Worker*, Library of Social Service.
Attlee, C. R. (1954), *As it Happened*, Heinemann.
Baker, E. F. (1964), *Technology and Women's Work*, Columbia University Press.
Barnett, Canon (1884), 'Universities and the Poor', *Nineteenth Century*, February, pp. 255–61.
Barnett, Mrs S. A. (1921), *Canon Barnett. His Life, Work and Friends. By his Wife*, John Murray.
Bartlett, F. C. (Ginsberg, M., Lindgren, E. J., Thouless, R. H.) (eds) (1939), *The Study of Society*, Kegan Paul, Trench, Trubner & Co.
Bartlett, H. M. (1961), *Analysing Social Work Practice by Fields*, National Association of Social Workers, New York.
Bartlett, H. M. (1970), *The Common Base of Social Work Practice*, National Association of Social Workers, New York.
Batten, E. M. (1939), *The Principles and Methods of Training Social Workers, with Special Reference to Hospital Almoners*, Hospital Almoners Association.
Beck, I. F. (1948), *The Almoner*, Council of Institute of Almoners.
Beveridge, Lord (1948), *Voluntary Action. A Report on Methods of Social Advance*, Allen & Unwin.
Bosanquet, Mrs B. (1896), *Rich and Poor*, Macmillan.
Bosanquet, Helen (1914), *Social Work in London, 1869–1912: A History of the Charity Organisation Society*, John Murray.

295

Boss, P. (1971), *Exploration into Child Care*, Routledge & Kegan Paul.
Bourdillon, A. F. C. (ed.) (1945), *Voluntary Social Services*, Methuen.
Bowley, A. L. (1921), *Prices and Wages in the United Kingdom 1914–20*, Clarendon Press.
British Federation of Social Workers (1941), *Wars and their Significance*.
Butler, J. E. (ed.) (1869), *Women's Work and Women's Culture*, Macmillan.
Butler, J. E. (1871), *The Constitution Violated: An Essay on the Contagious Diseases Act*, Hamilton.
Butrym, Z. (1968), *Medical Social Work in Action*, Bell & Sons.
Carpenter, J. Estlin (1881), *The Life and Work of Mary Carpenter*, Macmillan.
Carpenter, Mary (1857), 'Relation of Ragged Schools to the Educational Movement', *Transactions*, NAPSS, pp. 226–31.
Carpenter, Mary (1857), 'Reformatories for Convicted Girls', *Transactions*, NAPSS, pp. 338–42.
Cavenagh, W. E. (1950), *Four Decades of Students in Social Work*, University of Birmingham.
Chafetz, J. (1972), 'Women in Social Work', *Social Work* (USA), vol. 17, no. 5, September.
Chalmers, T. (1912), *Problems of Poverty, Selected Writings*, Nelson & Son.
Clement Brown, Sibyl (1939), 'Family Casework and Mental Health', *Charity Organisation Review*, vol. 13, no. 1, January, pp. 40ff.
Clement Brown, Sibyl (1939), 'The Methods of Social Caseworkers', ch. 15 in *The Study of Society*, ed. E. C. Bartlett.
Clement Brown, Sibyl (1970), 'Looking Backwards: Reminiscences, 1922–1946', *British Journal of Psychiatric Social Work*, vol. 10, no. 4, Autumn.
Clement Brown, Sibyl and Gloyne, E. R. (1966), *The Field Training of Social Workers*, Allen & Unwin.
Cohen, E. C. (1958), *Social Work in the American Tradition*, Dryden Press, New York.
Cosens, M. and Clement Brown, Sibyl (1936), *Developments in Psychiatric Social Work*, Association of Psychiatric Social Workers.
Cresswell, D'Arcy (1948), *Margaret McMillan, a Memoir*, Hutchinson.
Crosse, O. (1930), 'American Experiences', *Charity Organisation Quarterly*, January.
Curtis, Helen and Howell, Catherine (1965), *Part-time Social Work. A Study of Opportunities for the Employment of Trained Social Workers*, NCSS.
Curtis, Helen and Willmott, Phyllis (1962), *Part-time Employment, and Some Aspects of Recruitment: An Enquiry in London*, NCSS.
Dahlstrom, E. (ed.) (1962), *The Changing Roles of Men and Women*, Duckworth.
Davies, Emily (1866), *The Higher Education of Women*, Alexander Strahan.
Epstein, C. F. and Goale, W. J. (1970), *The Other Half: Roads to Women's Equality*, Prentice Hall.

Evans, D. (1934), *Women and the Civil Service*, Pitman.

Figes, Eva (1970), *Patriarchal Attitudes*, Faber & Faber.

Frere, M. (1903), 'The Charitable Work of a Local Manager in a Board School', *Charity Organisation Quarterly*, March, pp. 120–34.

Fulford, R. (1957), *Votes for Women*, Faber & Faber.

Gates, E. (ed.) (1924), *Women's Year Book 1923–4*, Women Publishers Ltd.

Gavron, H. (1968), *The Captive Wife*, Pelican.

Gilbert, B. B. (1970), *British Social Policy 1914–39*, Batsford.

Goldberg, E. M. (1970), *Helping the Aged*, Allen & Unwin.

Gray, K. R. (1964), 'Women's Contribution to Social Work', *Social Work*, vol. 21, no. 1, January.

Hall, M. P. and Howes, I. V. (1965), *The Church in Social Work*, Routledge & Kegan Paul.

Hardwicke, K. (1946), 'Regulation 33B and the Moral Welfare Worker', *Quarterly Leaflet of the Church of England Moral Welfare Council*, October, pp. 6–16.

Heywood, Jean S. (1959), *Children in Care*, Routledge & Kegan Paul.

Heywood, Jean S. (1964), *An Introduction to Teaching Casework*, Routledge & Kegan Paul.

Higson, J. E. (1955), *The Story of a Beginning: An Account of Pioneer Work for Moral Welfare*, SPCK.

Hutchinson, E. (1913), 'Women in the Police Courts', *The English Woman*, vol. 20, October, pp. 25–30.

Hill, Octavia (1884), 'Colour, Space and Music for the People', *Nineteenth Century*, May, pp. 741–52.

International Conference on Social Work (Third, London) (1938), *Report*, Le Ploy Press.

International Conference on Social Work (Fifth) (1950), *Proceedings*, Paris.

Jeffreys, Margot (1965), *An Anatomy of Social Welfare Services*, Michael Joseph.

Jones, Kathleen (1964), *The Teaching of Social Studies in British Universities*, Codicote Press.

Jones, Paula (1939), 'Some Memories of Octavia Hill', *Charity Organisation Quarterly*, vol. 13, no. 1, January, pp. 27–9.

Kamm, Josephine (1965), *Hope Deferred*, Methuen.

Kamm, Josephine (1966), *Rapiers and Battleaxes*, Allen & Unwin.

Kelsall, H. K. (1955), *Higher Civil Servants in Britain*, Routledge & Kegan Paul.

King, J. F. S. (1964), *The Probation Service*, Butterworth.

Kirkman Gray, B. (1905), *A History of English Philanthropy*, P. S. King & Son.

Kirkman Gray, B. (1908), *Philanthropy and the State of Social Politics*, P. S. King & Son.

Klein, Viola (1960), *Working Wives*, Institute of Personal Management.

Klein, Viola (1961), *Employing Married Women*, Institute of Personal Management.

Klein, Viola (1965), *Britain's Married Women Workers*, Routledge & Kegan Paul.

Klein, Viola (1966), 'The Demand for Professional Womanpower', *British Journal of Sociology*, vol. 17, no. 2, June, pp. 183–98.

Lady Margaret Hall Settlement (1939), *Social Services in North Lambeth and Kennington*, Oxford University Press.

Laroque, P. and Daley, A. (1956), *Health and Social Workers in England and France*, World Health Organisation.

Loch, C. S. (1892), 'The Confusion in Medical Charities', *Nineteenth Century*, August, pp. 298–310.

Loch, C. S. (1910), *Charity and Social Life*, Macmillan.

Lonsdale, M. (1884), 'Platform Women', *Nineteenth Century*, March.

Lubove, R. (1962), *The Progressives and the Slums*, Pittsburgh University Press.

Lubove, R. (1965), *The Professional Altruist*, Harvard University Press.

Macadam, Elizabeth (1925), *The Equipment of the Social Worker*, Allen & Unwin.

Macadam, Elizabeth (1934), *The New Philanthropy*, Allen & Unwin.

Macadam, Elizabeth (1945), *The Social Servant in the Making*, Allen & Unwin.

McDougall, K. (1969), 'The Eternal Ambivalence', *British Journal of Psychiatric Social Work*, vol. 10, no. 2.

Macey, J. P. (1965), *Housing Management*, Estates Gazette Ltd.

McIlquahan, Harriet (1906), *Local Government in England and Wales*, Women's Emancipation Union.

Madison, B. Q. (1965), *Social Welfare in the Soviet Union*, Stanford University Press.

Manchester University Settlement (1955), *Diamond Jubilee 1895–1955, Souvenir Brochure*.

Mansbridge, A. (1932), *Margaret McMillan, Prophet and Pioneer*, Dent & Sons.

Markham, Violet (1953), *Return Passage*, Oxford University Press.

Marsh, D. C. (1965), *The Changing Social Structure of England and Wales, 1871–1961*, Routledge & Kegan Paul.

Marshall, A. (1903), 'Economic Teaching at the Universities in Relation to Public Well Being', *Charity Organisation Review*, new series, no. 73, January.

Martindale, Hilda (1938), *Women Servants of the State 1870–1938*, Allen & Unwin.

Marx, Karl (1958), *Selected Works*, 2 vols, Foreign Languages Publishing House, Moscow.

Matheson, M. (1908), 'Training for Social Work', *Women's Employment*, 17 July.

Matheson, M. (1912), 'Opportunities for Training for Personal Services', *Women Workers*, vol. 22, no. 3, December, pp. 69–74.

Matheson, M. (1915), 'Birmingham Women's Settlement', *Charity Organisation Review*, January, pp. 24–30.

Matheson, M. (1916), 'Opportunities for Social Work Training', *Student Movement*, May, pp. 167–9.

Matheson, M. (1917), 'Why Social Workers Want Women's Suffrage', *Common Cause*, 16 February.

Matheson, M. (1917), 'The Poor Ye Have Always With You', *The Challenge*, 2 November.

Maurice, G. E. (1914), *Life of Octavia Hill*, Macmillan.

Mead, Margaret (1950), *Male and Female*, Gollancz.

Meier, Elizabeth G. (1954), *A History of the New York School of Social Work*, Columbia University Press.

Mess, H. A. (1947), *Voluntary Social Services since 1918*, Kegan Paul, Trench, Trubner & Co.

Mill, J. S. (1910 edn), *On Liberty* (1859), *Considerations on Representative Government* (1861), J. M. Dent, Everyman's Library.

Mill, J. S. (1929 edn), *On the Subjection of Women* (1869), J. M. Dent, Everyman's Library.

Milnes, N. (1929), 'The Difficulties Encountered in Recruiting and Training Voluntary and Professional Workers in a Social Case Agency', *COS Quarterly*, January, pp. 21–31.

Mitchell, Juliet (1971), *Women's Estate*, Pelican.

Moberley Bell, E. (1942), *Octavia Hill*, Constable.

Moberley Bell, E. (1961), *The Story of Hospital Almoners*, Faber & Faber.

Moberley Bell, E. (1962), *Josephine Butler, Flame of Fire*, Constable.

Morris, Cherry (ed.) (1955), *Social Casework in Great Britain*, 2nd edn, Faber & Faber.

Morris, M. (1969), *Voluntary Work in the Welfare State*, Routledge & Kegan Paul.

Mowat, C. L. (1955), *Britain Between the Wars*, Methuen.

Mowat, C. L. (1961), *The Charity Organisation Society, 1869–1913*, Methuen.

Myrdal, A. and Klein, Viola (1956), *Women's Two Roles*, Routledge & Kegan Paul.

National Association of Probation Officers (1966), *Seniority in the Probation Service*, Probation Papers, no. 4.

National Council of Social Service (1939), *Report of the Advisory Committee on Recruitment and Training*.

Nussey, H. G. (1903), 'The Work of the Hospital Almoner', *Charity Organisation Review*, no. 74, February, pp. 79–97.

Owen, D. (1965), *English Philanthropy*, Oxford University Press.

Parker, J. and Allen, R. (1969), 'Social Workers in Local Government', *Social and Economic Administration*, vol. 3, no. 1, January, pp. 17–38.

Parkes, B. R. (1860), 'Industrial Employment of Women', *Transactions*, NAPSS, pp. 811–19.

Political and Economic Planning (1937), *Report on the British Social Services*, PEP.

Pollard, Beatrice (1962), *Social Casework for the State*, Pall Mall Press.

Pringle, J. C. (1937), *Social Work of the London Churches*, Oxford University Press.

Robertson, W. (1964), *Welfare in Trust: A History of the Carnegie United Kingdom Trust 1913–63*, Carnegie United Kingdom Trust.

Rodgers, Barbara N. (1963), *A Follow-up Study of Social Administration Students at Manchester University 1940–60*, Manchester University Press.

Rodgers, Barbara N. (1964), *The Careers of Social Studies Students*, Codicote Press.

Rodgers, Barbara N. (1970), 'New Portrait of Social Work', *Social and Economic Administration*, vol. 4, no. 3, July.

Rodgers, Barbara N. and Dixon, Julia (1960), *Portrait of Social Work*, Oxford University Press.

Rooff, M. (1972), *One Hundred Years of Family Social Work, A Study of the Family Welfare Association 1869–1969*, Michael Joseph.

Rover, C. (1967), *Women's Suffrage and Party Politics in Britain 1866–1914*, Routledge & Kegan Paul.

Rover, C. (1970), *Love, Morals and the Feminists*, Routledge & Kegan Paul.

Ruskin, J. (1937 edn), *Sesame and Lilies* (1864), Nelson & Sons.

Salomon, A. (1937), *Education for Social Work*, Verlag fur Recht und Gesellschaft A.G., Zurich.

Sayles, A. (1924), *The Houses of the Workers*, T. Fisher Unwin.

Seed, P. (1973), *The Expansion of Social Work*, Routledge & Kegan Paul.

Simey, M. B. (1951), *Charitable Effort in Liverpool in the Nineteenth Century*, Liverpool University Press.

Simey, T. S. (1947), *Salaries and Conditions of Work of Social Workers*, NCSS.

Smith, Margaret (1965), *Professional Education for Social Work in Great Britain*, Allen & Unwin.

Snelling, J. (1970), *The Contribution of the Institute of Medical Social Workers to Education for Social Work*, Association of Social Work Teachers.

Stocks, Mary (1945), *Fifty Years in Every Street*, Manchester University Press.

Stocks, Mary (1949), *Eleanor Rathbone*, Gollancz.

Stocks, Mary (1960), *A Hundred Years of District Nursing*, Allen & Unwin.

Stocks, Mary (1970), *My Commonplace Book*, Peter Davies.

Stone, Gilbert (ed.) (1917), *Women War Workers*, Harrap.

Strachey, R. (1935), *Careers and Openings for Women*, Faber & Faber.

Timms, N. (1964a), *Psychiatric Social Work in Great Britain 1939–62*, Routledge & Kegan Paul.

Timms, N. (1964b), *Social Casework*, Routledge & Kegan Paul.

Timms, N. (1968), *The Language of Social Casework*, Routledge & Kegan Paul.

Timms, N. (1970), *Social Work: An Outline for the Intending Student*, Routledge & Kegan Paul.

Titmuss, R. M. (1963), 'The Position of Women', ch. 5 in *Essays on the Welfare State*, Allen & Unwin.

Tropp, Asher (1959), *The School Teachers: The Growth of the Teaching*

Profession in England and Wales from 1800 to the Present Day, Heinemann.

Turner, E. M. (n.d.), *Josephine Butler, her Place in History*, Association for Moral and Social Hygiene.

Twining, L. (1858), 'The Objects and Aims of the Workhouse Visiting Society', *Transactions*, NAPSS, pp. 666–71.

United Nations (1955), *Training for Social Work, Second International Survey*.

Urwick, E. J. (1903), 'Settlement Ideals', *Charity Organisation Review*, December, pp. 328–9.

Urwick, E. J. (1908), *Luxury and Waste of Life*, J. M. Dent.

Urwick, E. J. (1920), *A Philosophy of Social Progress*, Methuen.

Veblen, T. (1934), *Theory of the Leisure Class*, Random House.

Waldron, F. E. (1959), 'The Association of Social Workers', *Case Conference*, vol. 5, no. 7, January.

Walton, R. G. and Barber, E. (1968), 'Mature Students on a Child Care Course,' *Case Conference*, vol. 15, no. 4, August.

Wandor, M. (1972), *The Body Politic*, Stage 1.

White, Cynthia L. (1970), *Women's Magazines 1693–1968*, Michael Joseph.

Williams, B. E. (1942), 'On Knowing Oneself', *Quarterly Leaflet of the Church of England Moral Welfare Council*, March, pp. 4–6.

Williams, G. (1967), *Caring for People: Staffing Residential Homes*, Allen & Unwin.

Willmott, P. (1961), 'The Part-time Social Worker', *Case Conference*, vol. 7, no. 11, May.

Wollstonecraft, Mary (1954 edn), *The Rights of Women* (1792), J. M. Dent, Everyman's Library.

Wood, M. W. (1949), *The Pilgrimage of Perseverance*, NCSS.

Woodroofe, K. (1962), *From Charity to Social Work*, Routledge & Kegan Paul.

Wootton, B. (1959), *Social Science and Social Pathology*, Allen & Unwin.

Wootton, B. (1967), *In a World I Never Made: Autobiographical Reflections*, Allen & Unwin.

Young, A. F. and Ashton, E. T. (1956), *British Social Work in the Nineteenth Century*, Routledge & Kegan Paul.

Younghusband, Eileen (1947), *Report on the Employment and Training of Social Workers*, T. A. Constable.

Younghusband, Eileen (1951), *Social Work in Britain*, T. A. Constable.

Younghusband, Eileen (1964), *Social Work and Social Change*, Allen & Unwin.

Manuscript sources

Association of Child Care Officers, Annual Reports.

Bochel, D. (1963), 'The Development of the Probation Service in England and Wales', MA(Econ) thesis, University of Manchester.

Clement Brown, Sibyl (1933), A series of three lectures on 'Recent Advances in Applied Social Psychology': (1) 'Objects and Methods in Social Work'; (2) 'Research into the Cause of Individual Maladjustments and its Application to Social Casework'; (3) 'The Relation of Mental Hygiene to the Social Work of the Future'. Unpublished Manuscripts.

Clement Brown, Sibyl (1934), 'Social Casework in Action', unpublished.

Fox, E. (1934), 'Modern Developments in Work for Mental Defectives. A Historical Survey', paper delivered to the Conference on Mental Welfare, 23 November.

Home Office, Probation and After Care Statistics for 1969, England and Wales, unpublished.

Institute of Hospital Almoners, Annual Reports.

Letters by various people, housed in the Fawcett Library.

Ross, E. M. (1956), 'Women and Poor Law Administration 1857–1909', MA thesis, University of London.

Scott, J. C. (1970), 'Bradford Women in Organisation', MA thesis, University of Bradford.

Strachey, P. (n.d., circa 1920), speech delivered at a conference on Unemployment Amongst Women, manuscript, Fawcett Library.

Walton, R. G. (1967), 'The Development of the Residential Care of Deprived Children since 1900', MA thesis, University of Manchester.

Government publications

Census Reports, England and Wales.

Report of the Departmental Committee on the Training, Appointment and Payment of Probation Officers, Cmnd 1601, HMSO, 1922.

Report of the Departmental Committee on the Social Services in Courts of Summary Jurisdiction, Cmd 5122, HMSO, 1936.

Report of the Care of Children Committee (Curtis Report), Cmd 6922, HMSO, 1946.

Interim Report of the Care of Children Committee, Cmd 6760, HMSO, 1946.

Department of Health and Social Security, Children Act 1948.

Titmuss, R. M., *History of the Second World War. Problems of Social Policy*, HMSO, 1950.

Home Office, *Sixth Report of the Work of the Children's Department*, HMSO, 1951.

Ministry of Health, *Report of the Working Party on Social Workers in the Local Authority Health and Welfare Services* (Younghusband Report), HMSO, 1959.

Report of the Departmental Committee on the Probation Service (Morison Report), Cmnd 1650, HMSO, 1962.

University Grants Committee, *Report on the First Employment of University Graduates 1961–2*, HMSO, 1963.

Home Office, *Trends and Regional Comparisons in Probation*, HMSO, 1966.

Home Office, *Report on the Work of the Children's Department 1964–6*, HMSO, 1967.

Report of the Committee on Local Authority and Allied Personal Social Services (Seebohm Report), Cmnd 3703, HMSO, 1968.

Hunt, A., *A Survey of Women's Employment*, vol. 1, *Report*,
Government Social Survey, 55379, HMSO, 1968.

Department of Education and Science, *Student Numbers in Higher
Education in England and Wales*, Education Planning Paper No. 2,
HMSO, 1970.

University Grants Committee, *The First Employment of University
Graduates 1968-9*, HMSO, 1970.

Summary of Returns of Child Care Staff, DHSS, 1971.

Index

Abel-Smith, B., 32, 36
Addams, Jane, 52
Administrative skill in social work, 25, 29, 52, 154, 168, 179, 197, 199, 208, 219, 220, 223, 236, 237–8, 258–9
Almoners, see Medical Social work
American social work developments, 47, 98–100, 113, 128f, 161, 203
Ashdown, Margaret, 163
Association of Child Care Officers, 226, 244, 245
Association of Children's Officers, 244, 245
Association of Part-Time Social Workers, 247–8, 250–1, 252
Association of Psychiatric Social Workers, 130, 154, 155, 215, 240, 241
Association of Social Workers, 241
Attlee, Clement, 6, 7, 50, 113, 141, 146, 148
Aves, Geraldine, 145, 240

Barnardo, Dr, 5, 21, 239
Barker, Dame Lilian, 145
Barnett, Mrs Henrietta, 19, 52–4, 63, 69
Barnett, Canon Samuel A., 21, 50, 52–5
Barrett, Miss Rosa M., 21
Bartlett, Harriet, 3, 4
Becker, Lydia, 64
Birmingham Women's Settlement, 53, 74, 91–2
Blackwell, Dr Elizabeth, 16, 83
Boarding-out visitors, 198
Bosanquet, Bernard, 21
Bosanquet, Helen, 20, 29, 113
Bowlby, John, 253
Bradford, womens organisations in, 18, 42
Brill, Kenneth, 242
British Association of Social Workers, 242

British Federation of Social Workers, 154–5, 241
Bureaucracy, 208, 261–2
Butler, Josephine, 18, 23–4, 26, 42, 66, 261
Butrym, 2, 224–5, 261–2

Cabot, Dr, 47, 66f
Cadbury, Elizabeth, 15
Carnegie Trust, 155, 196, 205
Carpenter, Mary, 16, 19, 22–3, 25, 26, 66f, 261
Cavenagh, Winifred E., 208, 221
Caxton Hall Conference, 177f
Central Council for Education and Training in Social Work, 218, 239
Chalmers, Dr, 15
Charity Organisation Society, 2, 20, 27, 28–9, 35, 44, 50, 54, 55, 57–60, 61, 62, 82–3, 92, 108, 112, 128
Child care, 4, 20, 184–6, 213–15, 226–8
Child care officers, 213
Child guidance clinics, 132–3
Children's departments, 198, 199, 214, 235
Children's officers, 197, 235, 236, 244, 245
Church of England Children's Society, 21, 240
Church of England Temperance Society, 21, 47
Citizens' Advice Bureau, 182, 240, 248
Civil Service, women's appointments, 36–40, 143–5, 238–9
Clement Brown, Sybil, 107, 113, 149, 160–3, 172–3, 178, 179, 180, 185, 198, 238
Committees of charitable ladies, membership of, 27–8, 198

Commonwealth Fund, 128f, 181
Communist Manifesto, The, 43
Community work, 240
Cons, Emma, 53, 63
Contagious Diseases Acts, 23, 25, 42, 70
Cooper, Miss J., 238
Council for Training in Social Work, 212
Curtis, Myra, 185
Curtis Committee, 184–6, 196, 197, 236

Davis, Emily, 16–18
Department of Health and Social Security, 238
Directors of social services, 235f
Directors of welfare services, 244, 245
Dixon, Julia, 5
Dyson, Miss D. M., 178, 198

Edridge, S. G., 48
Education Act 1944, 186
Education services, 1, 14, 16–18, 63–5, 134–5, 186
Engels, Frederick, 84–5
English Woman's Journal, 15

Family Service Units, 183, 240
Family Welfare Association, 239
Fawcett, Professor H., 71
Forster Education Act, 1870, 63
Fox, Evelyn, 129, 136
Frere, Margaret, 64
Freud, Sigmund, 3
Freudian psychology, 61, 131, 133, 172
Fry, Margery, 73, 110, 176

Generic social work courses, 205, 215–16, 218
Green, Thomas Hill, 21, 67

Halmos, Paul, 262
Health and welfare departments, 212
Heywood, Dr Jean, 216–17
Higson, Miss J. E., 97, 98, 140–1
Hill, M. Davenport, 21
Hill, Miss Miranda, 59
Hill, Octavia, 5, 18–19, 22, 24, 26, 29, 51, 53, 54, 55, 57, 63, 64, 66f, 74, 98, 100

Home Office, 146, 185, 197, 207, 214, 238–9, 260
Hopkins, Ellice, 42–3
Hospital Almoners Association, 45
Housing management, 20, 63, 98, 137–9
Howard Association, 21
Hubbard, Mrs, 32
Hughes, Miss E. P., 21

Ideal of service, women's conception of, 82–4, 187, 220, 261–3
India, women's interest in, 71
Industrialisation, 1, 2
Inspectors, 36f, 143–5, 238–9
Institute of Hospital Almoners, 45
Institute of Medical Social Workers, 225–6, 241
International Congress of Women, 78
Irvine, Elizabeth, 216

Jeffrys, Margot, 231–4
Jehu, Professor Derek, 216
Jones, Professor Howard, 216
Jones, Professor Kathleen, 216, 219

Klein, Viola, 246–7

Lady Allen of Hurtwood, 184
Large scale organisations, women's antipathy to, 69–70
Lawrence, D. H., 3
Leadership, of women in social work, 81, 258–9
Liverpool, social work in, 73–4
Local Authority Social Services Act, 1970, 209, 235
Loch, Charles, 5, 21, 29, 44, 59, 61, 100
Lubove, R., 47

Macadam, Elizabeth, 74, 106, 115, 118, 119, 159–60, 168
McDougall, Kay, 163, 186, 215, 216, 242
McFie, Miss Bernice, 155, 241
McIlquahan, Mrs Harriet, 30
McMillan, Margaret, 64
Markham, Violet, 66, 72f, 110, 158
Martindale, Hilda, 37, 38
Marxism, 84–5
Mason, Miss M. H., 37–8

Material aid, 14, 46, 114, 202
Matheson, Miss Cecile, 49, 74f,
    81–2, 93–5, 109, 186
Matrons, 32–4
Medical social work, 4, 19, 20–1,
    43–7, 80, 91, 95–6, 108, 114f,
    135, 168–70, 206–7, 224–6
Mental health, 98–9
Mental hygiene and social work,
    98–9
Merrington, Martha Crawford, 30
Metropolitan Association for
    Befriending Young Servants,
    43, 53, 55
Mill, John Stuart, 2, 69–71, 85
Milnes, Nora, 149–50
Ministry of Health, 146, 168, 169,
    185, 207, 214, 238–9
Moral welfare, 4, 20, 40–3, 97–8,
    139–41, 240
Morison Committee, 228–9, 230
Morton, Miss T. M., 64, 132, 134
Motivation for social work, 82,
    186–7, 227–8, 257–8
Mowat, C. L., 20, 29, 44
Munitions work, 92–3, 98

Nassau Senior, Mrs, 32, 37, 73
National Assistance, 202
National Association for the
    Promotion of Social Science, 37,
    71
National Association of
    Probation Officers, 96, 175–6,
    228–9, 243
National Children's Home, 21
National Council of Social
    Service, 148, 182, 183
National Institute for Social
    Work Training, 215, 218–19
National Society for the Prevention
    of Cruelty to Children, 22
National Union of Women's
    Suffrage Societies, 74, 75, 92
National Union of Women Workers,
    49, 59, 75, 83
Nelson, G., 21
Nightingale, Florence, 16, 70, 71
North of England Council for
    Promoting the Higher
    Education of Women, 19, 23, 67
Nursing, 13–14, 32, 102–3,
    108, 121, 191–5

Parker, Julia, 232, 233, 244
Parker, Professor Roy, 216
Parkes, Miss B. R., 15–16
Parsloe, Professor Phyllida, 216
Part-time work, 247f
Pauperism, 1, 17, 32, 68
Penitentiaries, 18, 23, 40
Philanthropy
    and economic life, 85–7
    and education, 16–18
Police court missionaries, 47
Political and Economic Planning, 160
Politics, its relation to philanthropy
    and social work, 6–7, 17, 37,
    77, 85, 196, 209
Pollard, Beatrice, 231
Poor Law, 30–8, 55, 146, 202
Poor Law infirmaries, 38, 53
Population growth, 1, 12
Pringle, Rev. J. C., 110, 116, 152
Probation, 4, 21, 47–50, 80, 96–7,
    110–11, 122f, 174f, 206, 228–31
Professionalisation of social work,
    45, 48, 80–1, 83, 111, 149f,
    180–1
Prostitution, 125
Psychiatric social work, 4, 63, 128f,
    171f, 207, 223–4

Rainer, Frederick, 21
Rathbone, Eleanor, 73f, 85, 107,
    157
Reformatories, 17, 18, 23, 25, 39
Registration
    of doctors, 14
    of nurses, 14
    of social workers, 242
Relieving officers, 35, 198
Research in social work, 150–1, 159,
    161, 180, 205, 216, 219
Richmond, Mary, 99, 100, 113
Rodgers, Barbara, 5, 221, 232, 247,
    249
Rosling, Miss, 145, 174, 185
Royal Commission on the Poor
    Laws, 1909, 35, 55, 65
Rudolph, Prebendary, 21
Ruskin, John, 20, 67, 72

School Boards, 31, 54, 63, 64, 72
School Boards officers, 64
School care committees, 64–5, 134

Schoolmistresses, 12
Schools of social work, 203, 204
Seebohm Committee, 218, 250
Settlements, 4, 20, 21, 50–6, 57, 59, 141–3
Sewell, Margaret, 29, 57, 60
Sexual taboos, influence on social work roles, 127–8, 148
Sharpley, Mary McNicol, 59
Simey, T. S., 196, 198, 200–1
Social administration, 203
Social casework, 131, 149, 153, 154, 217, 240
Social insurance services, 47, 202
Social reform, 75–7, 84, 110, 137
Social studies courses, 203f, 209
Social work
  as a career, 2, 46, 66, 81–2, 93–5, 107–8, 120–1, 207–8
  definition of, 3–8, 154, 163, 178
Social work roles, 96, 100, 126, 207–8, 230–1, 245, 258, 260
Social work salaries, 94, 121, 123, 157, 170, 175, 199, 201, 246
Social work students, 45–6, 95, 209–11, 221–2, 227
Social work training, 16, 45–6, 53, 55, 57–65, 81, 100, 118–19, 147, 155–7, 170, 179, 209f
Social work values, 6, 7, 83–4, 98, 100, 149–50, 261–3
Social workers, 82–3, 108–11, 189f, 221–3
Society for Promoting the Return of Women as Poor Law Guardians, 31
Spencer, Herbert, 53, 67
Stansfield, Miss, 38
Stansfield, James, 37
Statutory social services, development of, 146, 152
Statutory social work, growth of, 119, 209
Stephenson, Dr, 5, 21
Stewart, Miss, 29, 44
Stocks, Mary, 64, 106, 110
Strachey, Pauline, 104–6
Strachey, Roy, 107–8

Teaching, 12, 13–14, 102–3, 108, 121, 191–5
Timms, Noel, 3, 216, 217, 223–4
Titmuss, Richard M., 167, 181, 205

Training officers, 217–18
Twining, Louisa, 15, 30, 31, 36, 66, 71

Universities
  attitude to social work, 59–62, 63, 147, 179, 181, 203–6
  extension movement, 21
University Women's Part-Time Employment Agency, 248
Urban growth, 1, 2
Urwick, E. J., 45, 54, 61, 62

Veblen, Thorstein, 84f
Venereal disease, 97, 183–4
Vincent, Howard, 21
Visiting, charitable, 14–15, 17, 27, 44, 57–8, 80
Visiting teachers, 134–5
Voluntary organisations, 27, 182–3, 185, 239–41
Volunteers, 1, 14, 49, 134, 182, 239–41

War, impact on social work, 91–2, 167, 176, 186
Warren, Enid, 242
Waugh, Benjamin, 22
Weber, Max, 261
Webb, Beatrice, 55, 73, 74, 85
Welfare State, 196, 199
Whitaker, Professor Dorothy Stork, 216
Williams Committee, 218
Winnicot, Clare, 163, 238
Wollstonecraft, Mary, 2
Women
  employment of, 12–13, 68, 102–7, 188f, 246f
  sexual and social roles, 3, 15, 25, 78–9, 84–7, 103, 189
  social class of, 12, 35
Women, married, 79
  problems of, 247f
  proportion of, 188
Women, single
  contribution to social work, 186–7
  employment of, 46, 78
  proportion of, 80
Women relieving officers, 35
Women's Employment Bureau, 116, 122
Women's Employment Federation, 248

Women's entry to professions,
    12–13, 77–8, 81–2, 102f, 188f
Women's guardians, 30–1
Women's Group on Public Welfare,
    182, 184
Women's liberation, 255–6
Women's Local Government
    Society, 31
Women's rights and women
    social workers, 66f, 102–3, 122
Women's suffrage, 66f, 100–1

Women's Voluntary Service,
    49–50, 181–2
Wootton, Barbara, 107, 109–10,
    236–7
Workhouse Visiting Society, 30
Workhouses, 17, 30, 32, 34–5

Younghusband, Dame Eileen, 163,
    196, 198–200, 203–6, 210, 211,
    219, 220

Routledge Social Science Series

Routledge & Kegan Paul   London and Boston

68–74 Carter Lane   London EC4V 5EL
9 Park Street   Boston   Mass 02108

Contents

International Library of Sociology 3
General Sociology 3
Foreign Classics of Sociology 4
Social Structure 4
Sociology and Politics 4
Foreign Affairs 5
Criminology 5
Social Psychology 5
Sociology of the Family 6
Social Services 7
Sociology of Education 7
Sociology of Culture 8
Sociology of Religion 9
Sociology of Art and Literature 9
Sociology of Knowledge 9
Urban Sociology 9
Rural Sociology 10
Sociology of Industry and Distribution 10
Documentary 11
Anthropology 11
Sociology and Philosophy 12
International Library of Anthropology 12
International Library of Social Policy 12
International Library of Welfare and Philosophy 13
Primary Socialization, Language and Education 13
Reports of the Institute of Community Studies 13
Reports of the Institute for Social Studies in Medical Care 14
Medicine, Illness and Society 14
Monographs in Social Theory 14
Routledge Social Science Journals 15

Authors wishing to submit manuscripts for any series in
this catalogue should send them to the Social Science Editor,
Routledge & Kegan Paul Ltd, 68–74 Carter Lane,
London EC4V 5EL

●*Books so marked are available in paperback*
All books are in Metric Demy 8vo format (216×138mm approx.)

International Library of Sociology

General Editor John Rex

GENERAL SOCIOLOGY

Barnsley, J. H. The Social Reality of Ethics. *464 pp.*
Belshaw, Cyril. The Conditions of Social Performance. *An Exploratory Theory. 144 pp.*
Brown, Robert. Explanation in Social Science. *208 pp.*
● Rules and Laws in Sociology. *192 pp.*
Bruford, W. H. Chekhov and His Russia. *A Sociological Study. 244 pp.*
Cain, Maureen E. Society and the Policeman's Role. *326 pp.*
Gibson, Quentin. The Logic of Social Enquiry. *240 pp.*
Glucksmann, M. Structuralist Analysis in Contemporary Social Thought. *212 pp.*
Gurvitch, Georges. Sociology of Law. *Preface by Roscoe Pound. 264 pp.*
Hodge, H. A. Wilhelm Dilthey. *An Introduction. 184 pp.*
Homans, George C. Sentiments and Activities. *336 pp.*
Johnson, Harry M. Sociology: *a Systematic Introduction. Foreword by Robert K. Merton. 710 pp.*
Mannheim, Karl. Essays on Sociology and Social Psychology. *Edited by Paul Keckskemeti. With Editorial Note by Adolph Lowe. 344 pp.*
 Systematic Sociology: *An Introduction to the Study of Society. Edited by J. S. Erös and Professor W. A. C. Stewart. 220 pp.*
Martindale, Don. The Nature and Types of Sociological Theory. *292 pp.*
●**Maus, Heinz.** A Short History of Sociology. *234 pp.*
Mey, Harald. Field-Theory. *A Study of its Application in the Social Sciences. 352 pp.*
Myrdal, Gunnar. Value in Social Theory: *A Collection of Essays on Methodology. Edited by Paul Streeten. 332 pp.*
Ogburn, William F., and **Nimkoff, Meyer F.** A Handbook of Sociology. *Preface by Karl Mannheim. 656 pp. 46 figures. 35 tables.*
Parsons, Talcott, and **Smelser, Neil J.** Economy and Society: *A Study in the Integration of Economic and Social Theory. 362 pp.*
●**Rex, John.** Key Problems of Sociological Theory. *220 pp.*
 Discovering Sociology. *278 pp.*
 Sociology and the Demystification of the Modern World. *282 pp.*
●**Rex, John** (Ed.) Approaches to Sociology. *Contributions by Peter Abell, Frank Bechhofer, Basil Bernstein, Ronald Fletcher, David Frisby, Miriam Glucksmann, Peter Lassman, Herminio Martins, John Rex, Roland Robertson, John Westergaard and Jock Young. 302 pp.*
Rigby, A. Alternative Realities. *352 pp.*
Roche, M. Phenomenology, Language and the Social Sciences. *374 pp.*
Sahay, A. Sociological Analysis. *220 pp.*
Urry, John. Reference Groups and the Theory of Revolution. *244 pp.*
Weinberg, E. Development of Sociology in the Soviet Union. *173 pp.*

FOREIGN CLASSICS OF SOCIOLOGY

●**Durkheim, Emile.** Suicide. *A Study in Sociology. Edited and with an Intro-duction by George Simpson. 404 pp.*
Professional Ethics and Civic Morals. *Translated by Cornelia Brookfield. 288 pp.*
●**Gerth, H. H.,** and **Mills, C. Wright.** From Max Weber: *Essays in Sociology. 502 pp.*
●**Tönnies, Ferdinand.** Community and Association. (*Gemeinschaft und Gesellschaft.) Translated and Supplemented by Charles P. Loomis. Foreword by Pitirim A. Sorokin. 334 pp.*

SOCIAL STRUCTURE

Andreski, Stanislav. Military Organization and Society. *Foreword by Professor A. R. Radcliffe-Brown. 226 pp. 1 folder.*
Coontz, Sydney H. Population Theories and the Economic Interpretation. *202 pp.*
Coser, Lewis. The Functions of Social Conflict. *204 pp.*
Dickie-Clark, H. F. Marginal Situation: *A Sociological Study of a Coloured Group. 240 pp. 11 tables.*
Glaser, Barney, and **Strauss, Anselm L.** Status Passage. *A Formal Theory. 208 pp.*
Glass, D. V. (Ed.) Social Mobility in Britain. *Contributions by J. Berent, T. Bottomore, R. C. Chambers, J. Floud, D. V. Glass, J. R. Hall, H. T. Himmelweit, R. K. Kelsall, F. M. Martin, C. A. Moser, R. Mukherjee, and W. Ziegel. 420 pp.*
Jones, Garth N. Planned Organizational Change: *An Exploratory Study Using an Empirical Approach. 268 pp.*
Kelsall, R. K. Higher Civil Servants in Britain: *From 1870 to the Present Day. 268 pp. 31 tables.*
König, René. The Community. *232 pp. Illustrated.*
●**Lawton, Denis.** Social Class, Language and Education. *192 pp.*
McLeish, John. The Theory of Social Change: *Four Views Considered. 128 pp.*
Marsh, David C. The Changing Social Structure of England and Wales, 1871-1961. *288 pp.*
Mouzelis, Nicos. Organization and Bureaucracy. *An Analysis of Modern Theories. 240 pp.*
Mulkay, M. J. Functionalism, Exchange and Theoretical Strategy. *272 pp.*
Ossowski, Stanislaw. Class Structure in the Social Consciousness. *210 pp.*
Podgórecki, Adam. Law and Society. *About 300 pp.*

SOCIOLOGY AND POLITICS

Acton, T. A. Gypsy Politics and Social Change. *316 pp.*
Hechter, Michael. Internal Colonialism. *The Celtic Fringe in British National Development, 1536-1966. About 350 pp.*
Hertz, Frederick. Nationality in History and Politics: *A Psychology and Sociology of National Sentiment and Nationalism. 432 pp.*

Kornhauser, William. The Politics of Mass Society. *272 pp. 20 tables.*

Laidler, Harry W. History of Socialism. *Social-Economic Movements: An Historical and Comparative Survey of Socialism, Communism, Co-operation, Utopianism; and other Systems of Reform and Reconstruction. 992 pp.*

Lasswell, H. D. Analysis of Political Behaviour. *324 pp.*

Mannheim, Karl. Freedom, Power and Democratic Planning. *Edited by Hans Gerth and Ernest K. Bramstedt. 424 pp.*

Mansur, Fatma. Process of Independence. *Foreword by A. H. Hanson. 208 pp.*

Martin, David A. Pacifism: *an Historical and Sociological Study. 262 pp.*

Myrdal, Gunnar. The Political Element in the Development of Economic Theory. *Translated from the German by Paul Streeten. 282 pp.*

Wootton, Graham. Workers, Unions and the State. *188 pp.*

FOREIGN AFFAIRS: THEIR SOCIAL, POLITICAL AND ECONOMIC FOUNDATIONS

Mayer, J. P. Political Thought in France from the Revolution to the Fifth Republic. *164 pp.*

CRIMINOLOGY

Ancel, Marc. Social Defence: *A Modern Approach to Criminal Problems. Foreword by Leon Radzinowicz. 240 pp.*

Cain, Maureen E. Society and the Policeman's Role. *326 pp.*

Cloward, Richard A., and **Ohlin, Lloyd E.** Delinquency and Opportunity: *A Theory of Delinquent Gangs. 248 pp.*

Downes, David M. The Delinquent Solution. *A Study in Subcultural Theory. 296 pp.*

Dunlop, A. B., and **McCabe, S.** Young Men in Detention Centres. *192 pp.*

Friedlander, Kate. The Psycho-Analytical Approach to Juvenile Delinquency: *Theory, Case Studies, Treatment. 320 pp.*

Glueck, Sheldon, and **Eleanor.** Family Environment and Delinquency. *With the statistical assistance of Rose W. Kneznek. 340 pp.*

Lopez-Rey, Manuel. Crime. *An Analytical Appraisal. 288 pp.*

Mannheim, Hermann. Comparative Criminology: *a Text Book. Two volumes. 442 pp. and 380 pp.*

Morris, Terence. The Criminal Area: *A Study in Social Ecology. Foreword by Hermann Mannheim. 232 pp. 25 tables. 4 maps.*

Rock, Paul. Making People Pay. *338 pp.*

●**Taylor, Ian, Walton, Paul,** and **Young, Jock.** The New Criminology. *For a Social Theory of Deviance. 325 pp.*

SOCIAL PSYCHOLOGY

Bagley, Christopher. The Social Psychology of the Epileptic Child. *320 pp.*

Barbu, Zevedei. Problems of Historical Psychology. *248 pp.*

Blackburn, Julian. Psychology and the Social Pattern. *184 pp.*

●**Brittan, Arthur.** Meanings and Situations. *224 pp.*

Carroll, J. Break-Out from the Crystal Palace. *200 pp.*

●**Fleming, C. M.** Adolescence: Its Social Psychology. *With an Introduction to recent findings from the fields of Anthropology, Physiology, Medicine, Psychometrics and Sociometry. 288 pp.*

● The Social Psychology of Education: *An Introduction and Guide to Its Study. 136 pp.*

Homans, George C. The Human Group. *Foreword by Bernard DeVoto. Introduction by Robert K. Merton. 526 pp.*

● Social Behaviour: *its Elementary Forms. 416 pp.*

●**Klein, Josephine.** The Study of Groups. *226 pp. 31 figures. 5 tables.*

Linton, Ralph. The Cultural Background of Personality. *132 pp.*

●**Mayo, Elton.** The Social Problems of an Industrial Civilization. *With an appendix on the Political Problem. 180 pp.*

Ottaway, A. K. C. Learning Through Group Experience. *176 pp.*

Ridder, J. C. de. The Personality of the Urban African in South Africa. *A Thermatic Apperception Test Study. 196 pp. 12 plates.*

●**Rose, Arnold M.** (Ed.) Human Behaviour and Social Processes: *an Interactionist Approach. Contributions by Arnold M. Rose, Ralph H. Turner, Anselm Strauss, Everett C. Hughes, E. Franklin Frazier, Howard S. Becker, et al. 696 pp.*

Smelser, Neil J. Theory of Collective Behaviour. *448 pp.*

Stephenson, Geoffrey M. The Development of Conscience. *128 pp.*

Young, Kimball. Handbook of Social Psychology. *658 pp. 16 figures. 10 tables.*

SOCIOLOGY OF THE FAMILY

Banks, J. A. Prosperity and Parenthood: *A Study of Family Planning among The Victorian Middle Classes. 262 pp.*

Bell, Colin R. Middle Class Families: *Social and Geographical Mobility. 224 pp.*

Burton, Lindy. Vulnerable Children. *272 pp.*

Gavron, Hannah. The Captive Wife: *Conflicts of Household Mothers. 190 pp.*

George, Victor, and **Wilding, Paul.** Motherless Families. *220 pp.*

Klein, Josephine. Samples from English Cultures.
1. Three Preliminary Studies and Aspects of Adult Life in England. *447 pp.*
2. Child-Rearing Practices and Index. *247 pp.*

Klein, Viola. Britain's Married Women Workers. *180 pp.*

The Feminine Character. *History of an Ideology. 244 pp.*

McWhinnie, Alexina M. Adopted Children. *How They Grow Up. 304 pp.*

● **Myrdal, Alva,** and **Klein, Viola.** Women's Two Roles: *Home and Work. 238 pp. 27 tables.*

Parsons, Talcott, and **Bales, Robert F.** Family: Socialization and Interaction Process. *In collaboration with James Olds, Morris Zelditch and Philip E. Slater. 456 pp. 50 figures and tables.*

SOCIAL SERVICES

Bastide, Roger. The Sociology of Mental Disorder. *Translated from the French by Jean McNeil. 260 pp.*

Carlebach, Julius. Caring For Children in Trouble. *266 pp.*

Forder, R. A. (Ed.) Penelope Hall's Social Services of England and Wales. *352 pp.*

George, Victor. Foster Care. *Theory and Practice. 234 pp.*
Social Security: *Beveridge and After. 258 pp.*

George, V., and **Wilding, P.** Motherless Families. *248 pp.*

●**Goetschius, George W.** Working with Community Groups. *256 pp.*

Goetschius, George W., and **Tash, Joan.** Working with Unattached Youth. *416 pp.*

Hall, M. P., and **Howes, I. V.** The Church in Social Work. *A Study of Moral Welfare Work undertaken by the Church of England. 320 pp.*

Heywood, Jean S. Children in Care: *the Development of the Service for the Deprived Child. 264 pp.*

Hoenig, J., and **Hamilton, Marian W.** The De-Segregation of the Mentally Ill. *284 pp.*

Jones, Kathleen. Mental Health and Social Policy, 1845-1959. *264 pp.*

King, Roy D., Raynes, Norma V., and **Tizard, Jack.** Patterns of Residential Care. *356 pp.*

Leigh, John. Young People and Leisure. *256 pp.*

Morris, Mary. Voluntary Work and the Welfare State. *300 pp.*

Morris, Pauline. Put Away: *A Sociological Study of Institutions for the Mentally Retarded. 364 pp.*

Nokes, P. L. The Professional Task in Welfare Practice. *152 pp.*

Timms, Noel. Psychiatric Social Work in Great Britain (1939-1962). *280 pp.*

● Social Casework: *Principles and Practice. 256 pp.*

Young, A. F. Social Services in British Industry. *272 pp.*

Young, A. F., and **Ashton, E. T.** British Social Work in the Nineteenth Century. *288 pp.*

SOCIOLOGY OF EDUCATION

Banks, Olive. Parity and Prestige in English Secondary Education: a Study in Educational Sociology. *272 pp.*

Bentwich, Joseph. Education in Israel. *224 pp. 8 pp. plates.*

●**Blyth, W. A. L.** English Primary Education. *A Sociological Description.*
1. Schools. *232 pp.*
2. Background. *168 pp.*

Collier, K. G. The Social Purposes of Education: *Personal and Social Values in Education. 268 pp.*

Dale, R. R., and **Griffith, S.** Down Stream: *Failure in the Grammar School.* *108 pp.*

Dore, R. P. Education in Tokugawa Japan. *356 pp. 9 pp. plates.*

Evans, K. M. Sociometry and Education. *158 pp.*

●**Ford, Julienne.** Social Class and the Comprehensive School. *192 pp.*

Foster, P. J. Education and Social Change in Ghana. *336 pp. 3 maps.*

Fraser, W. R. Education and Society in Modern France. *150 pp.*

Grace, Gerald R. Role Conflict and the Teacher. *About 200 pp.*

Hans, Nicholas. New Trends in Education in the Eighteenth Century. *278 pp. 19 tables.*

● Comparative Education: *A Study of Educational Factors and Traditions.* *360 pp.*

Hargreaves, David. Interpersonal Relations and Education. *432 pp.*

● Social Relations in a Secondary School. *240 pp.*

Holmes, Brian. Problems in Education. *A Comparative Approach. 336 pp.*

King, Ronald. Values and Involvement in a Grammar School. *164 pp.*

School Organization and Pupil Involvement. *A Study of Secondary Schools.*

●**Mannheim, Karl,** and **Stewart, W. A. C.** An Introduction to the Sociology of Education. *206 pp.*

Morris, Raymond N. The Sixth Form and College Entrance. *231 pp.*

●**Musgrove, F.** Youth and the Social Order. *176 pp.*

●**Ottaway, A. K. C.** Education and Society: An Introduction to the Sociology of Education. *With an Introduction by W. O. Lester Smith. 212 pp.*

Peers, Robert. Adult Education: *A Comparative Study. 398 pp.*

Pritchard, D. G. Education and the Handicapped: *1760 to 1960. 258 pp.*

Richardson, Helen. Adolescent Girls in Approved Schools. *308 pp.*

Stratta, Erica. The Education of Borstal Boys. *A Study of their Educational Experiences prior to, and during, Borstal Training. 256 pp.*

Taylor, P. H., Reid, W. A., and **Holley, B. J.** The English Sixth Form. *A Case Study in Curriculum Research. 200 pp.*

SOCIOLOGY OF CULTURE

Eppel, E. M., and **M.** Adolescents and Morality: *A Study of some Moral Values and Dilemmas of Working Adolescents in the Context of a changing Climate of Opinion. Foreword by W. J. H. Sprott. 268 pp. 39 tables.*

●**Fromm, Erich.** The Fear of Freedom. *286 pp.*

● The Sane Society. *400 pp.*

Mannheim, Karl. Essays on the Sociology of Culture. *Edited by Ernst Mannheim in co-operation with Paul Kecskemeti. Editorial Note by Adolph Lowe. 280 pp.*

Weber, Alfred. Farewell to European History: *or The Conquest of Nihilism. Translated from the German by R. F. C. Hull. 224 pp.*

SOCIOLOGY OF RELIGION

Argyle, Michael and **Beit-Hallahmi, Benjamin.** The Social Psychology of Religion. *About 256 pp.*
Nelson, G. K. Spiritualism and Society. *313 pp.*
Stark, Werner. The Sociology of Religion. *A Study of Christendom.*
  Volume I. *Established Religion. 248 pp.*
  Volume II. *Sectarian Religion. 368 pp.*
  Volume III. *The Universal Church. 464 pp.*
  Volume IV. *Types of Religious Man. 352 pp.*
  Volume V. *Types of Religious Culture. 464 pp.*
Turner, B. S. Weber and Islam. *216 pp.*
Watt, W. Montgomery. Islam and the Integration of Society. *320 pp.*

SOCIOLOGY OF ART AND LITERATURE

Jarvie, Ian C. Towards a Sociology of the Cinema. *A Comparative Essay on the Structure and Functioning of a Major Entertainment Industry. 405 pp.*
Rust, Frances S. Dance in Society. *An Analysis of the Relationships between the Social Dance and Society in England from the Middle Ages to the Present Day. 256 pp. 8 pp. of plates.*
Schücking, L. L. The Sociology of Literary Taste. *112 pp.*
Wolff, Janet. Hermeneutic Philosophy and the Sociology of Art. *About 200 pp.*

SOCIOLOGY OF KNOWLEDGE

Diesing, P. Patterns of Discovery in the Social Sciences. *262 pp.*
●**Douglas, J. D.** (Ed.) Understanding Everyday Life. *370 pp.*
●**Hamilton, P.** Knowledge and Social Structure. *174 pp.*
Jarvie, I. C. Concepts and Society. *232 pp.*
Mannheim, Karl. Essays on the Sociology of Knowledge. *Edited by Paul Kecskemeti. Editorial Note by Adolph Lowe. 353 pp.*
Remmling, Gunter W. (Ed.) Towards the Sociology of Knowledge. *Origin and Development of a Sociological Thought Style. 463 pp.*
Stark, Werner. The Sociology of Knowledge: *An Essay in Aid of a Deeper Understanding of the History of Ideas. 384 pp.*

URBAN SOCIOLOGY

Ashworth, William. The Genesis of Modern British Town Planning: *A Study in Economic and Social History of the Nineteenth and Twentieth Centuries. 288 pp.*
Cullingworth, J. B. Housing Needs and Planning Policy: *A Restatement of the Problems of Housing Need and 'Overspill' in England and Wales. 232 pp. 44 tables. 8 maps.*

Dickinson, Robert E. City and Region: *A Geographical Interpretation* *608 pp. 125 figures.*

The West European City: *A Geographical Interpretation. 600 pp. 129 maps. 29 plates.*

● The City Region in Western Europe. *320 pp. Maps.*

Humphreys, Alexander J. New Dubliners: *Urbanization and the Irish Family. Foreword by George C. Homans. 304 pp.*

Jackson, Brian. Working Class Community: *Some General Notions raised by a Series of Studies in Northern England. 192 pp.*

Jennings, Hilda. Societies in the Making: *a Study of Development and Redevelopment within a County Borough. Foreword by D. A. Clark. 286 pp.*

●**Mann, P. H.** An Approach to Urban Sociology. *240 pp.*

Morris, R. N., and **Mogey, J.** The Sociology of Housing. *Studies at Berinsfield. 232 pp. 4 pp. plates.*

Rosser, C., and **Harris, C.** The Family and Social Change. *A Study of Family and Kinship in a South Wales Town. 352 pp. 8 maps.*

RURAL SOCIOLOGY

Chambers, R. J. H. Settlement Schemes in Tropical Africa: *A Selective Study. 268 pp.*

Haswell, M. R. The Economics of Development in Village India. *120 pp.*

Littlejohn, James. Westrigg: *the Sociology of a Cheviot Parish. 172 pp. 5 figures.*

Mayer, Adrian C. Peasants in the Pacific. *A Study of Fiji Indian Rural Society. 248 pp. 20 plates.*

Williams, W. M. The Sociology of an English Village: *Gosforth. 272 pp. 12 figures. 13 tables.*

SOCIOLOGY OF INDUSTRY AND DISTRIBUTION

Anderson, Nels. Work and Leisure. *280 pp.*

●**Blau, Peter M.,** and **Scott, W. Richard.** Formal Organizations: *a Comparative approach. Introduction and Additional Bibliography by J. H. Smith. 326 pp.*

Eldridge, J. E. T. Industrial Disputes. *Essays in the Sociology of Industrial Relations. 288 pp.*

Hetzler, Stanley. Applied Measures for Promoting Technological Growth. *352 pp.*

Technological Growth and Social Change. *Achieving Modernization. 269 pp.*

Hollowell, Peter G. The Lorry Driver. *272 pp.*

Jefferys, Margot, *with the assistance of Winifred Moss.* Mobility in the Labour Market: *Employment Changes in Battersea and Dagenham. Preface by Barbara Wootton. 186 pp. 51 tables.*

Millerson, Geoffrey. The Qualifying Associations: *a Study in Professionalization. 320 pp.*

Smelser, Neil J. Social Change in the Industrial Revolution: *An Application of Theory to the Lancashire Cotton Industry, 1770-1840. 468 pp. 12 figures. 14 tables.*

Williams, Gertrude. Recruitment to Skilled Trades. *240 pp.*

Young, A. F. Industrial Injuries Insurance: *an Examination of British Policy. 192 pp.*

DOCUMENTARY

Schlesinger, Rudolf (Ed.) Changing Attitudes in Soviet Russia.
 2. The Nationalities Problem and Soviet Administration. *Selected Readings on the Development of Soviet Nationalities Policies. Introduced by the editor. Translated by W. W. Gottlieb. 324 pp.*

ANTHROPOLOGY

Ammar, Hamed. Growing up in an Egyptian Village: *Silwa, Province of Aswan. 336 pp.*

Brandel-Syrier, Mia. Reeftown Elite. *A Study of Social Mobility in a Modern African Community on the Reef. 376 pp.*

Crook, David, and **Isabel.** Revolution in a Chinese Village: *Ten Mile Inn. 230 pp. 8 plates. 1 map.*

Dickie-Clark, H. F. The Marginal Situation. *A Sociological Study of a Coloured Group. 236 pp.*

Dube, S. C. Indian Village. *Foreword by Morris Edward Opler. 276 pp. 4 plates.*
 India's Changing Villages: *Human Factors in Community Development. 260 pp. 8 plates. 1 map.*

Firth, Raymond. Malay Fishermen. *Their Peasant Economy. 420 pp. 17 pp. plates.*

Firth, R., Hubert, J., and **Forge, A.** Families and their Relatives. *Kinship in a Middle-Class Sector of London: An Anthropological Study. 456 pp.*

Gulliver, P. H. Social Control in an African Society: a Study of the Arusha, Agricultural Masai of Northern Tanganyika. *320 pp. 8 plates. 10 figures.*
 Family Herds. *288 pp.*

Ishwaran, K. Shivapur. *A South Indian Village. 216 pp.*
 Tradition and Economy in Village India: *An Interactionist Approach. Foreword by Conrad Arensburg. 176 pp.*

Jarvie, Ian C. The Revolution in Anthropology. *268 pp.*

Jarvie, Ian C., and **Agassi, Joseph.** Hong Kong. *A Society in Transition. 396 pp. Illustrated with plates and maps.*

Little, Kenneth L. Mende of Sierra Leone. *308 pp. and folder.*
 Negroes in Britain. *With a New Introduction and Contemporary Study by Leonard Bloom. 320 pp.*

Lowie, Robert H. Social Organization. *494 pp.*

Mayer, Adrian,C. Caste and Kinship in Central India: *A Village and its Region. 328 pp. 16 plates. 15 figures. 16 tables.*

Peasants in the Pacific. *A Study of Fiji Indian Rural Society. 248 pp.*

Smith, Raymond T. The Negro Family in British Guiana: *Family Structure and Social Status in the Villages. With a Foreword by Meyer Fortes. 314 pp. 8 plates. 1 figure. 4 maps.*

SOCIOLOGY AND PHILOSOPHY

Barnsley, John H. The Social Reality of Ethics. *A Comparative Analysis of Moral Codes. 448 pp.*

Diesing, Paul. Patterns of Discovery in the Social Sciences. *362 pp.*

● **Douglas, Jack D.** (Ed.) Understanding Everyday Life. *Toward the Reconstruction of Sociological Knowledge. Contributions by Alan F. Blum. Aaron W. Cicourel, Norman K. Denzin, Jack D. Douglas, John Heeren, Peter McHugh, Peter K. Manning, Melvin Power, Matthew Speier, Roy Turner, D. Lawrence Wieder, Thomas P. Wilson and Don H. Zimmerman. 370 pp.*

Jarvie, Ian C. Concepts and Society. *216 pp.*

Pelz, Werner. The Scope of Understanding in Sociology. *Towards a more radical reorientation in the social humanistic sciences. 283 pp.*

Roche, Maurice. Phenomenology, Language and the Social Sciences. *371 pp.*

Sahay, Arun. Sociological Analysis. *212 pp.*

Sklair, Leslie. The Sociology of Progress. *320 pp.*

International Library of Anthropology

General Editor Adam Kuper

Brown, Paula. The Chimbu. *A Study of Change in the New Guinea Highlands. 151 pp.*

Lloyd, P. C. Power and Independence. *Urban Africans' Perception of Social Inequality. 264 pp.*

Pettigrew, Joyce. Robber Noblemen. *A Study of the Political System of the Sikh Jats. 284 pp.*

Van Den Berghe, Pierre L. Power and Privilege at an African University. *278 pp.*

International Library of Social Policy

General Editor Kathleen Jones

Bayley, M. Mental Handicap and Community Care. *426 pp.*

Butler, J. R. Family Doctors and Public Policy. *208 pp.*

Holman, Robert. Trading in Children. *A Study of Private Fostering. 355 pp.*

Jones, Kathleen. History of the Mental Health Service. *428 pp.*
Thomas, J. E. The English Prison Officer since 1850: *A Study in Conflict.*
258 pp.
Woodward, J. To Do the Sick No Harm. *A Study of the British Voluntary
Hospital System to 1875. About 220 pp.*

International Library of Welfare and Philosophy

General Editors Noel Timms and David Watson

● **Plant, Raymond.** Community and Ideology. *104 pp.*

Primary Socialization, Language and Education

General Editor Basil Bernstein

Bernstein, Basil. Class, Codes and Control. *2 volumes.*
   1. *Theoretical Studies Towards a Sociology of Language. 254 pp.*
   2. *Applied Studies Towards a Sociology of Language. About 400 pp.*
Brandis, W., and **Bernstein, B.** Selection and Control. *176 pp.*
Brandis, Walter, and **Henderson, Dorothy.** Social Class, Language and
   Communication. *288 pp.*
Cook-Gumperz, Jenny. Social Control and Socialization. *A Study of Class
   Differences in the Language of Maternal Control. 290 pp.*
● **Gahagan, D. M.,** and **G. A.** Talk Reform. *Exploration in Language for Infant
   School Children. 160 pp.*
Robinson, W. P., and **Rackstraw, Susan D. A.** A Question of Answers.
   2 volumes. 192 pp. and 180 pp.
Turner, Geoffrey J., and **Mohan, Bernard A.** A Linguistic Description and
   Computer Programme for Children's Speech. *208 pp.*

Reports of the Institute of Community Studies

Cartwright, Ann. Human Relations and Hospital Care. *272 pp.*
● Parents and Family Planning Services. *306 pp.*
   Patients and their Doctors. *A Study of General Practice. 304 pp.*
● **Jackson, Brian.** Streaming: *an Education System in Miniature. 168 pp.*
Jackson, Brian, and **Marsden, Dennis.** Education and the Working Class:
   *Some General Themes raised by a Study of 88 Working-class Children
   in a Northern Industrial City. 268 pp. 2 folders.*
Marris, Peter. The Experience of Higher Education. *232 pp. 27 tables.*
   Loss and Change. *192 pp.*

13

Marris, Peter, and **Rein, Martin.** Dilemmas of Social Reform. *Poverty and Community Action in the United States. 256 pp.*

Marris, Peter, and **Somerset, Anthony.** African Businessmen. *A Study of Entrepreneurship and Development in Kenya. 256 pp.*

Mills, Richard. Young Outsiders: *a Study in Alternative Communities. 216 pp.*

Runciman, W. G. Relative Deprivation and Social Justice. *A Study of Attitudes to Social Inequality in Twentieth-Century England. 352 pp.*

Willmott, Peter. Adolescent Boys in East London. *230 pp.*

Willmott, Peter, and **Young, Michael.** Family and Class in a London Suburb. *202 pp. 47 tables.*

Young, Michael. Innovation and Research in Education. *192 pp.*

●**Young, Michael,** and **McGeeney, Patrick.** Learning Begins at Home. *A Study of a Junior School and its Parents. 128 pp.*

Young, Michael, and **Willmott, Peter.** Family and Kinship in East London. *Foreword by Richard M. Titmuss. 252 pp. 39 tables.*
The Symmetrical Family. *410 pp.*

Reports of the Institute for Social Studies in Medical Care

Cartwright, Ann, Hockey, Lisbeth, and **Anderson, John L.** Life Before Death. *310 pp.*

Dunnell, Karen, and **Cartwright, Ann.** Medicine Takers, Prescribers and Hoarders. *190 pp.*

Medicine, Illness and Society

General Editor W. M. Williams

Robinson, David. The Process of Becoming Ill. *142 pp.*

Stacey, Margaret, *et al.* Hospitals, Children and Their Families. *The Report of a Pilot Study. 202 pp.*

Monographs in Social Theory

General Editor Arthur Brittan

●**Barnes, B.** Scientific Knowledge and Sociological Theory. *About 200 pp.*

Bauman, Zygmunt. Culture as Praxis. *204 pp.*

● **Dixon, Keith.** Sociological Theory. *Pretence and Possibility. 142 pp.*

●**Smith, Anthony D.** The Concept of Social Change. *A Critique of the Functionalist Theory of Social Change. 208 pp.*

Routledge Social Science Journals

The British Journal of Sociology. *Edited by Terence P. Morris. Vol. 1, No. 1, March 1950 and Quarterly. Roy. 8vo. Back numbers available. An international journal with articles on all aspects of sociology.*

Economy and Society. *Vol. 1, No. 1. February 1972 and Quarterly. Metric Roy. 8vo. A journal for all social scientists covering sociology, philosophy, anthropology, economics and history. Back numbers available.*

Year Book of Social Policy in Britain, The. *Edited by Kathleen Jones. 1971. Published annually.*

Printed in Great Britain by Unwin Brothers Limited
The Gresham Press Old Woking Surrey
A member of the Staples Printing Group

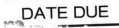